WELCOME TO *CHARACTER DESIGN QUARTERLY 06*

One of the things I love about CDQ (and there are many things on that list) is finding out about the different paths that lead our artists and designers into their careers. Most will have enjoyed making art as a child, or admired the work of others through books, comics, films, and cartoons, but that is often where the similarities end.

In this issue we learn about Amanda MacFarlane's journey into professional character design as a self-taught freelance artist, while Floriane Marchix reveals that she originally trained as an animator before finding that visual development actually suits her perfectly. Lois van Baarle, this issue's fabulous cover artist, has seen the growth of art communities online and social media having a massive impact on her freelance career. Meanwhile, James A. Castillo is looking to the future, including new developments in the animation industry. It is clear that wherever you are in you career, persuing character design with passion is what matters. Enjoy!

ANNIE MOSS
EDITOR

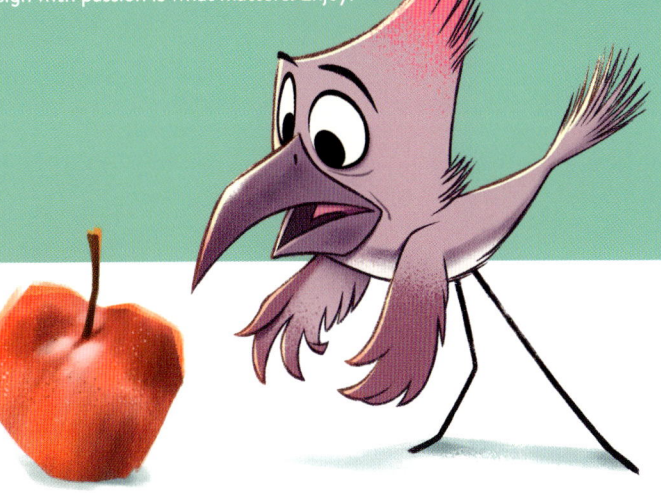

Image © Luis Gadea

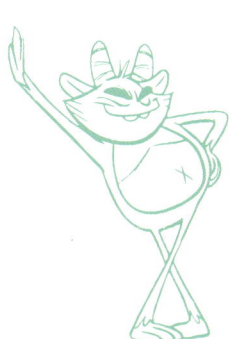
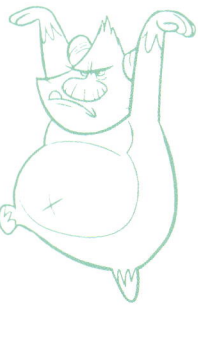

Lois van Baarle

BEHIND THE COVER ART

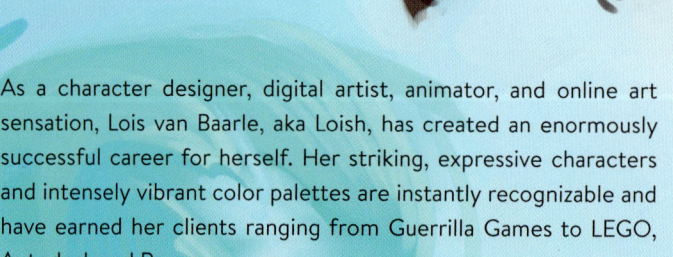

As a character designer, digital artist, animator, and online art sensation, Lois van Baarle, aka Loish, has created an enormously successful career for herself. Her striking, expressive characters and intensely vibrant color palettes are instantly recognizable and have earned her clients ranging from Guerrilla Games to LEGO, Autodesk and Psyop.

Although she originally studied animation at Utrecht School of Arts, Lois's career has surpassed her ambitions and she now works as a freelance artist creating character designs for a wide variety of projects and making personal digital paintings for herself and her followers. Having created this issue's magnificent cover art, Lois talks to us about how her online presence has influenced her career, why she restricts her studio time to office hours, and shares her experience of the key skills you need to have to build a successful freelance career.

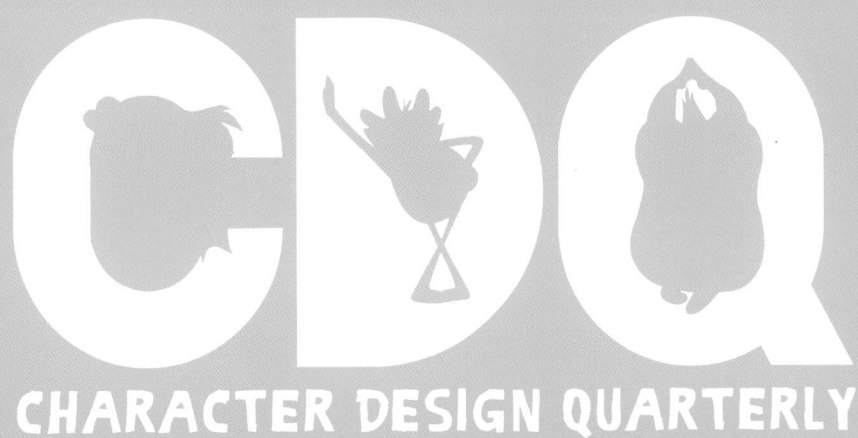

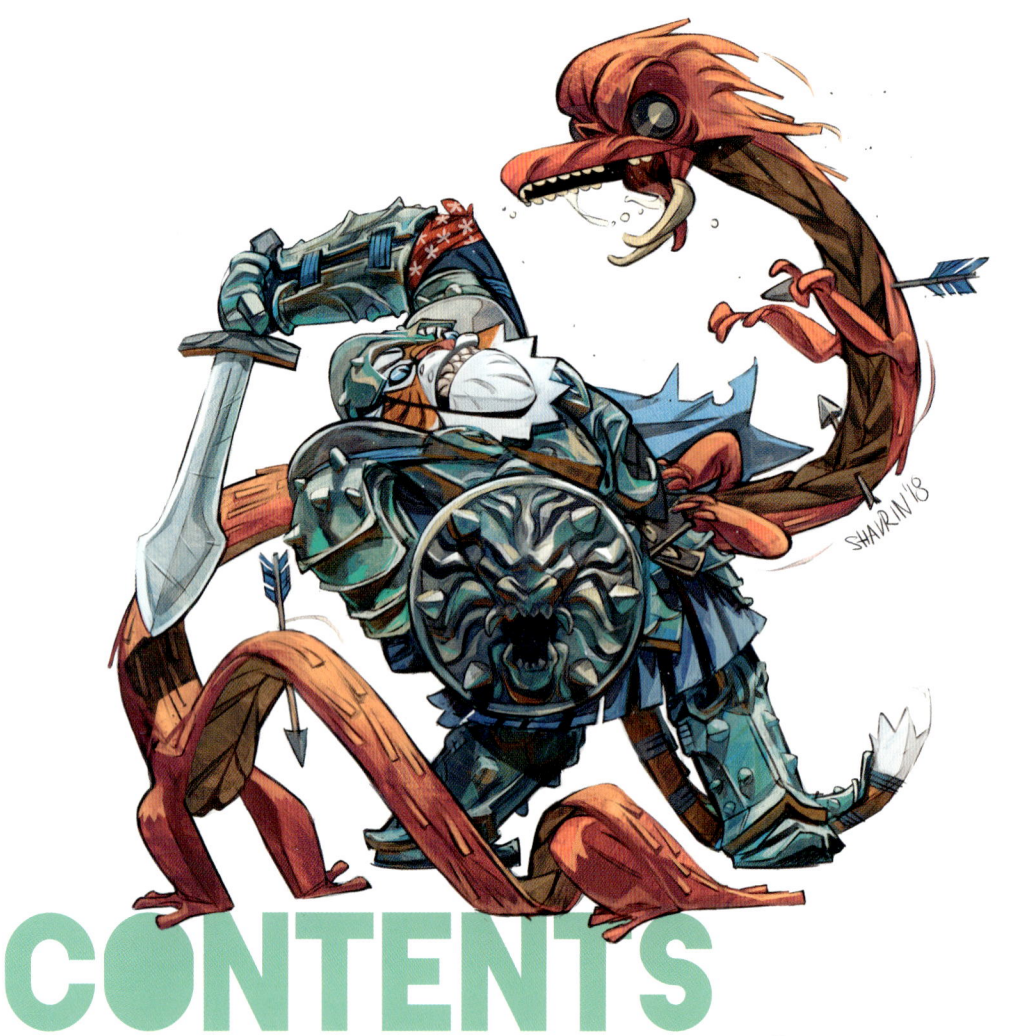

Image © Ivan Shavrin

CONTENTS

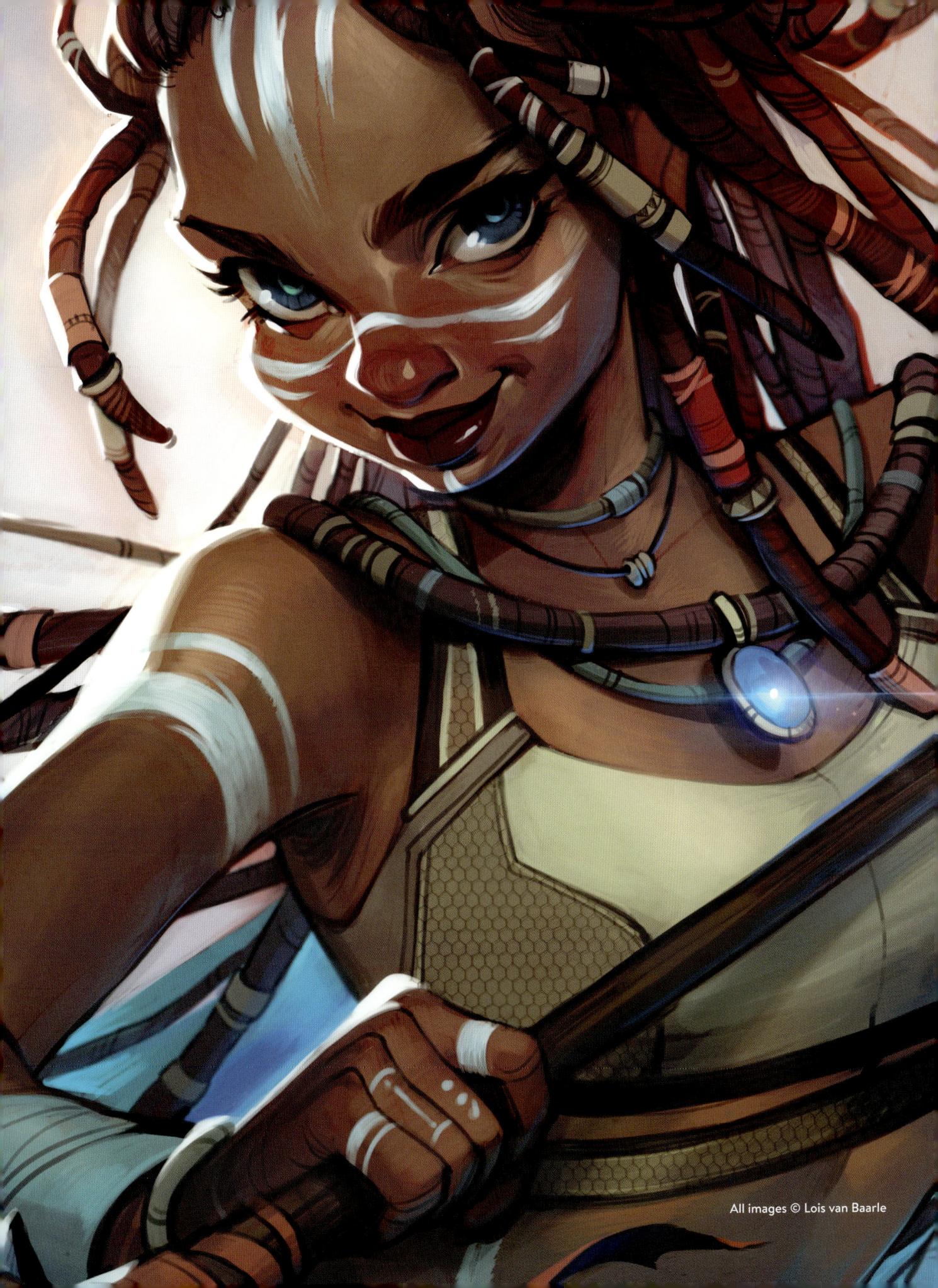

Hi Lois! Thank you for chatting with CDQ. Please could you start by telling us a bit about yourself and your background?

I'm Lois van Baarle, otherwise known as Loish! Depending on the context, I consider myself to be different things; on one hand I am a digital artist, but on the other hand I'm a character designer, and I also focus heavily on sharing my work online.

As a digital artist I paint and share knowledge about creating digital art through tutorials, workshops, and sharing as many resources as I can with others. However, as a character designer I also work on various projects, creating characters for clients. I have worked on the *Horizon Zero Dawn* franchise for Guerrilla Games, as well as created character designs for LEGO, particularly their line of toys aimed at a female audience, like *Friends*, *Elves*, and *DC Super Heroes*. I've also made character designs for animated films, 3D models for virtual reality, besides many other projects. Finally, I share my work online on social media and maintain my online presence on a daily basis.

What are your favorite digital tools to use when painting?

Currently, my favorite tool to quickly add color to a sketch is Procreate on an iPad Pro. Procreate is very quick and intuitive software, and because it can be used on a tablet it is easy to carry around and work when I am traveling.

My all-time favorite software however will always be Photoshop. I've been using it since I was fifteen and because I've been using it for over a decade it now feels like the most natural way to work for me. When using Photoshop I work with a Wacom Cintiq 27QHD tablet.

This page: *Huntress*

Opposite page: The process of creating this issue's amazing cover art!

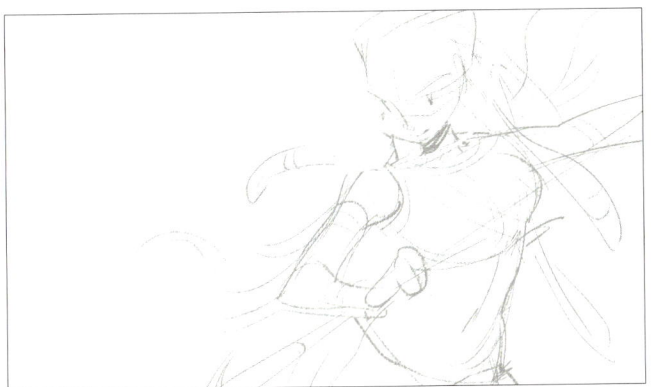
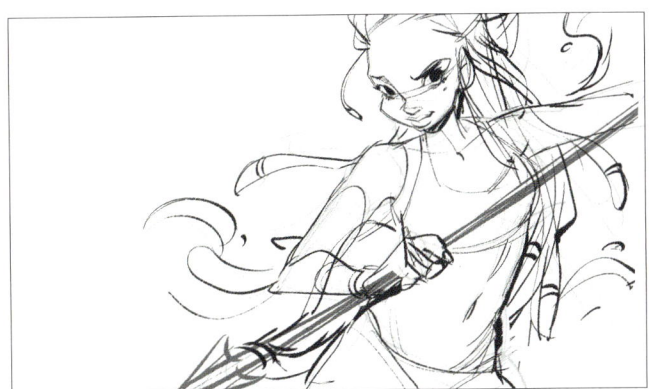
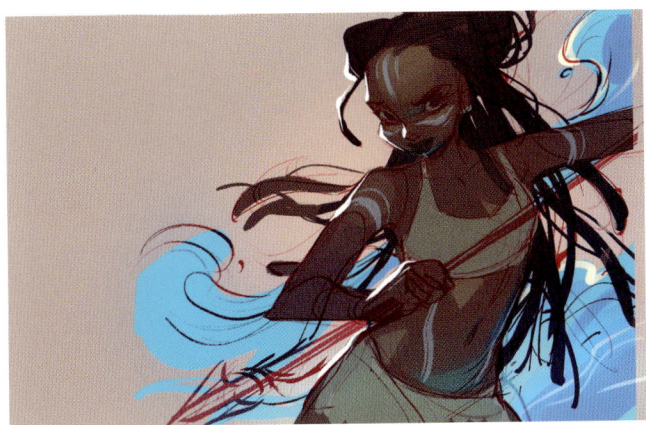
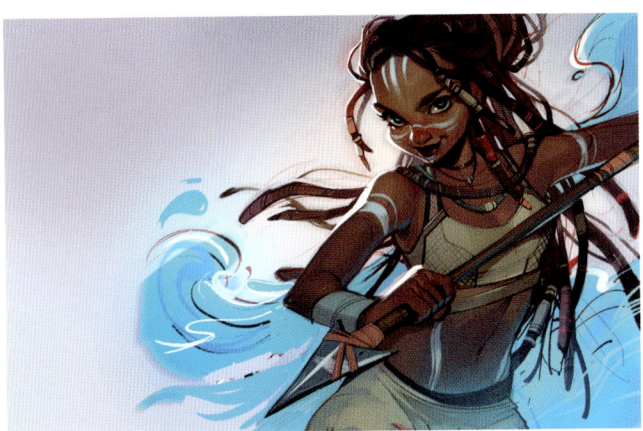

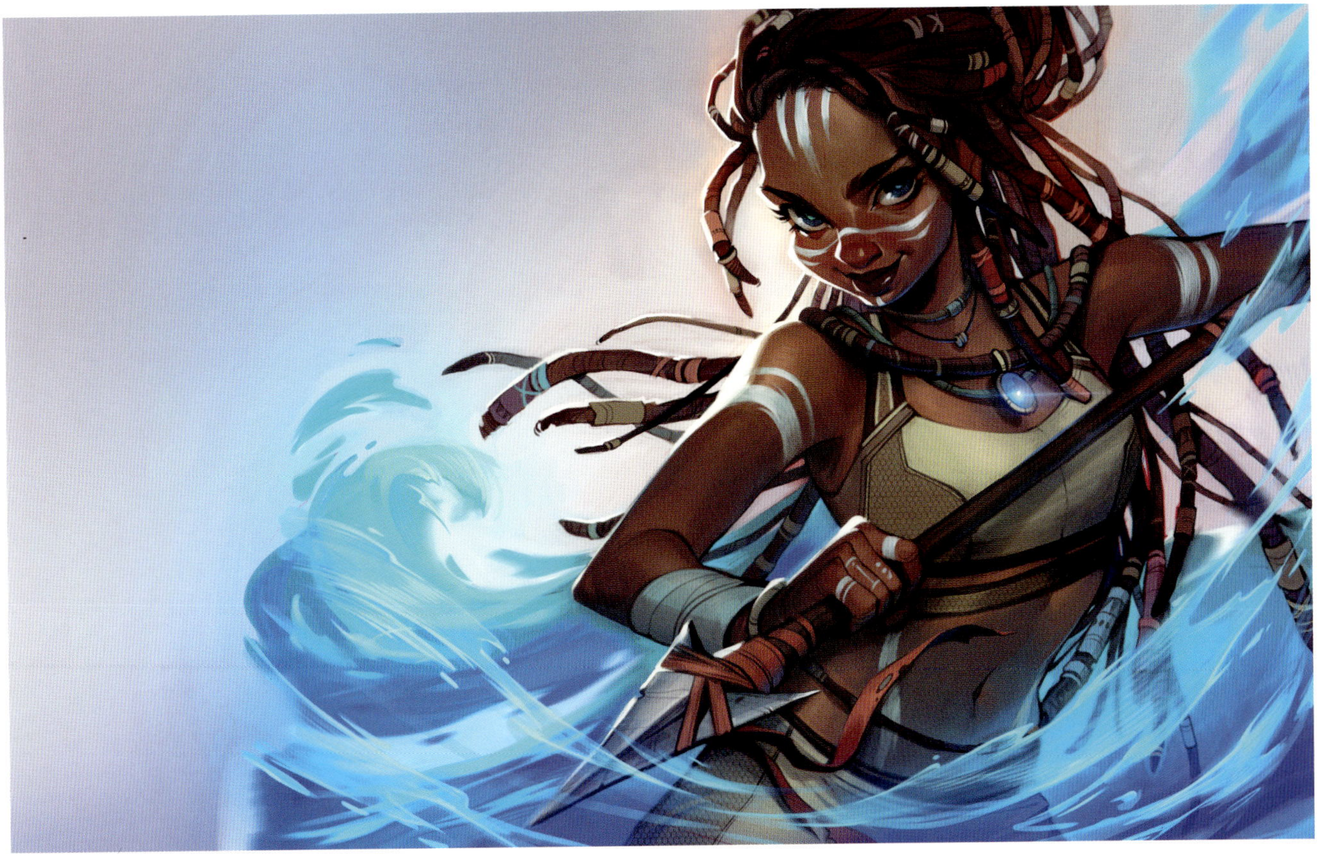

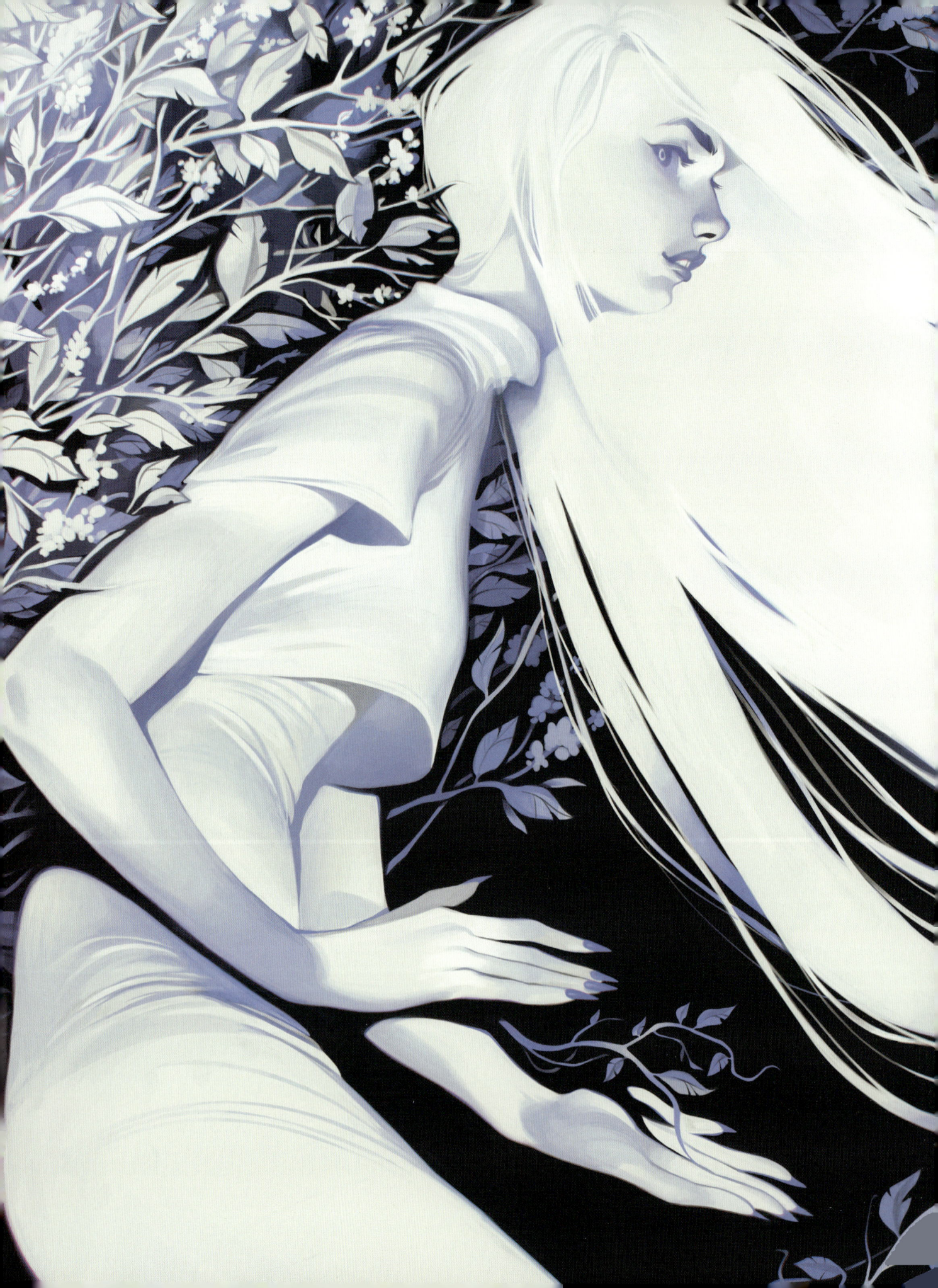

"I wanted to create a mix of that classic and elegant decorativeness of Art Nouveau, the flowing and sweet femininity of Disney, and the contemporary look and colors of Manga art"

Where do you find inspiration for your gorgeous characters and arresting color palettes?

This definitely derives from a mix of inspirations that I have built up over time! Initially I was hugely inspired by a mix of Art Nouveau, Disney, and various Manga styles. I wanted to create a mix of that classic and elegant decorativeness of Art Nouveau, the flowing and sweet femininity of Disney, and the contemporary look and colors of Manga art. Over time I have discovered many new artists that inspire me in new ways, like James Jean, and Andrew Hem. I have also found inspiration in the Sky Doll comic book series, particularly the detailed covers of each issue.

My work evolves slowly as I discover new artists, but nostalgia always plays a huge role; I'm always trying to find ways to get my color palettes to resonate emotionally with the viewer. I find that channeling colors that have a nostalgic feeling about them works best to generate an emotional response. For my color palettes I reference things like old, faded photographs or the look of the colorful '80s cartoons that I grew up with. I'm also enormously inspired by nature which can create a strong emotional response: the colors of a beautiful sunset, for example, can be deeply affecting.

Besides an affinity for art, what skills or qualities do you think an artist needs if they aspire to a freelance career?

It really depends on what direction an artist wants to pursue. I have learned that skills vary enormously across the board, and artists come in so many different forms. The main skill that is useful for any freelance work is the skill to communicate and connect with your clients and fellow artists. There is so much communication involved in making a project successful, and if you are open, engaged, and friendly to your clients, it can make the process so much more enjoyable. A positive, communicative relationship with your clients also makes it much more likely that they will approach you again for future projects.

Opposite page: *Moon*

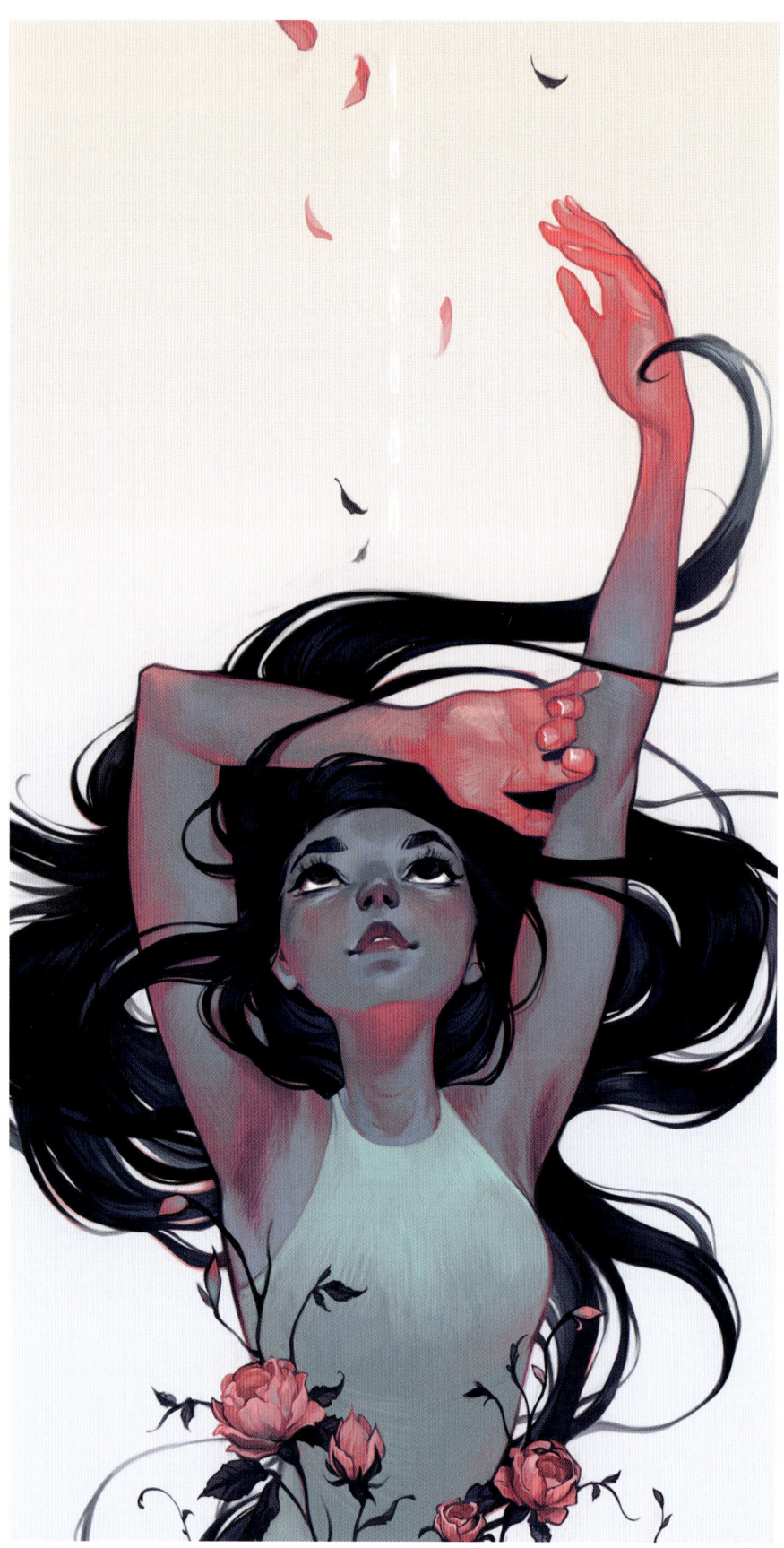

It is also really important to be dependable. Follow through on your side of the agreement, deliver work on time, and invest in communicating clearly and professionally, with reasonable boundaries. There is a stereotype that artists are quirky and difficult to work with, and conforming to this stereotype has a negative effect on both artists and the people who hire them. If you can reassure your client that you are a professional businessperson, your projects will run more smoothly.

How has the development of the internet shaped your career?

Being online has had a gigantic impact on my career. I would go so far as to say it is responsible for the career I have today! Through the internet my artwork is viewed by many people around the world and because of this clients reach out to me for work. Because of this dynamic, I have been able to discover what I can offer as an artist.

As a result of my online presence I have been approached for projects I would never have thought to aim for, and these unexpected ventures have ended up being a wonderful fit with my skill set, helping me grow artistically. I studied animation, but have ended up doing character design, which is a development that would never have happened if it were not for the internet and the opportunities it has presented me. I have found that character design is a perfect fit for me, even though I didn't know it when I started as a freelancer.

Opposite page: *Citrus*

This page: An image created to celebrate Lois reaching one million Facebook likes

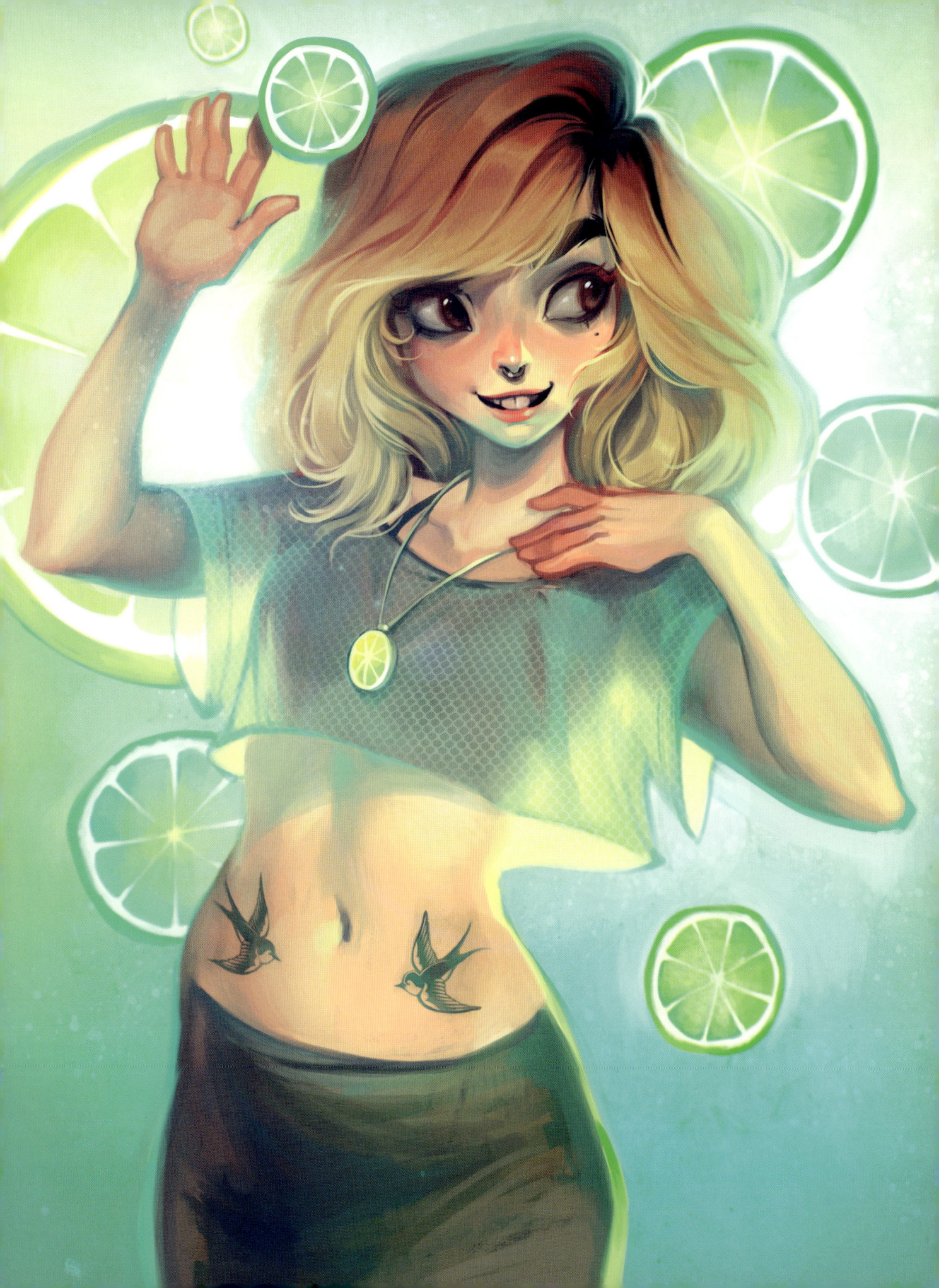

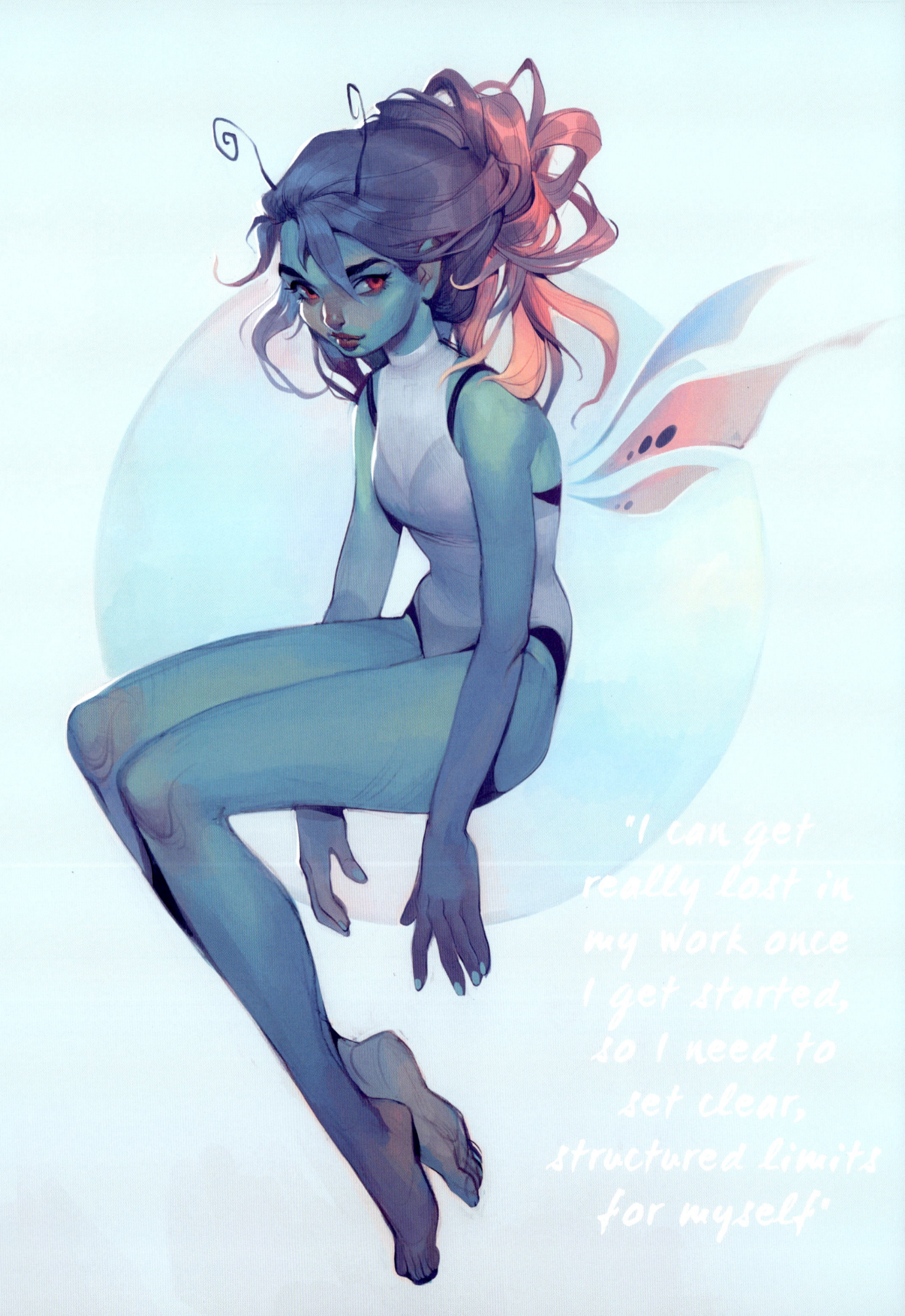

"I can get really lost in my work once I get started, so I need to set clear, structured limits for myself"

How does it feel to look back on the early days of sharing your work on DeviantArt?

It is surreal because things have changed so much in such a short time. I can fall into the trap of getting very nostalgic, because to me, things were more "pure" in the early days of internet art communities and forums.

Today's social media accounts are dominated by influencers and very unforgiving algorithms, whereas before, it was much more about the art and having small, dedicated communities. I think it is inevitable though that when looking back on the past people start to feel nostalgic that things were better before, so I try not to focus on those changes too much!

You've been a busy, freelance artist for a long time now. Could you walk us through your average day at work?

I have a studio space separate to my home and my working day usually starts there at around ten in the morning, always with a huge cup of coffee! I always start by going through my emails and doing some social media-related tasks, such as planning my posts for the day or going through my messages. I then either get started on client work, or I start on some personal art if I do not have client work scheduled for that day. I will work on my art for the rest of the day.

I end the working day by posting on social media; the evening is the best time for me to do this because the majority of my followers are online then. When I have finished my social media posts I am officially done for the day and I go home to relax!

That may sound pretty boring but I try to maintain as much structure as I can, and limit my working days to "normal" office-like hours (usually 10 am to 6 pm). Otherwise, the risk of injuring my arm from over-work or burning out becomes too great. I can get really lost in my work once I get started, so I need to set clear, structured limits for myself.

Below left: *Breathe*

Below right: *Smoulder*

Opposite: *Butterfly Girl*

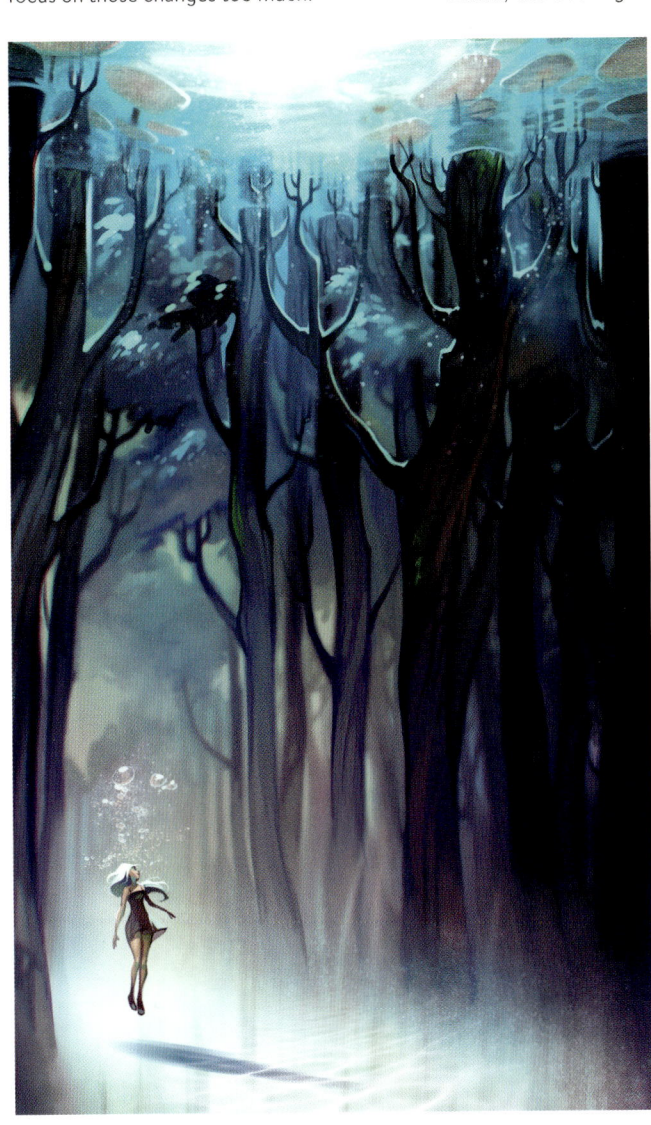

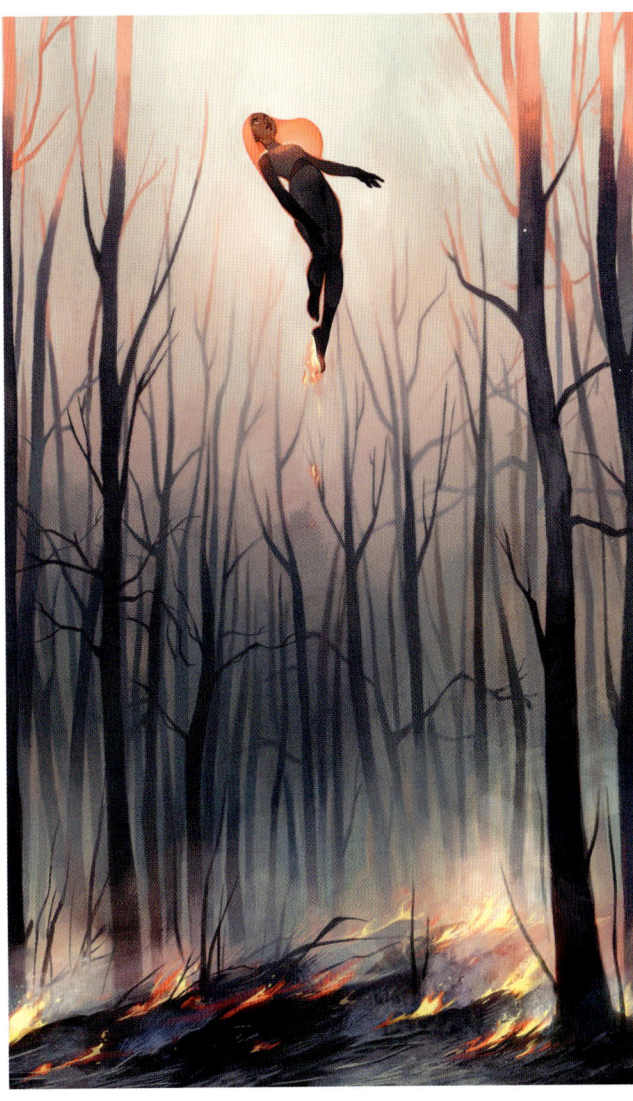

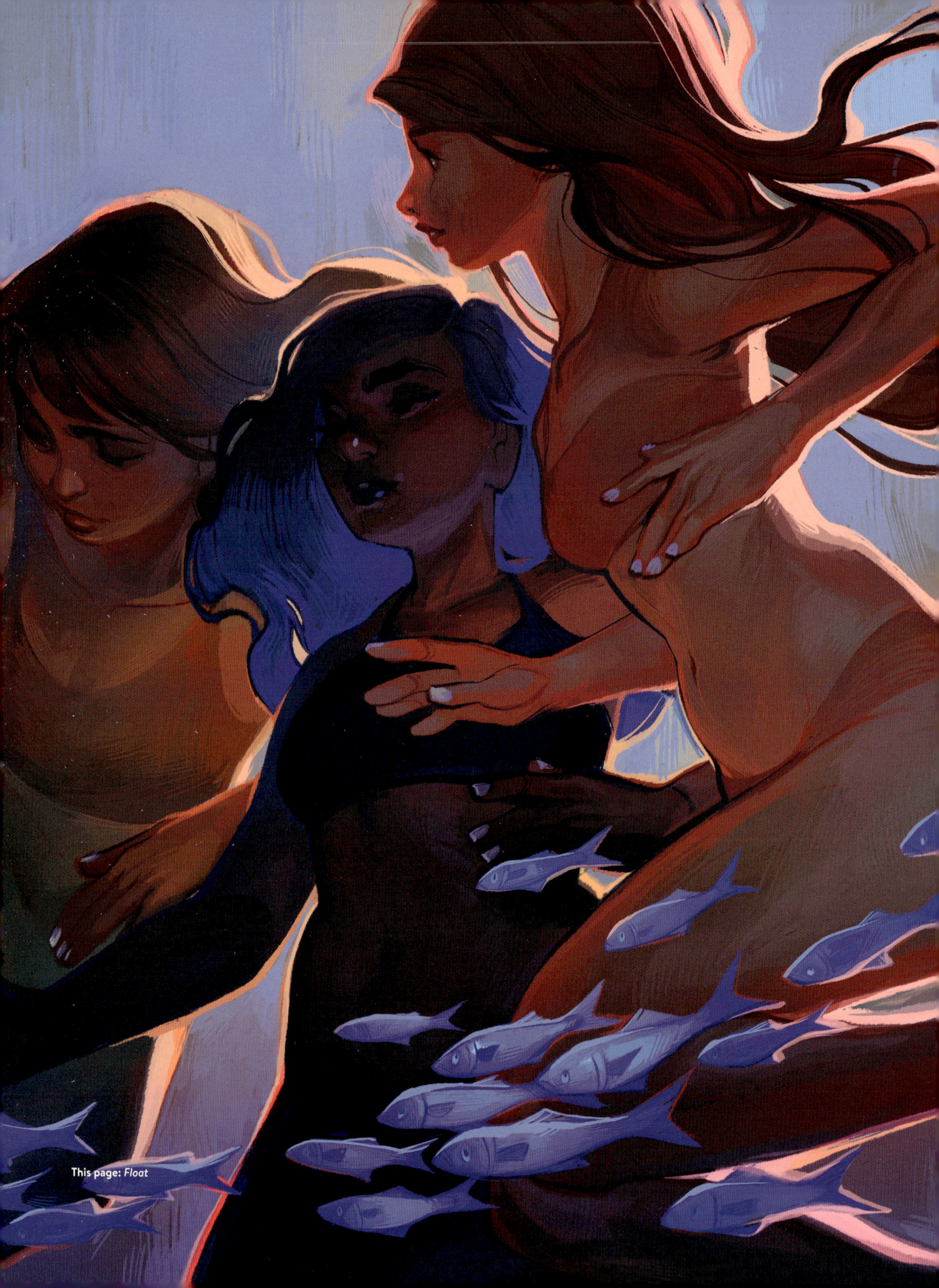

This page: *Float*

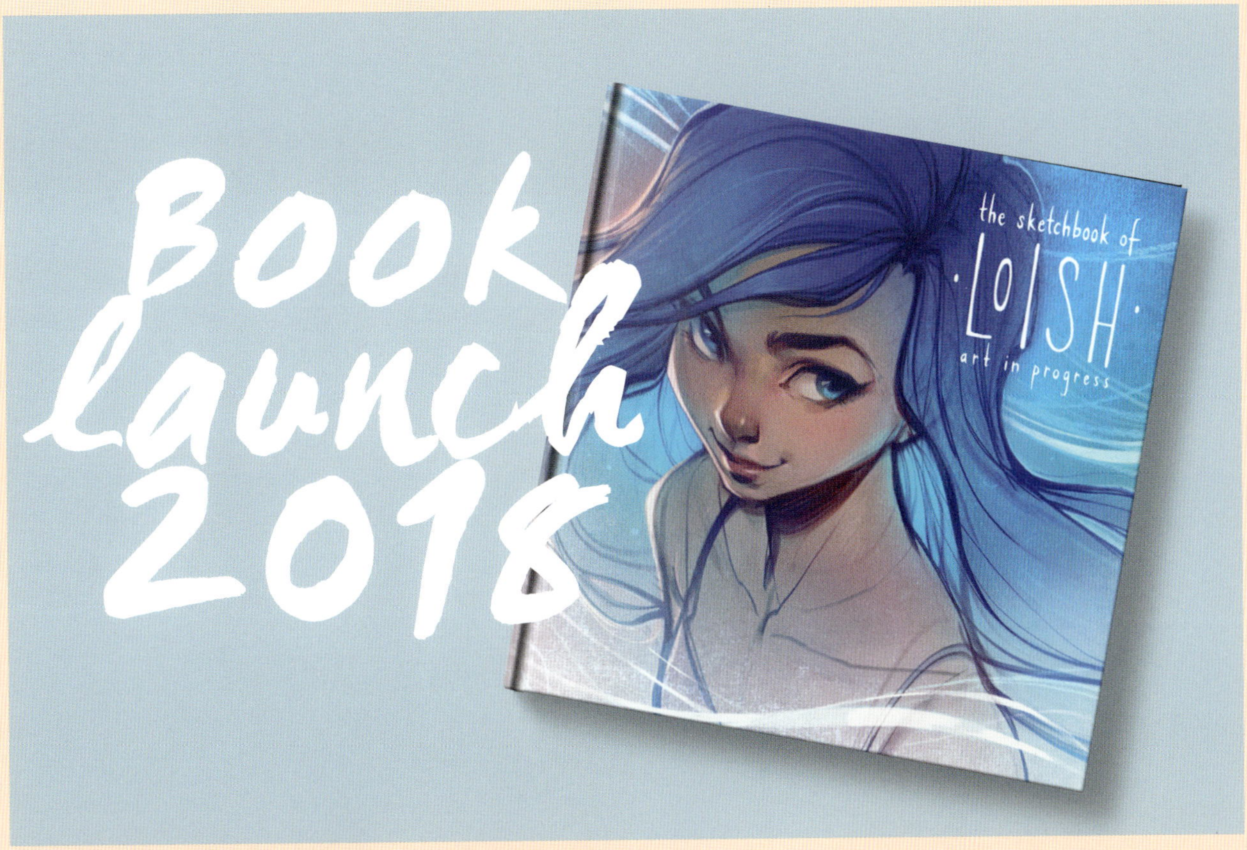

Book launch 2018

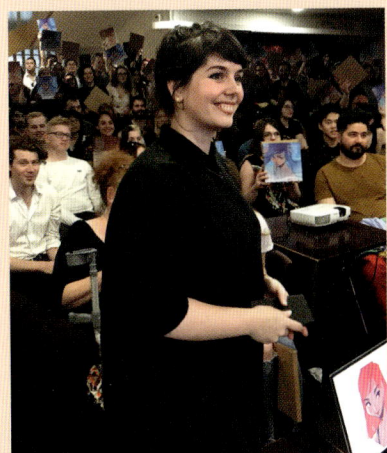

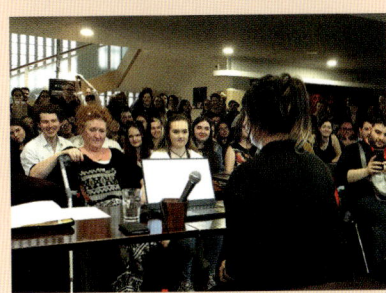

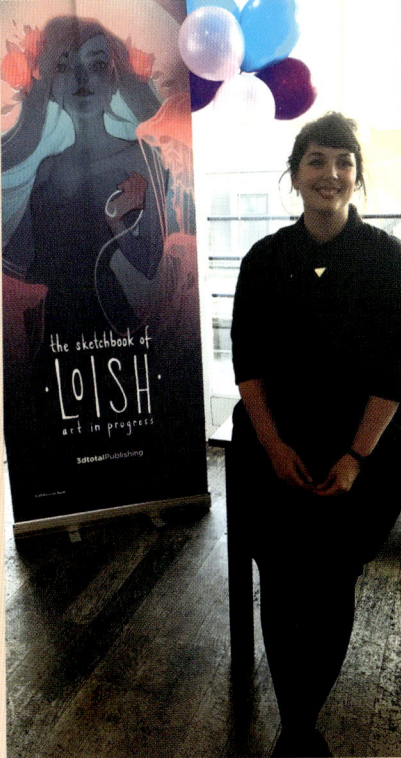

To celebrate the release of Lois's second book, *The Sketchbook of Loish: Art in Progress,* an inspiring and insightful look at her traditional and digital sketches, 3dtotal Publishing threw a spectacular launch party at Europe's largest bookstore in London. Overlooking the famous London skyline and river Thames, Lois's fans were invited to this special event to meet Lois and have their books signed. In addition to chatting to every attendee Lois also showed her process and answered questions about her work in a live digital painting demonstration. Thank you to everyone who came to meet Lois and support her work!

Find out about future events Lois is attending on her social media channels. Instagram: @loisvb, Twitter: @loishh, and Facebook: @loish.fans. You can buy a copy of *The Sketchboook of Loish: Art in Progress* or her first book, *The Art of Loish: A Look Behind the Scenes,* by going to shop.3dtotal.com.

DESIGNING FOR CHILDREN'S BOOKS

Julia Christians

Designing characters for children can be easy and fun because you can use almost anything that comes to mind to make the characters stand out. It is important to make your main character highly recognizable, to allow young readers to spot them easily in the story. Here are my tips to give your characters the originality and quirkiness that will help you to achieve this.

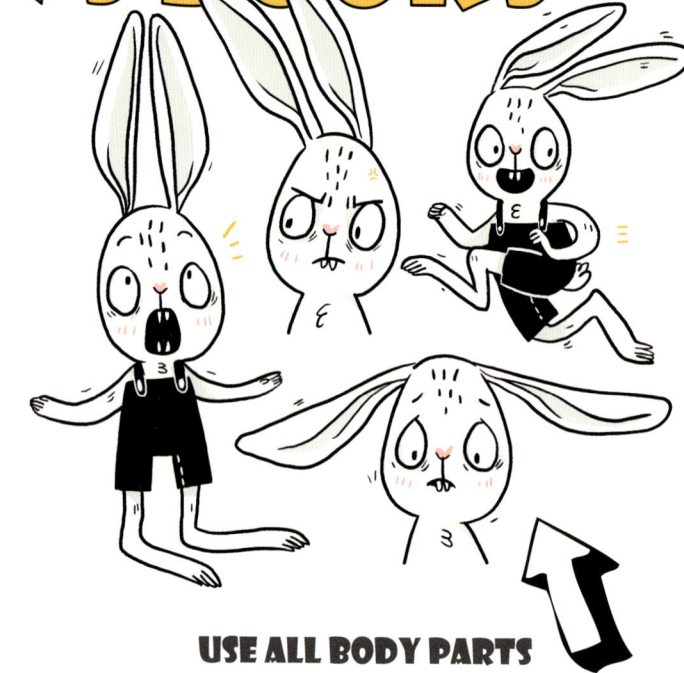

USE ALL BODY PARTS

Does your character have a tail? If so, use it! Do they have big floppy ears? Great! Use every part of the character you can to make the pose or gesture show movement, energy, and emotion.

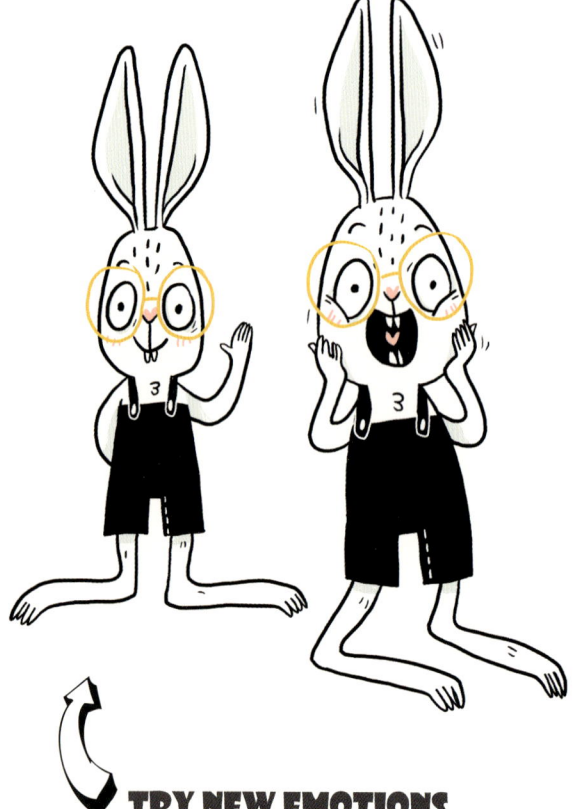

TRY NEW EMOTIONS

Experiment with different emotions and poses frequently. If you usually draw only smiling characters in a standing pose, it can be quite boring for others to look at. Have fun trying out extreme emotions, like anger, but also more obscure expressions such as curiosity or sleepiness.

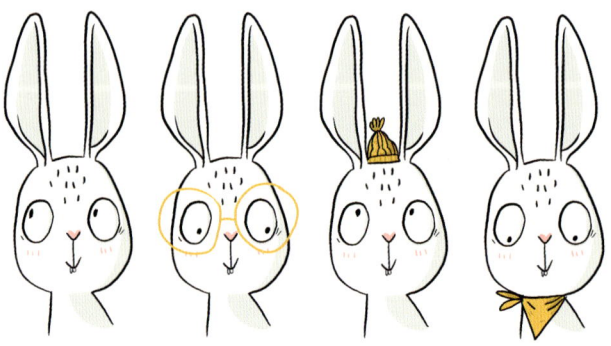

ACCESSORIZE

Add accessories to give your character a unique touch, make the design worthy of remark, and to emphasize the character's personality. Do not always go with the obvious choice either as choosing something a little unusual can make the design stand out even more.

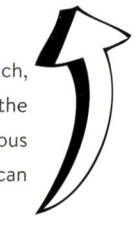

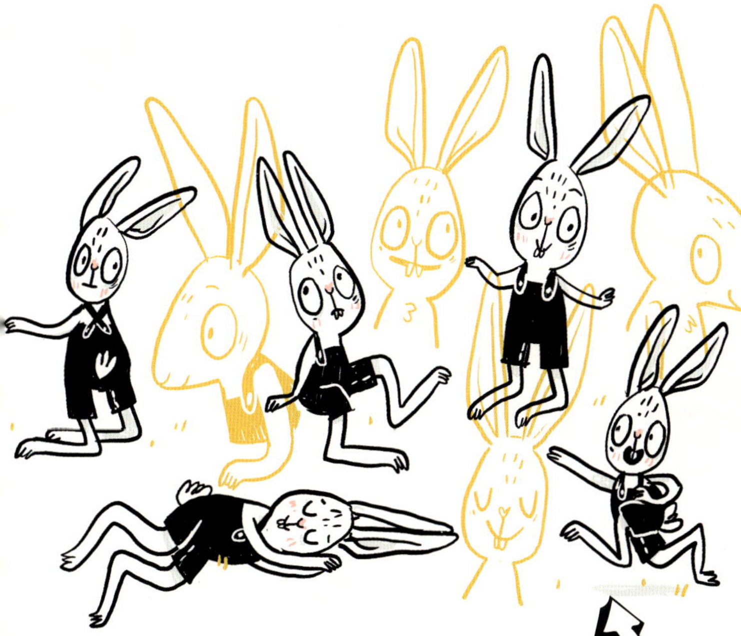

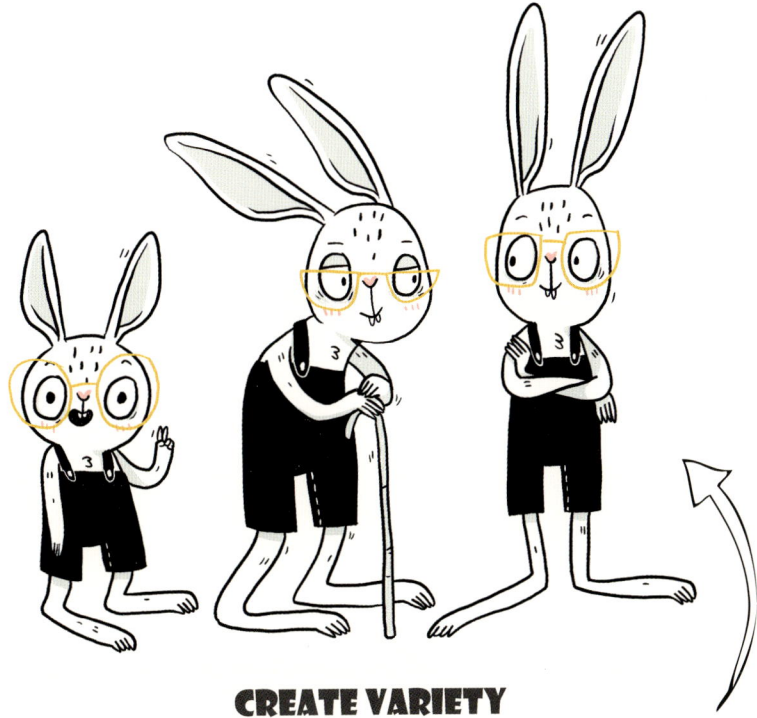

PRACTICE REPETITION

Sketch your character a lot! And I really mean a lot. The more you draw it, the more the design will develop. Even when you are satisfied with how the character looks, draw it even more to get consistency in your drawings.

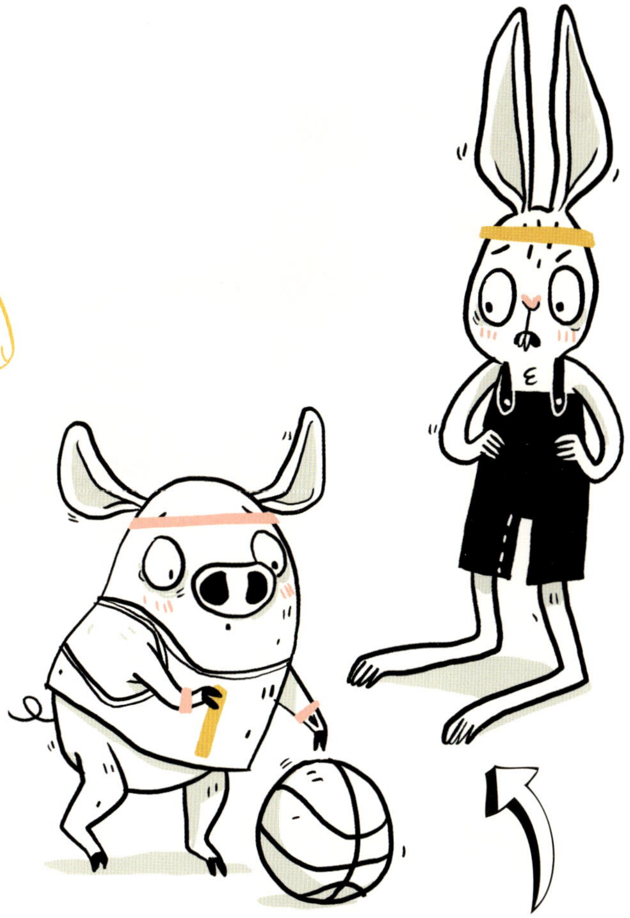

MAKE ADJUSTMENTS

When working on an animal character, think of everything your character must do in the story and how it might do those things. For example; if it is a pig, can it play basketball? How? If not, what changes can you make to your design for the story to work? The character must be functional as well as engaging.

CREATE VARIETY

Use different body shapes, races, and ages in your designs to add variety between your characters. The people you see in real life do not all look the same, so your characters should not look identical either. It is always a good idea to go outside and do some life drawing to get new ideas for character types.

PRESENTING TO ART DIRECTORS

When you apply for an illustration job in the children's book industry, show the art director you can handle your characters in any situation. Draw lots of different emotions and poses, and even show interactions with other characters or objects. Do not always go for your first idea; draw more options to see if you can push your character a little further.

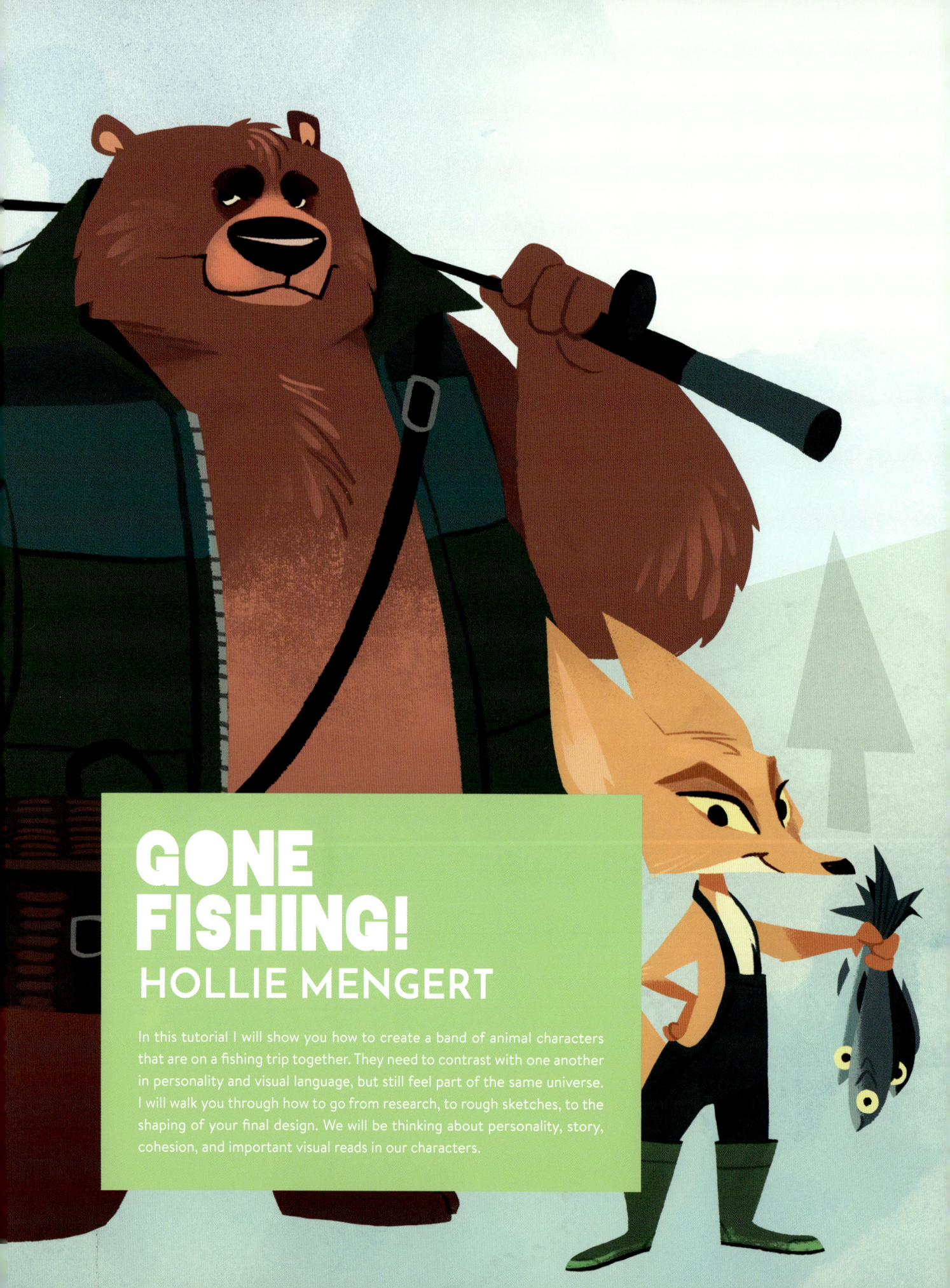

GONE FISHING!
HOLLIE MENGERT

In this tutorial I will show you how to create a band of animal characters that are on a fishing trip together. They need to contrast with one another in personality and visual language, but still feel part of the same universe. I will walk you through how to go from research, to rough sketches, to the shaping of your final design. We will be thinking about personality, story, cohesion, and important visual reads in our characters.

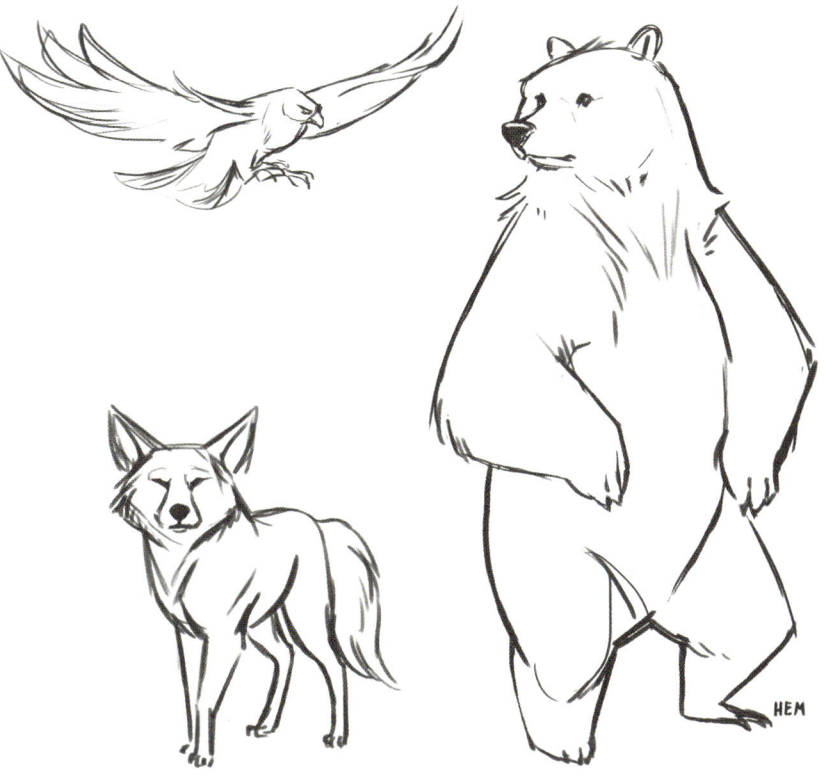

WHO AND WHAT ARE THEY?

This may seem like an obvious step, but knowing the story that you want to tell with your characters is half the battle. What they are will inform their personalities and the story, and therefore their design. This step is where I do research, find photo references, and create initial sketches. I live in the Pacific Northwest where both fish and mammals abound. The idea of a group of animal friends that would not normally be seen together sounds fun, so let's create a group with a bear, a coyote, and a hawk. Now we can start to think about the personalities of each character in our group.

INITIAL SKETCHES

This is where we test drive our initial ideas. Is Bear short or tall? Is he thin and hungry for fish? Or rotund because he is so well practiced at catching them? It is important to experiment with a variety of designs. Rarely will you find that the first design you try will be the best one. My first few sketches are fine, but they do not have the right personalities yet. I want Bear to be the leader of the group, Coyote to be mischievous, and Hawk to be intelligent and capable. Creating variety in my initial sketches helps to see what is working and what is not.

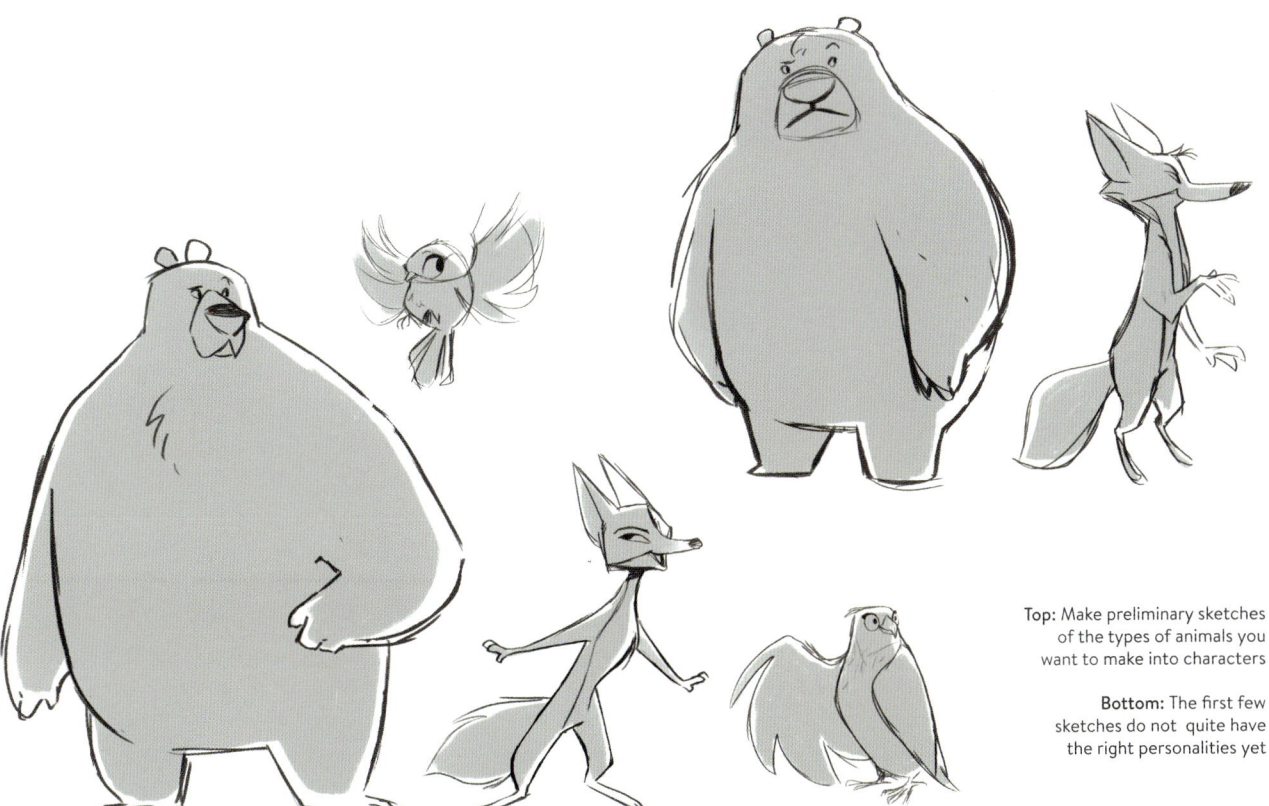

Top: Make preliminary sketches of the types of animals you want to make into characters

Bottom: The first few sketches do not quite have the right personalities yet

Right: The silhouettes clearly read as different species, but could be pushed further

Below: The characters will not perfectly hold these shapes in every pose, but being aware of them will guide the way you draw them

Opposite page: To create an interesting and dynamic grouping, each character should feel rhythmically different

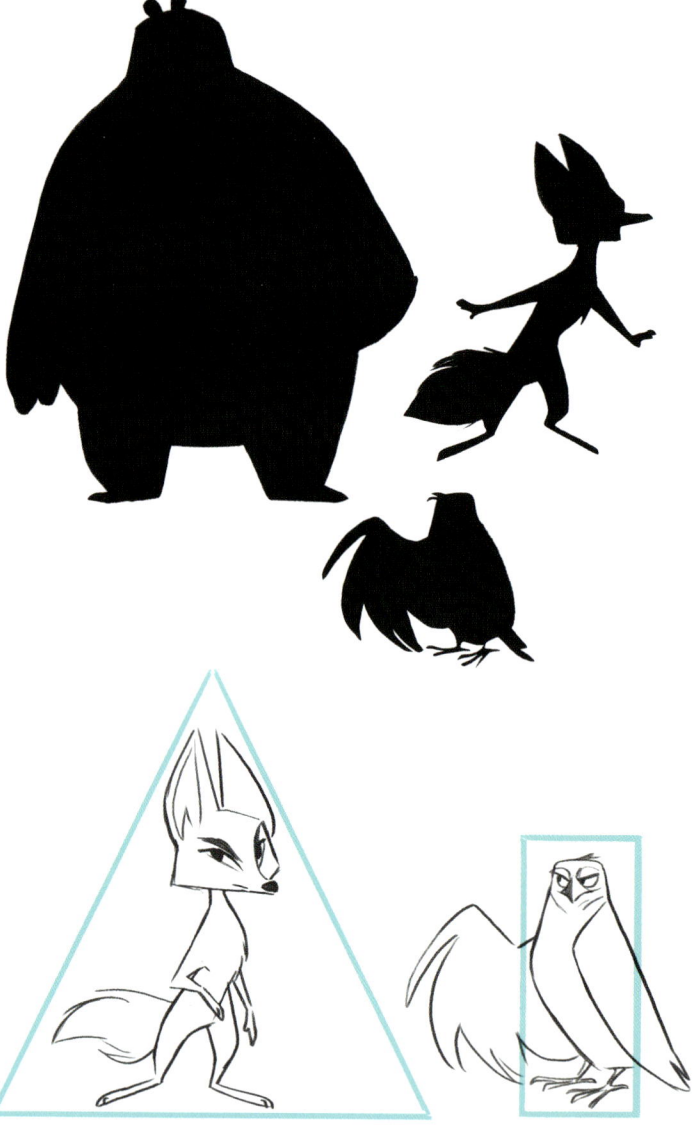

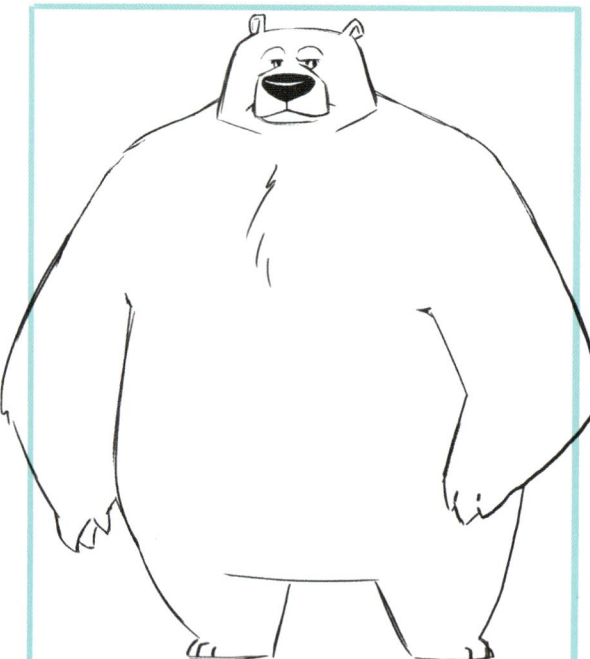

✚ INTERACTION THROUGH SHAPE

Variety in shape will keep the group dynamic and provide creative narrative options to play with. Maybe Hawk always likes to sit on Bear's head to get the best view of the lake. Maybe Coyote can barely contain his excitement in the boat, and Bear's weight is the only thing keeping them from capsizing. If they were all the same size and shape this part of the design would not be nearly as fun!

SILHOUETTES

I take my favorites of the initial sketches, convert each character into silhouette, and ask myself: Do the designs read as well in silhouette? Do they contrast with one another? This step will not take long, and will reveal problems in the design at a stage when they are simple to adjust. It is easier to make corrections at this stage than to wait until you have rendered and painted a variety of details. Here, I can tell that I want to make Bear a little broader, and Coyote a little shorter. Hawk's silhouette can be simplified and made more angular. Introducing more visual contrast between the characters will help to support the design details later in the process.

SHAPES

In character design, shape is key. If you lose their basic shape, you lose the readability of the character. Also, not every character should be the same shape. Bear should be dependable and strong, but seeing him in silhouette he does not seem sturdy enough, so I make him squarer. Coyote is almost a triangle, especially if I push his ears to be larger and more angular. These sharp angles suit his mischievous nature. Hawk is a smart, inquisitive, and agile character. I want to push him into more of a self-contained rectangle. However, this will be in contrast to his shape when he spreads his wings, showing his physical agility in addition to his mental prowess.

PROPORTIONS

Now that we have established the overall shape of each character, it is time to think more about the proportions. It is important that the proportions of characters are not too even; changing the distances between body parts will keep things interesting. Bear's head is small, his torso large and sturdy, and his legs short and grounded, emphasizing his strength and dependability. The huge ears, refined snout, and long thin torso of Coyote hint at his intelligence and awareness of the world around him. Hawk's head and body is a combined shape, his legs short, and wings broad.

If you divide the character into sections with lines, you will find them unevenly spaced, both within in each individual character, and across the whole group. These different rhythms keep each character unique and interesting. Composition is as important in character design as it is in any art artform.

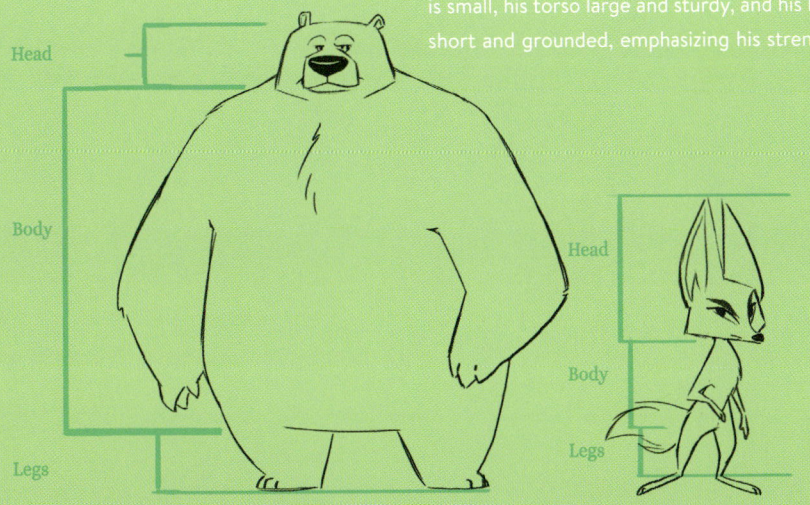

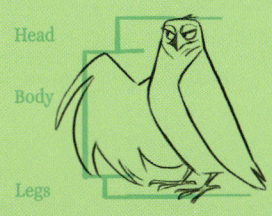

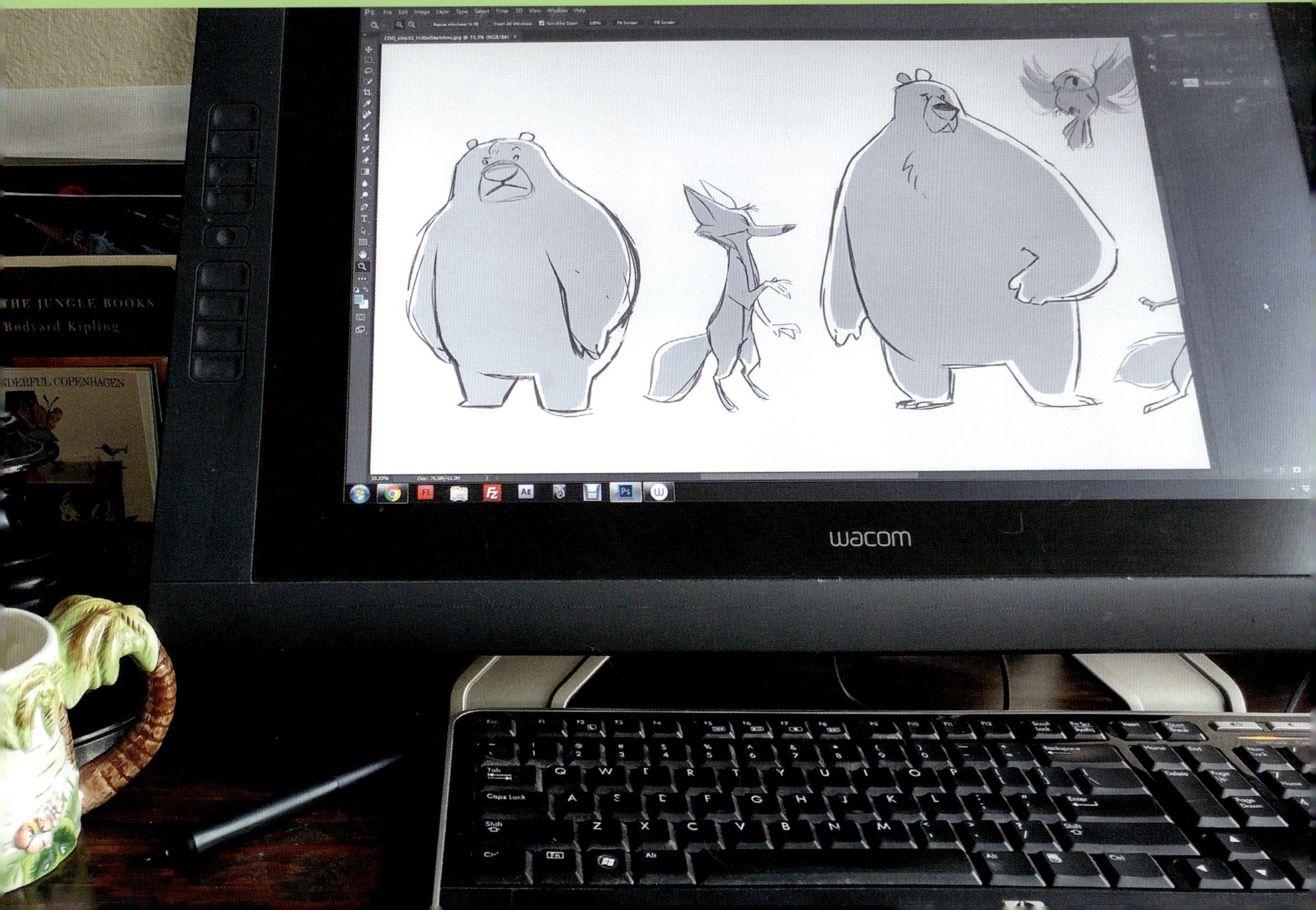

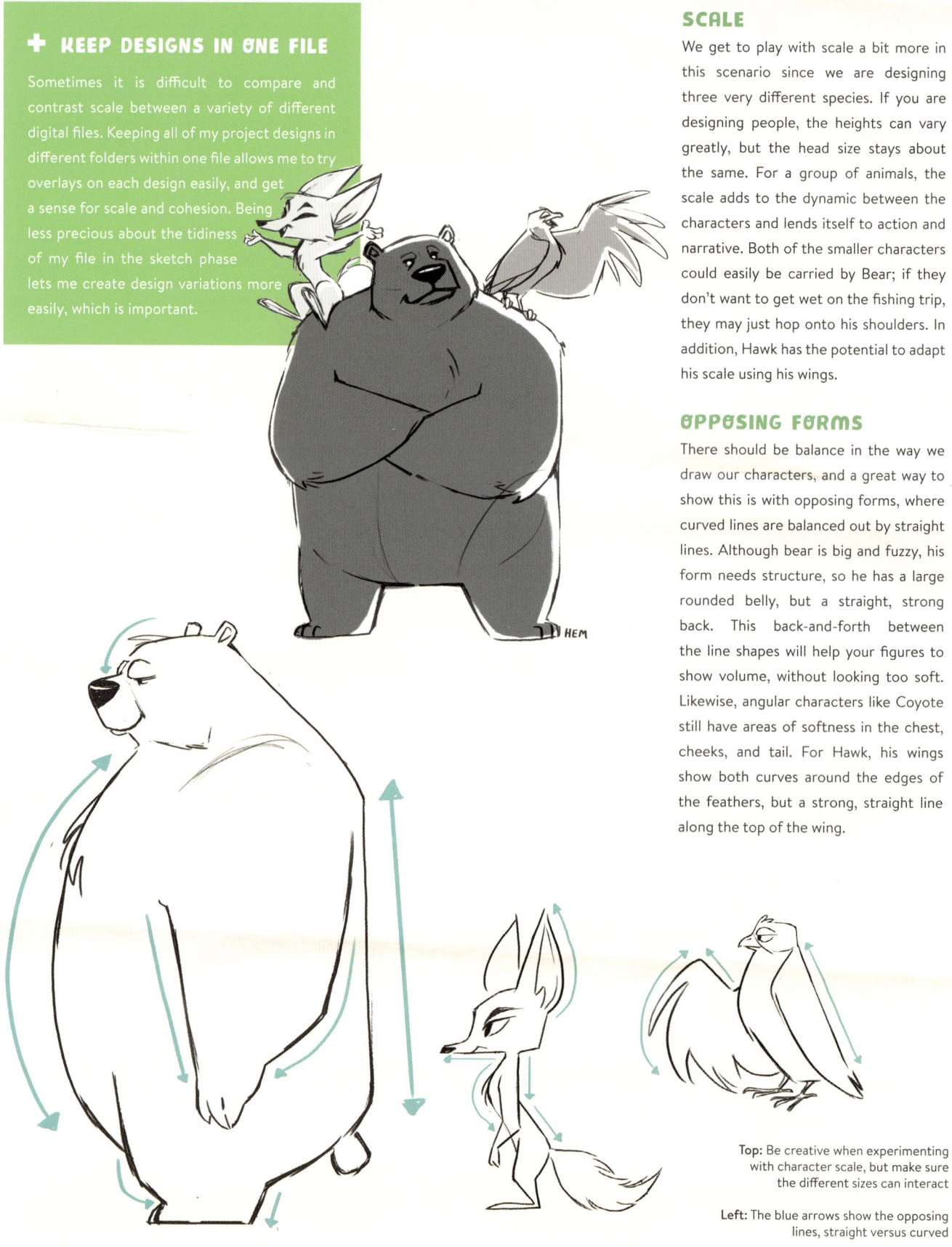

+ KEEP DESIGNS IN ONE FILE

Sometimes it is difficult to compare and contrast scale between a variety of different digital files. Keeping all of my project designs in different folders within one file allows me to try overlays on each design easily, and get a sense for scale and cohesion. Being less precious about the tidiness of my file in the sketch phase lets me create design variations more easily, which is important.

SCALE

We get to play with scale a bit more in this scenario since we are designing three very different species. If you are designing people, the heights can vary greatly, but the head size stays about the same. For a group of animals, the scale adds to the dynamic between the characters and lends itself to action and narrative. Both of the smaller characters could easily be carried by Bear; if they don't want to get wet on the fishing trip, they may just hop onto his shoulders. In addition, Hawk has the potential to adapt his scale using his wings.

OPPOSING FORMS

There should be balance in the way we draw our characters, and a great way to show this is with opposing forms, where curved lines are balanced out by straight lines. Although bear is big and fuzzy, his form needs structure, so he has a large rounded belly, but a straight, strong back. This back-and-forth between the line shapes will help your figures to show volume, without looking too soft. Likewise, angular characters like Coyote still have areas of softness in the chest, cheeks, and tail. For Hawk, his wings show both curves around the edges of the feathers, but a strong, straight line along the top of the wing.

Top: Be creative when experimenting with character scale, but make sure the different sizes can interact

Left: The blue arrows show the opposing lines, straight versus curved

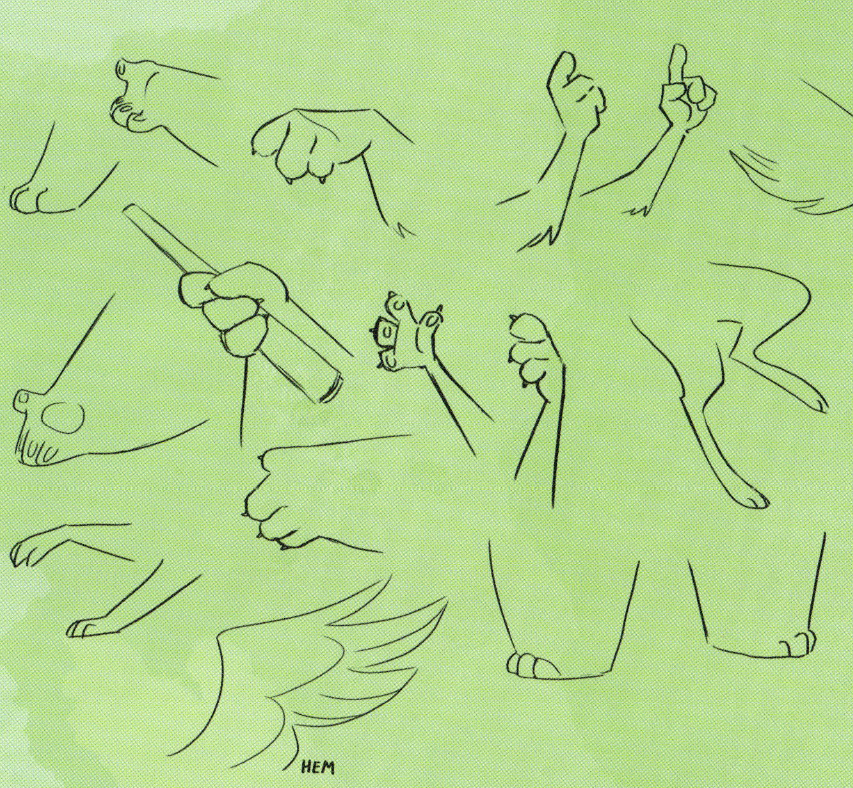

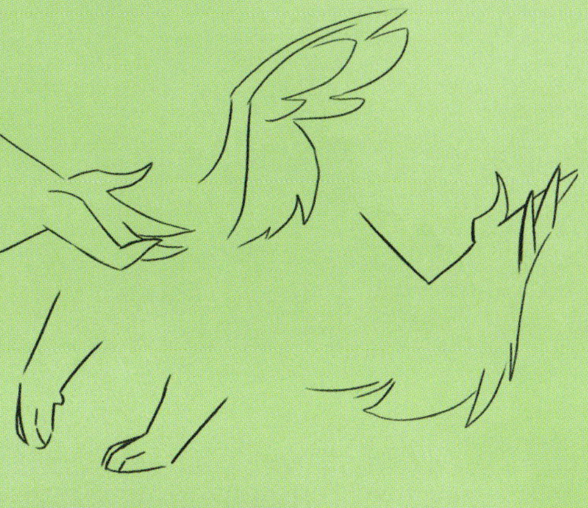

HEM

HANDS AND FEET

Whether designing animals or people, hands and feet are important. They are highly expressive of moods and action, and it is important to carry their detail through the design process. Is your story grounded in reality, or does your character have fewer fingers or toes than usual? The number of fingers, toes, nails, and claws must stay consistent throughout your character's poses, especially if they are to be animated. This group of characters needs to handle fishing gear. Making each character equally capable helps to ground them in the same universe.

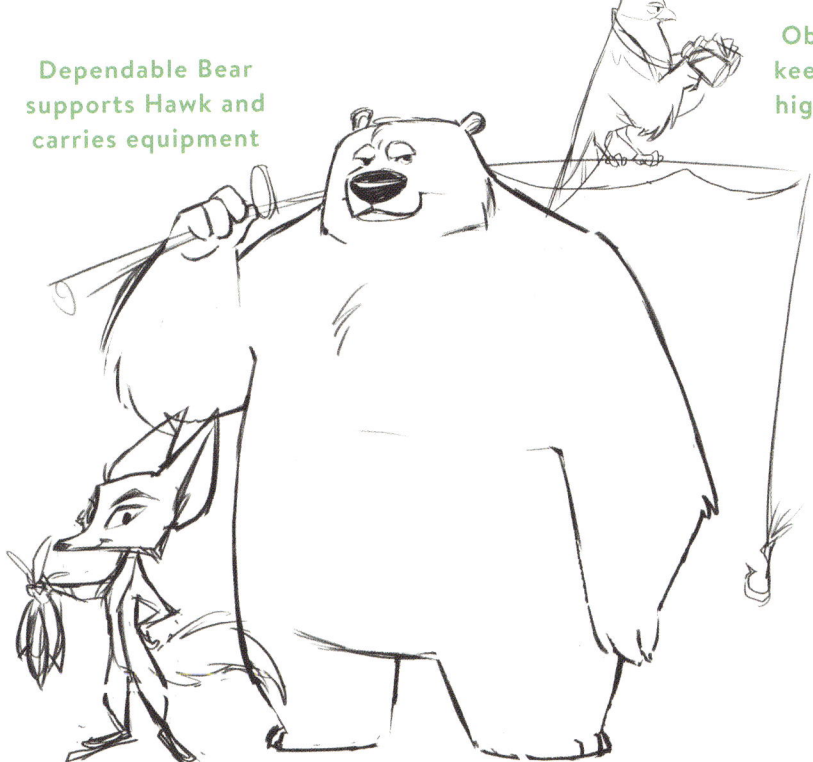

Dependable Bear supports Hawk and carries equipment

Observant Hawk keeps watch from high for the team

Adventurous Coyote leads the team from the front

POSING

Posing is tricky as you are not only establishing the best looking pose, but are also conveying the attitude of the character. Posing is the time to show everything we know about our characters and tell the whole story. It can take a lot of explorations before you find something that you feel expresses the character exactly. For this scenario, I wanted poses that made our animals feel like a team. Hawk is small so he prefers to be up high to keep an eye on things. Coyote is full of enthusiasm out in front, striking a reassured pose, while Bear is the more relaxed-looking anchor of the group.

Top: Create a page of hand and feet explorations to allow you to observe the same choices from different angles

Left: The close stance, while showing that each character has their own role, shows the formation of a team

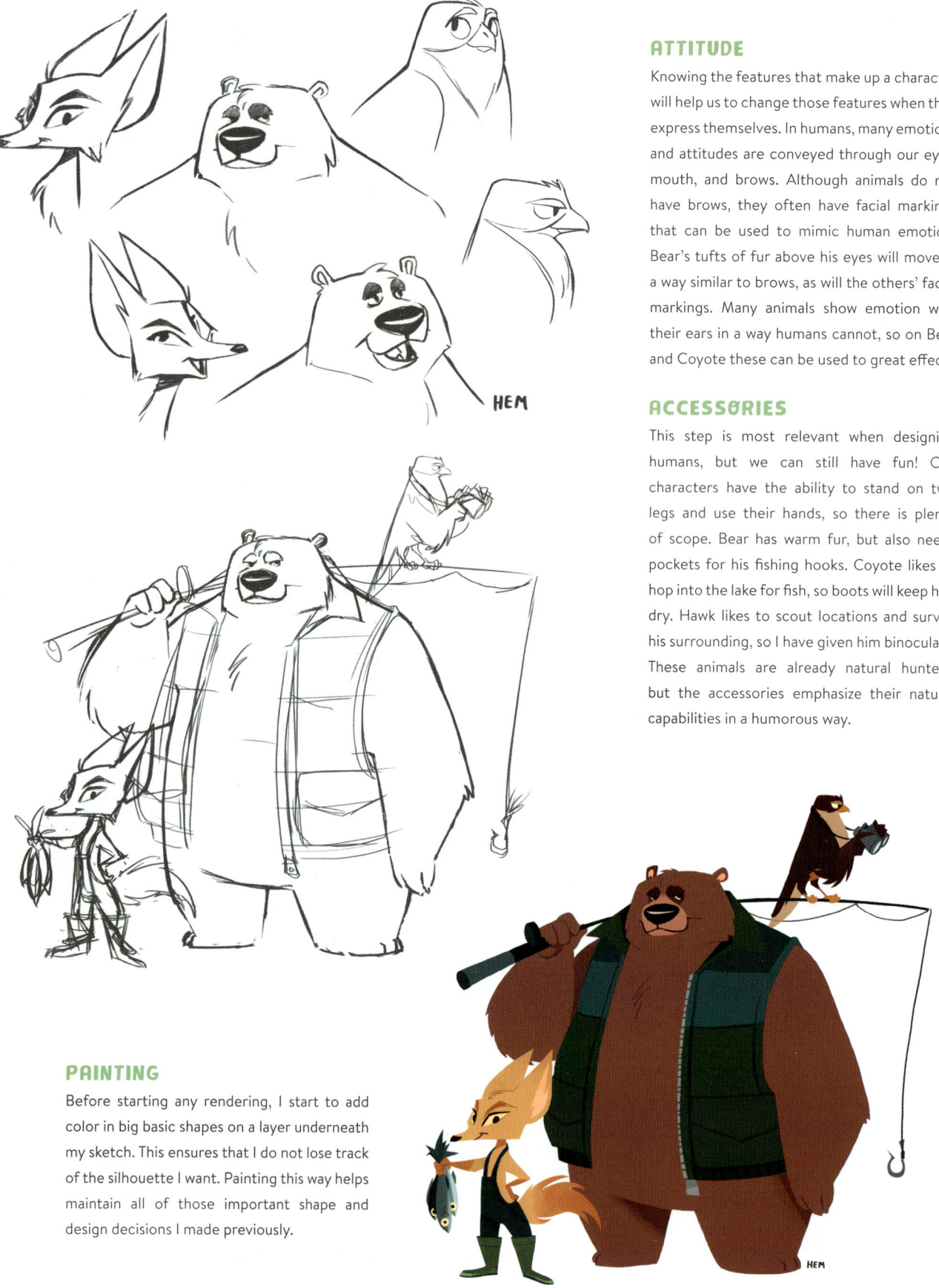

ATTITUDE

Knowing the features that make up a character will help us to change those features when they express themselves. In humans, many emotions and attitudes are conveyed through our eyes, mouth, and brows. Although animals do not have brows, they often have facial markings that can be used to mimic human emotion. Bear's tufts of fur above his eyes will move in a way similar to brows, as will the others' facial markings. Many animals show emotion with their ears in a way humans cannot, so on Bear and Coyote these can be used to great effect.

ACCESSORIES

This step is most relevant when designing humans, but we can still have fun! Our characters have the ability to stand on two legs and use their hands, so there is plenty of scope. Bear has warm fur, but also needs pockets for his fishing hooks. Coyote likes to hop into the lake for fish, so boots will keep him dry. Hawk likes to scout locations and survey his surrounding, so I have given him binoculars. These animals are already natural hunters, but the accessories emphasize their natural capabilities in a humorous way.

PAINTING

Before starting any rendering, I start to add color in big basic shapes on a layer underneath my sketch. This ensures that I do not lose track of the silhouette I want. Painting this way helps maintain all of those important shape and design decisions I made previously.

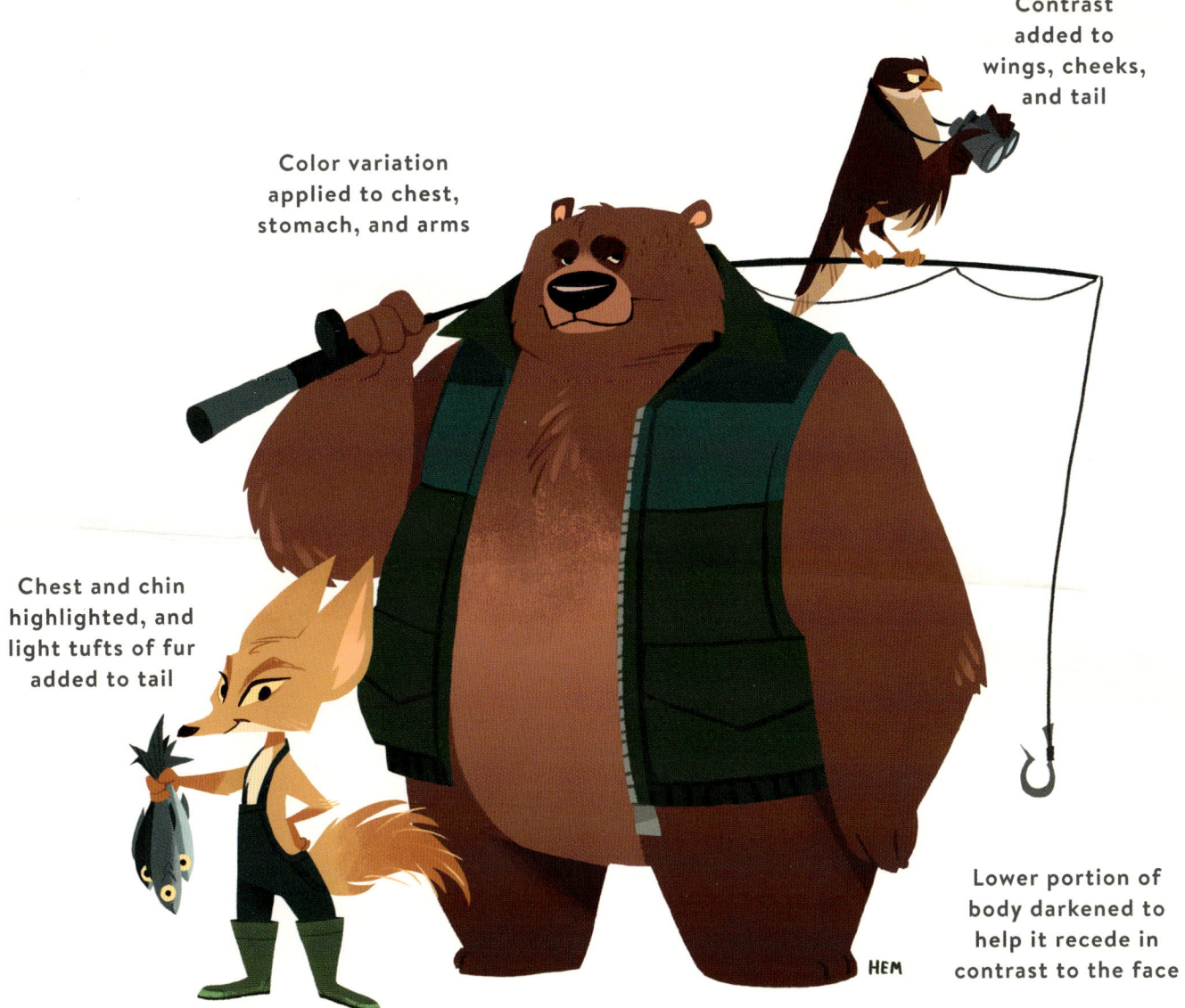

Contrast added to wings, cheeks, and tail

Color variation applied to chest, stomach, and arms

Chest and chin highlighted, and light tufts of fur added to tail

Lower portion of body darkened to help it recede in contrast to the face

HEM

Opposite top: Draw several different expressions before committing to one for each character

Opposite middle: Roughly block in the accessories over the group sketch

Opposite bottom: Once the base colors are blocked in, hide the sketch layer

Above: Use contast within individual designs to direct the viewer's focus

FOCUS

What do you want the viewer to look at most? What should be their first impression of each character? It is important to exaggerate the areas in which your character will be communicating with the audience. I keep my focal reads around the face, and recede detail on the lower parts of the body. This helps to make facial expressions the primary focus. I add color variation to both Bear and Coyote to give them more contrast. I darken Bear's lower body to help it recede more than his face and shoulders. For Hawk, I add color variation to his wings, cheeks, and tail feathers.

+ VALUE JUDGMENTS

I always view my paintings in black and white at stages during the coloring process. Ensuring you have contrasting values will make your illustrations pop, and keep them readable. Whenever color or design starts to feel too even or muddy, view your paintings in black and white to check the values. This will usually reveal the problem and help you to fix it.

DETAILS

Much of what we have covered so far will help create details that are motivated by the characters and scene we have created, instead of the other way around. Zoom out or stand back from your artwork. Are there areas on your character that look empty? Are there areas that have too much going on? If the characters read well from a distance, then you have been successful! If they are getting lost from a distance then it is time to edit your painting to make the character's faces and features read more clearly.

COLOR COHESION

Finally, I adjust the tonal levels and experiment with different hue adjustments to brighten my painting and unify the characters. Different variations of the same color scheme tie the three characters together. I made this palette full of earth tones, because these characters are nature lovers after all.

Right: To add more detail to balance out the composition, a lure is added to Bear's fishing line, and he is given a fishing basket

Opposite page: Here is the finished group!

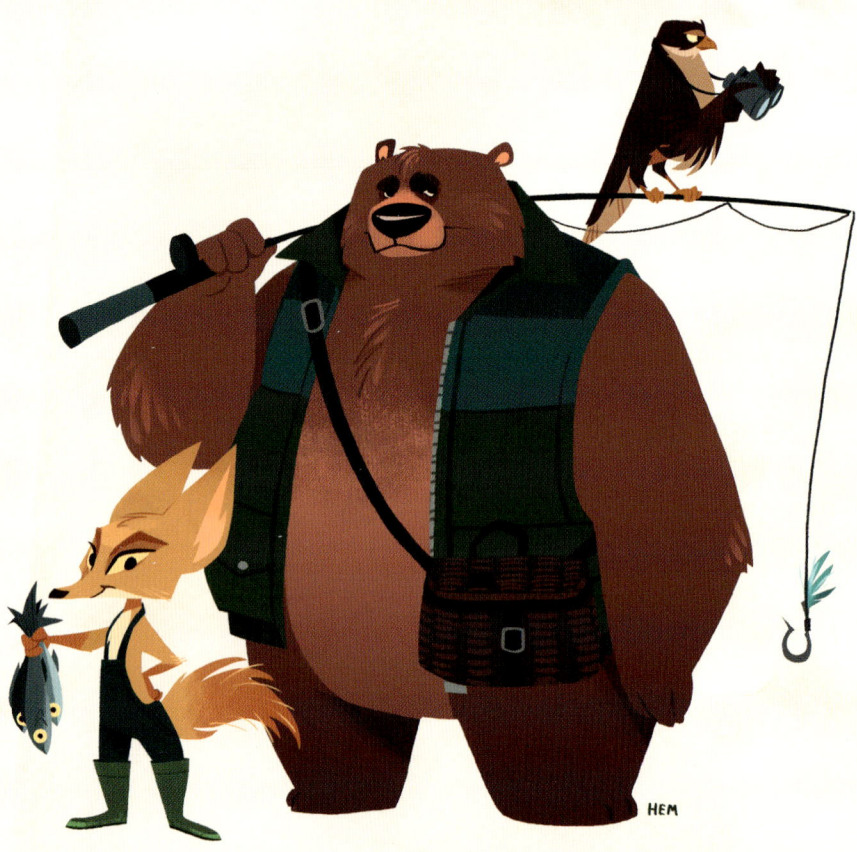

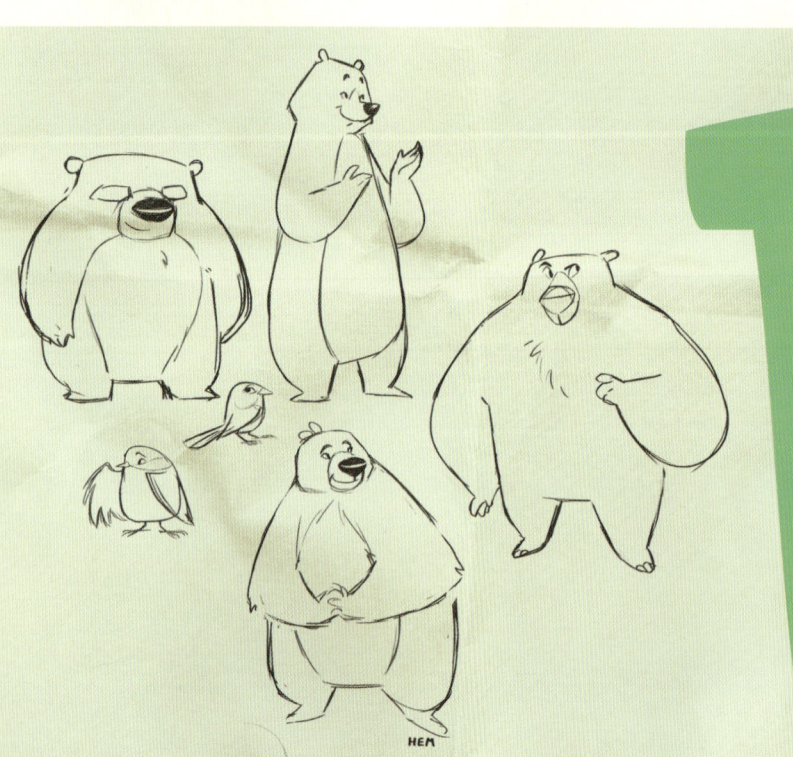

IDEAS TRASH CAN

Sometimes you need to explore what does not work in order to find something that does. In this case my Bear designs varied from too old to too friendly. Instead I chose one that looked like a capable fisherman. For Hawk, I wanted to play with his size, however making the design small and round made him unreadable as this particular type of bird. In the end, I thought it was more valuable to choose animal designs that looked as if they could embark upon a successful fishing trip.

"DIFFERENT VARIATIONS OF THE SAME COLOR SCHEME TIE THE THREE CHARACTERS TOGETHER"

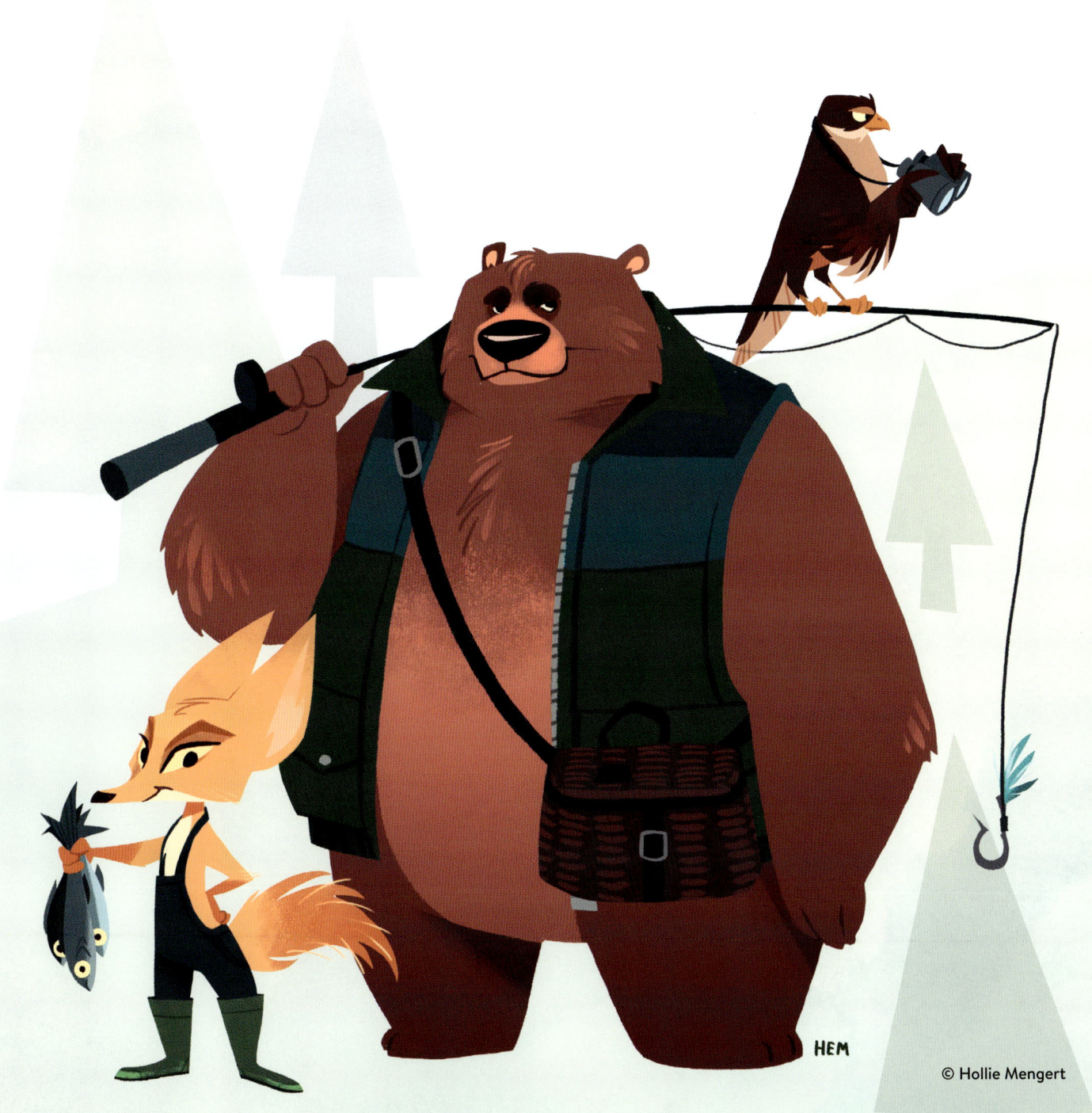

MEET THE ARTIST
James A. Castillo

After taking a seat in the big top to watch his captivating circus troupe
come to life in the previous issue, we wanted to chat further to Art Director
and Character Designer, James A. Castillo about his route into the industry
and what he's working on at the moment. In addition to sharing his current
project, *Madrid Noir*, James also talks to us about the essential skills he
needs as an Art Director, the future of the animation industry, and why it's
important to engage with your surroundings, wherever you are in the world.

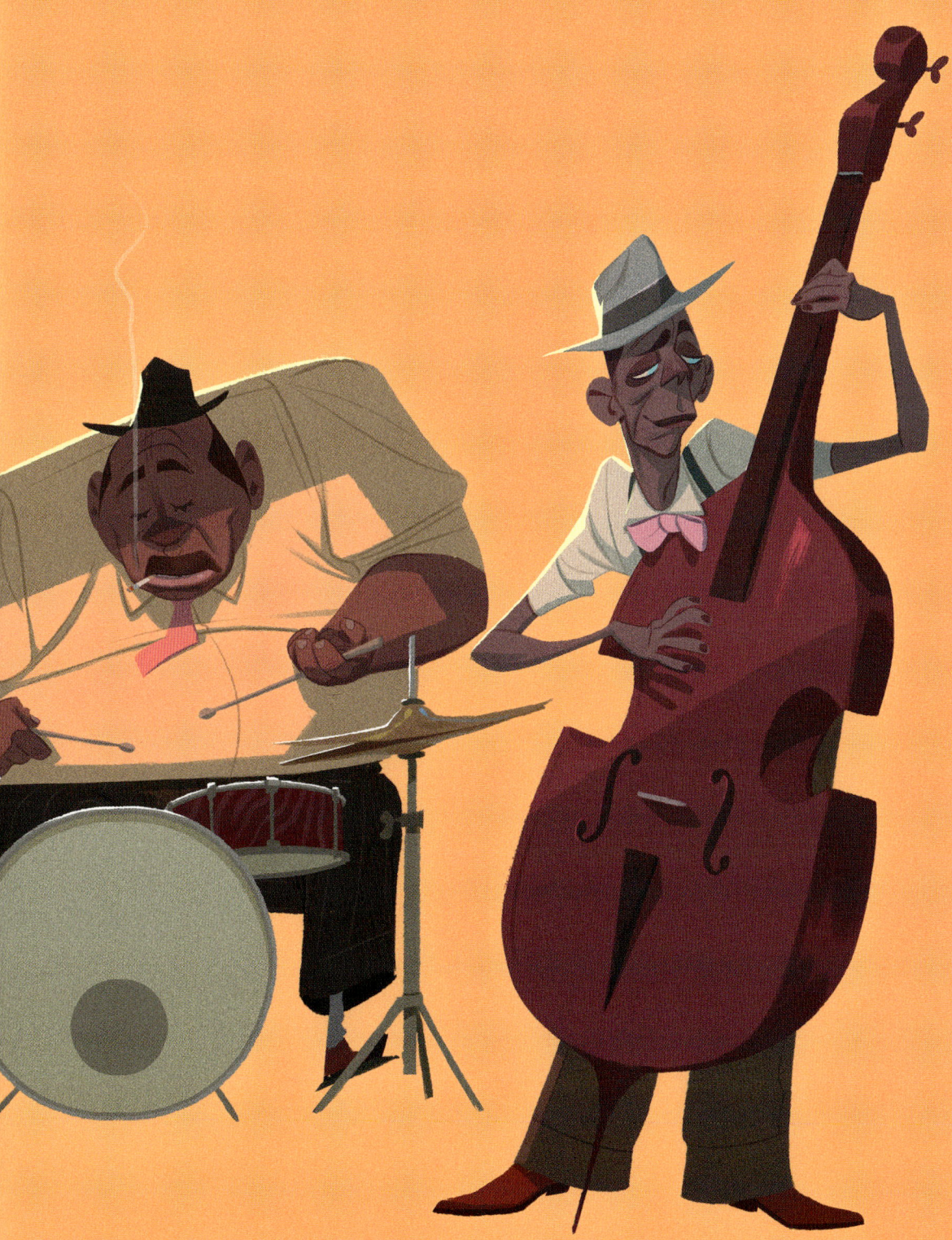

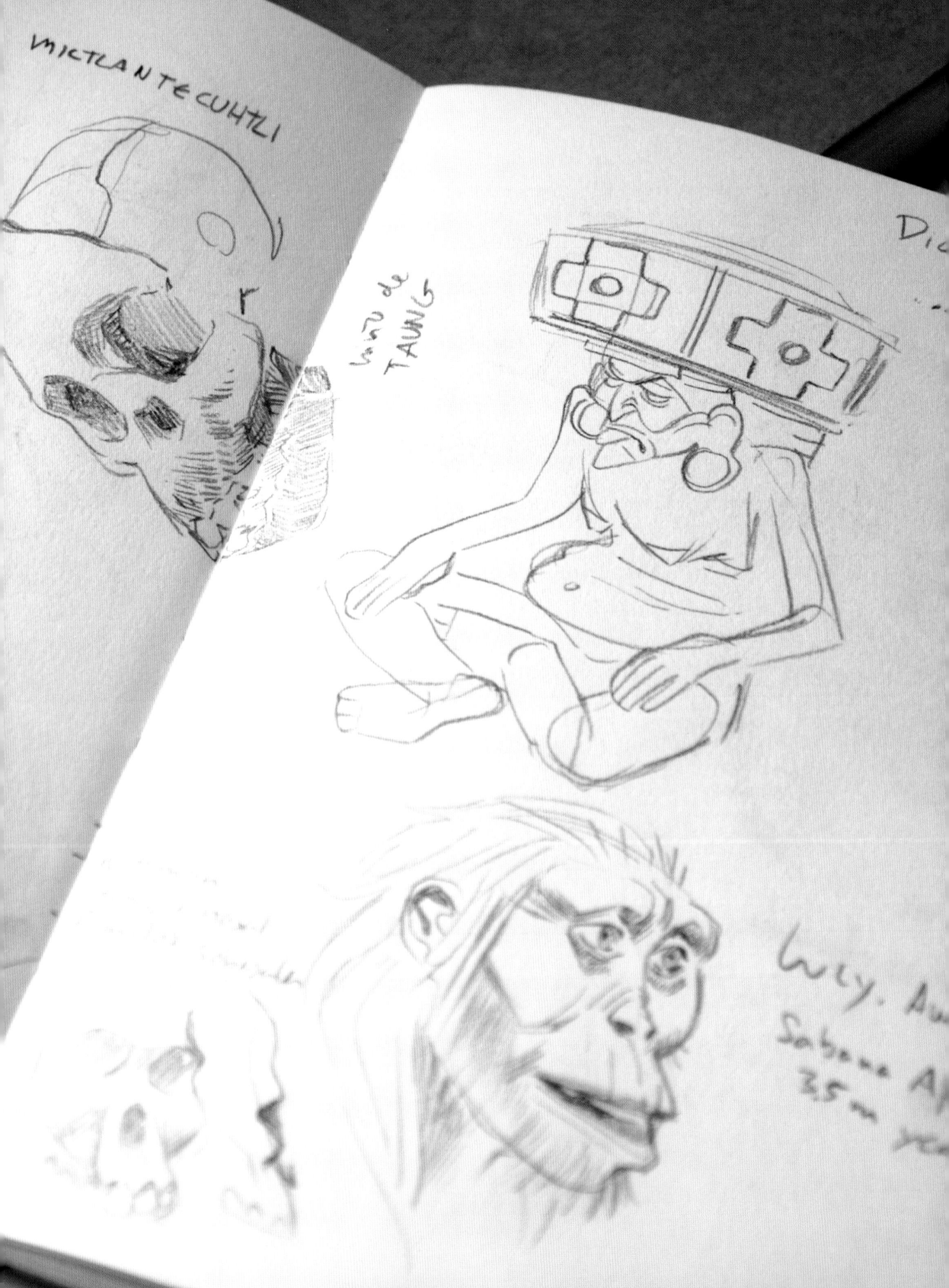

VMICTLAN TECUHTLI

main de
TAUNG

Di

Lucy. Au
Sabana A
35 m
y

HI JAMES! FOR ANYONE WHO ISN'T YET FAMILIAR WITH YOU AND YOUR WORK, COULD YOU INTRODUCE YOURSELF?

¡Hola a todos! It's a pleasure to talk with you guys. My name is James A. Castillo, and I was born and raised in Madrid, Spain. I always wanted to draw comics as a child, but ended up taking a course in 2D Animation in a local school, where they had a collection of animation art books. That opened my eyes to the artistic underbelly of animation production and I fell in love with it.

I went on to study animation at 3D Sense Media School in Singapore. During my studies I also worked as a freelancer for a variety of projects in my free time which, after I finished school, gave me something of a portfolio.

When I started working for mobile game companies, I spent my free time learning and investing in online courses to develop my skills further. In 2015 I moved to London to pursue my career as a character designer. Since then I have been very lucky to have worked with clients such as Paramount Pictures, Sony Pictures, and Nexus Studios among others.

IN YOUR EXPERIENCE, DOES THE EDUCATION AND TRAINING OF A CANDIDATE INFLUENCE THEIR CHANCES OF PICKING UP A GOOD ROLE?

That's a tricky question to answer. So much in this industry is about timing, with no "good" or "bad" way of getting into the industry. Once you have achieved a high standard of work, no one cares where or how you were taught.

There is so much information online, so many amazing teachers creating content of the highest quality that schools have a hard time competing with that. However, the one thing that schools have that's irreplaceable is the network of contacts you make – internships, classmates, teachers, and others.

Also, go to events! Save money to attend international festivals and local workshops. Meet people, say "Hi," and show your work. Invest in your career. I didn't go to a big school and couldn't do internships while studying, but still found a consistent flow of work. In the end, we all get to the same place: we have a good enough portfolio, we know a few people in the industry, and we have the passion to work hard. That's where your career starts.

"GO TO EVENTS! SAVE MONEY TO ATTEND INTERNATIONAL FESTIVALS AND LOCAL WORKSHOPS. MEET PEOPLE, SAY "HI," AND SHOW YOUR WORK"

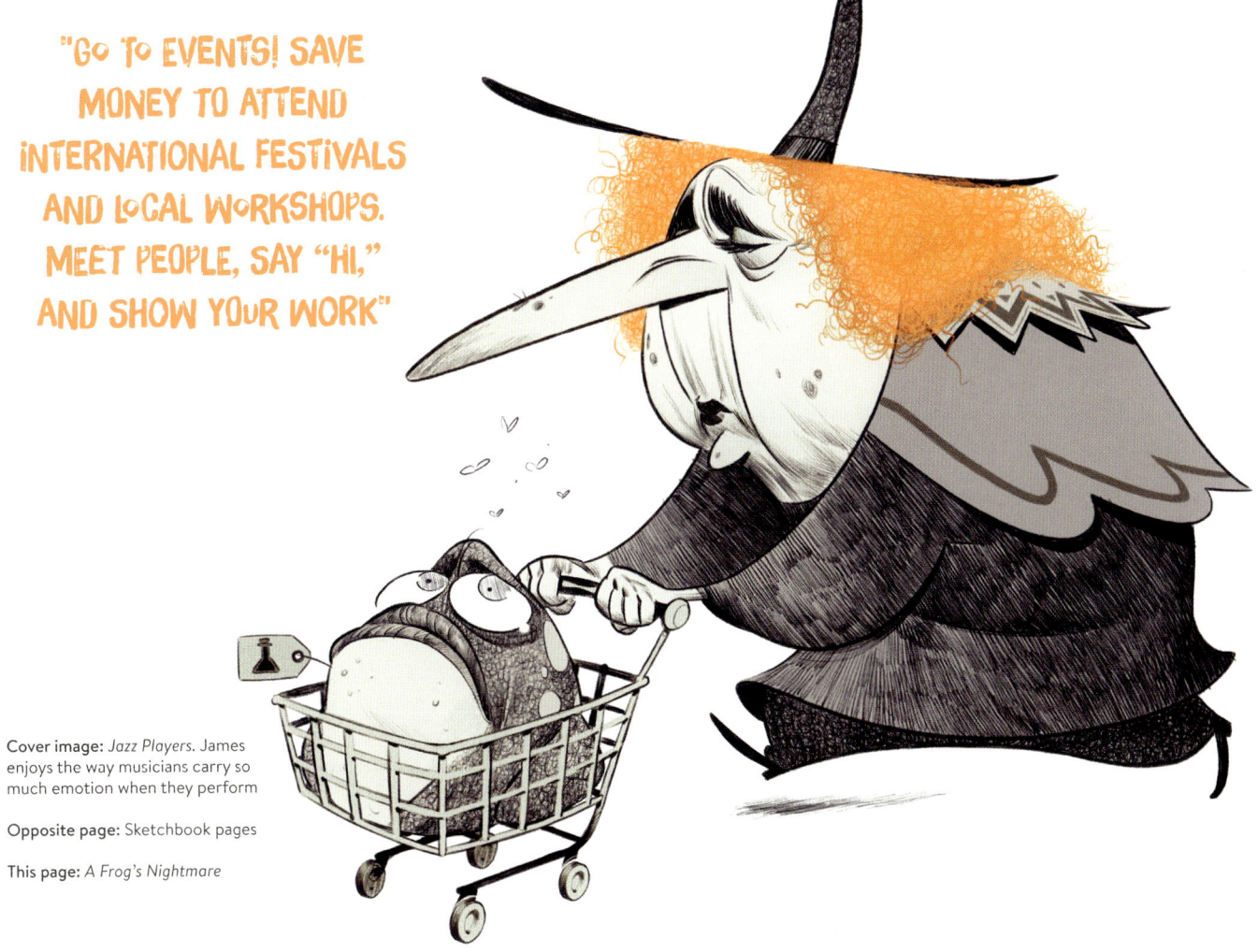

Cover image: *Jazz Players*. James enjoys the way musicians carry so much emotion when they perform

Opposite page: Sketchbook pages

This page: *A Frog's Nightmare*

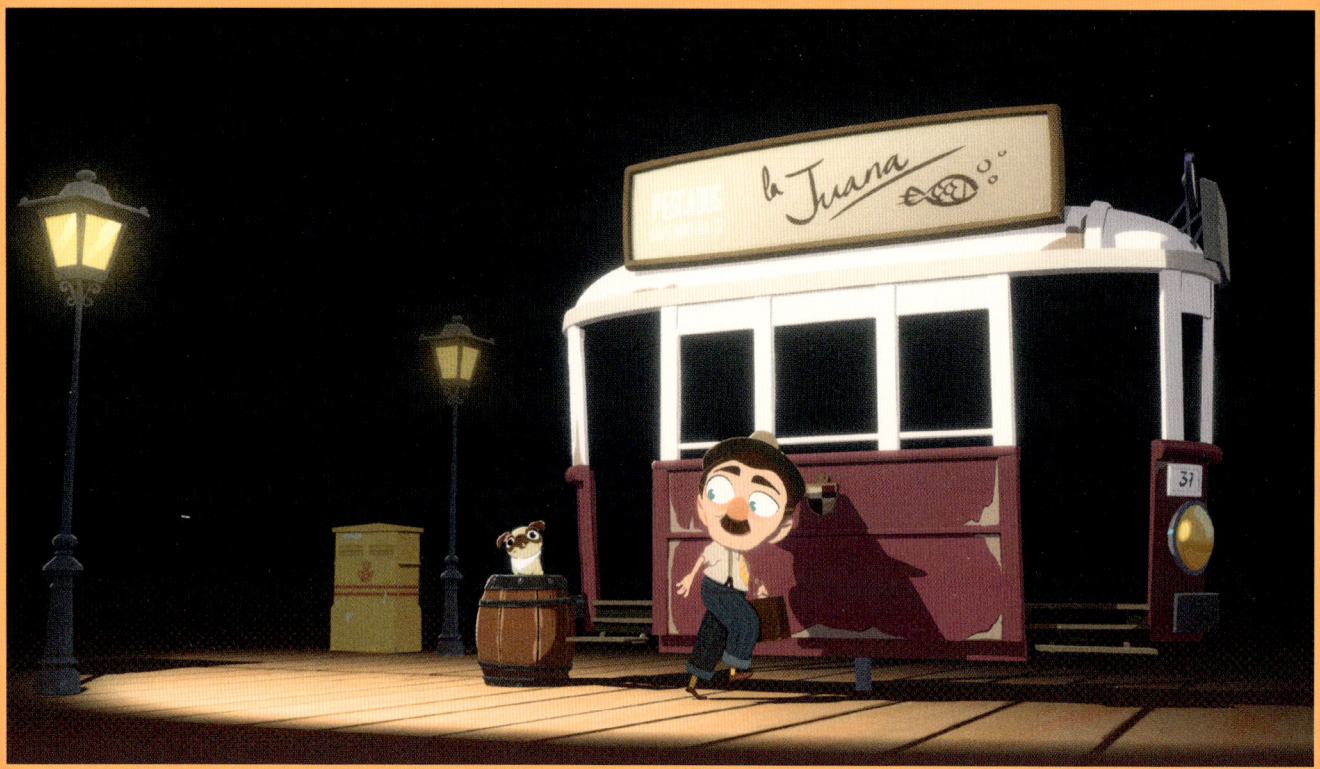

ON YOUR INSTAGRAM ACCOUNT, YOU DESCRIBE YOURSELF AS AN ART DIRECTOR. CAN YOU GIVE US SOME INSIGHT INTO HOW THAT ROLE WORKS FOR YOU AS AN ARTIST?

Art directing is a bit tricky to describe – an animation production is a very complex beast and each production needs Art Directors with different skills. As a general rule, an Art Director is responsible for defining and maintaining a cohesive artistic style through all the aspects that define a production. This means researching and communicating with all the artists, modelers, shading artists, character designers, and others to make sure that everyone has a clear idea of what you are trying to accomplish.

There is a management element to the role of Art Director; you are in constant communication with producers, directors, and leads, so you have to have a clear understanding of the pipeline and what each department needs from you. This means that you won't necessarily be drawing all the time, but creating mood boards and briefs for others in the team to follow.

Creating less art while doing more management can make frustration a real issue, depending on the size of the production. In a project like *Madrid Noir* (more on this later), which is a five-minute virtual reality experience with three characters and a theater set, I get to do a lot of the drawing work. I have a small team of artists that help me out with color keys and production design, but I get to be at the drawing board a lot.

In a bigger production, you probably won't be able to draw much, especially as the production picks up speed. In the early months of development, you get to be very involved and draw often. This part of the process will define the look of the show, and create the foundations for the art team to build up an

art bible. But after that, you are managing expectations and teams, trying to make the director and producers happy.

You really have to be an artist to art-direct, and having a matured taste and very strong understanding of what will appeal to an audience is important. Also, you talk with artists all day, so you need to speak their language, talking about aspects such as values, shape language, lighting set-ups, silhouettes, and storytelling.

> ## "YOU TALK WITH ARTISTS ALL DAY, SO YOU NEED TO SPEAK THEIR LANGUAGE"

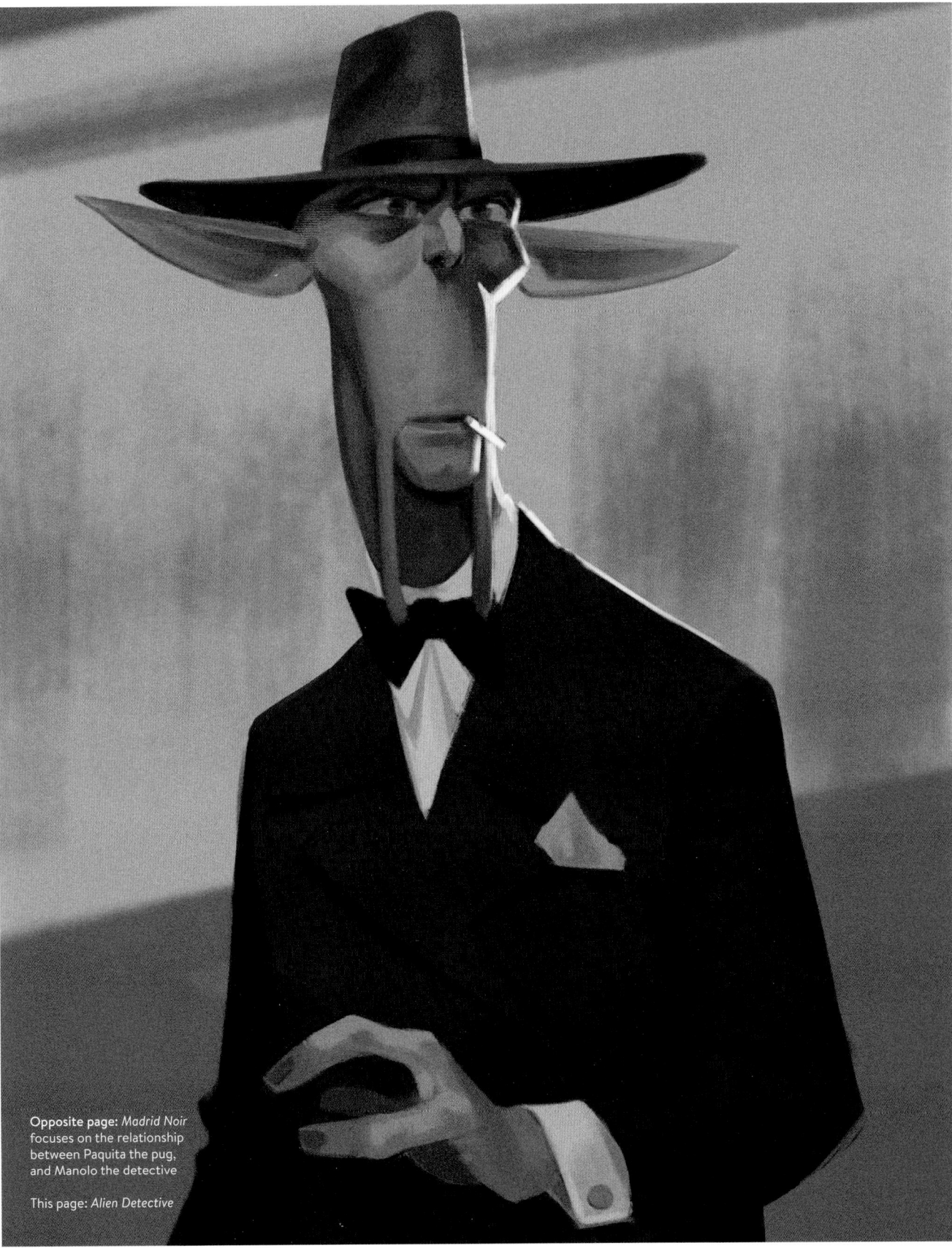

Opposite page: *Madrid Noir* focuses on the relationship between Paquita the pug, and Manolo the detective

This page: *Alien Detective*

WAS THERE A POINT IN YOUR DEVELOPMENT AS AN ARTIST WHERE EVERYTHING SUDDENLY "CLICKED" AND YOU FELT AS IF DESIGNS STARTED COMING TO YOU MORE ORGANICALLY?

I couldn't pinpoint exactly when it happened, because it was a very gradual process, but my approach to design definitely started changing when I moved to London in 2015. It wasn't about learning a new skill or new tools, or anything like that. Like most things in life, it was a change in mentality.

For a long time, I was obsessed with certain artists who had very particular skills or defining styles. I wanted to try and get to their level of rendering, or try to capture the sensibility in their strokes; it was a very frustrating process. It came from being insecure about my own work, and I thought that by trying to imitate them I would find some sort of validation for my efforts. That never happened, or if it did, it didn't fix anything. So, I redirected my attention away from other people's work, and into the world around me. We all have a way of experiencing the world around us, and we all have our own tastes – if you manage to tap into that, your work will be more genuine. It might not be what you expected, or it might not have the qualities that you appreciate in other artists, but it will be yours. My recent trip to the National Museum of Anthropology illustrates this exactly (see opposite). Once I started redirecting my attention from my Instagram feed to the people in my street, my designs became more unique and interesting.

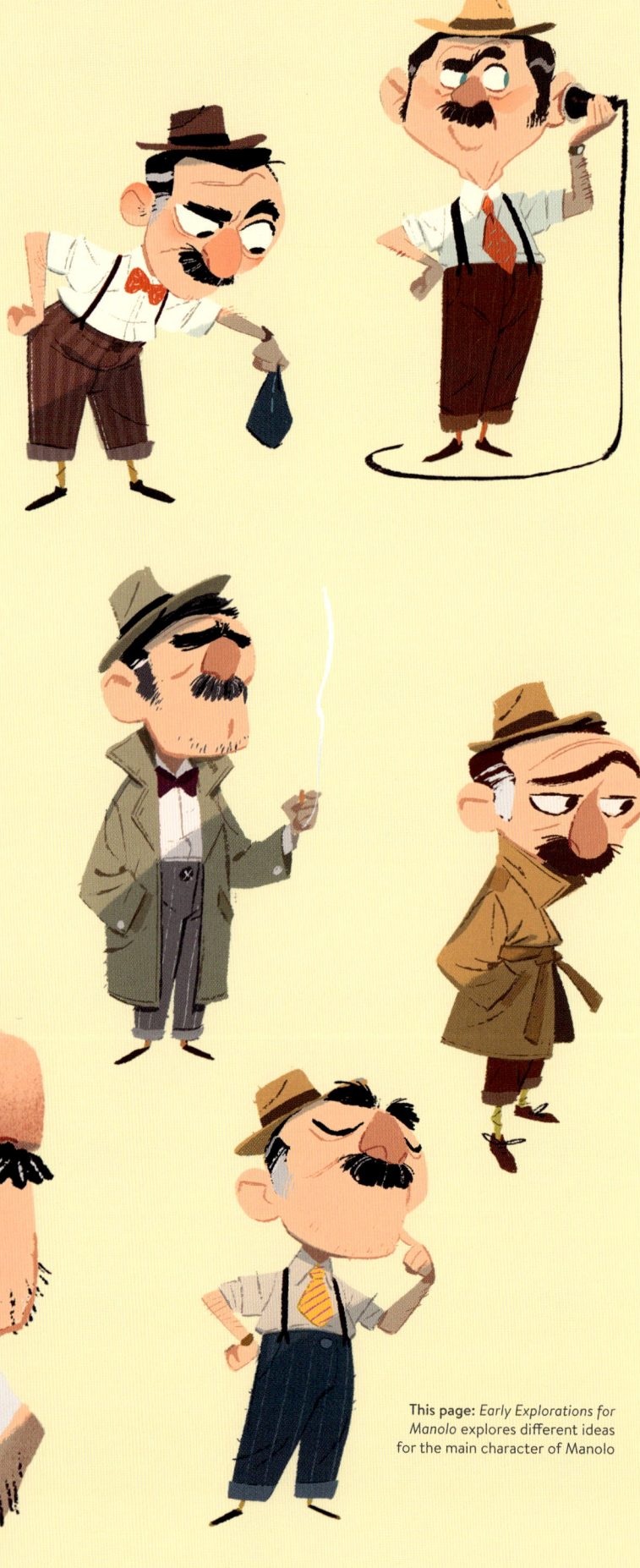

This page: *Early Explorations for Manolo* explores different ideas for the main character of Manolo

Observe The World Around You

There is an idea running around that escapism is how you find inspiration. However, it's amazing to think that the people, places, and objects immediately around you are what can help you the most.

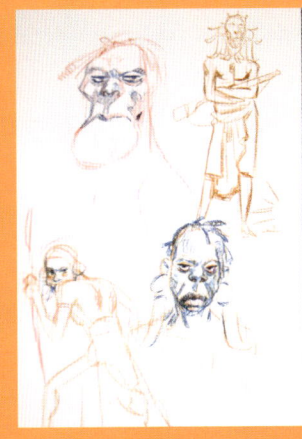
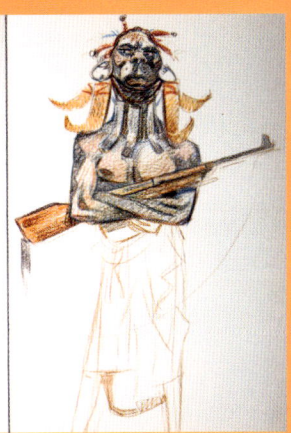

It is through specificity that you find relatability, which is essential when creating a character. No matter where you are, human nature is the same, and when captured in a drawing we can all recognize it. The only way to learn how to capture that is through observation and listening, simply engaging with the world around you.

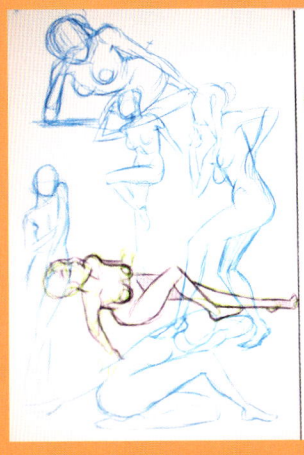
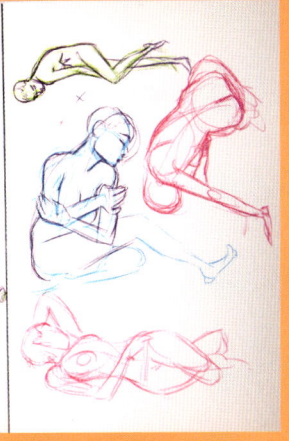

I admit that I don't do this enough, and mostly do it when I travel because I find that I have time on my hands, in trains, planes, buses, museums, even on the streets of a new city. If you find an interesting character, vehicle, building, or other fascinating subject that catches your attention, take a minute and try to draw it.

When translating what you see into your sketching, at first draw quickly, be economic, and reject detail. Try to use the least number of lines to find an expression, be gestural when defining a figure, and focus on overall shapes and direction lines.

Recently, I was in Mexico City and ended up spending almost nine hours wandering around the National Museum of Anthropology. Every single subject was inspiring and perfect for this exercise.

This page: A selection of pages from James' sketchbooks

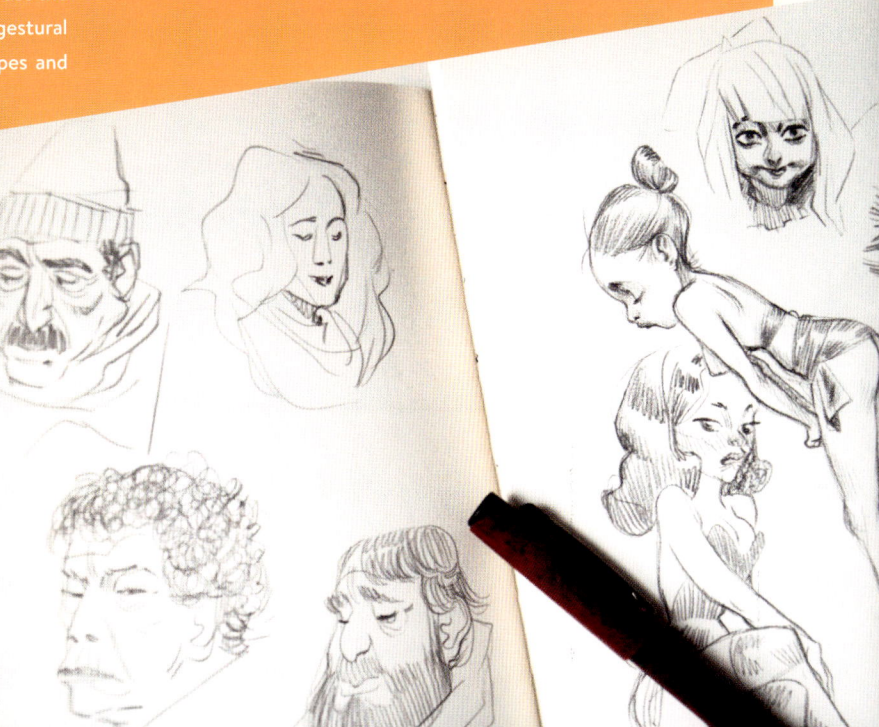

"IN VR, THE VIEWER IS IN A 360-DEGREE WORLD, SO CAN CHOOSE TO LOOK AT WHATEVER THEY WANT FROM ANY ANGLE. IN OTHER WORDS, IT IS A DIRECTOR'S NIGHTMARE"

EARLIER, YOU MENTIONED *MADRID NOIR*, IN WHICH THE CHARACTERS HAVE A VERY UNIQUE AESTHETIC. HOW DOES YOUR APPROACH CHANGE WHEN THE DESIGNS WILL BE VIEWED IN VR?

Thanks for the compliment! *Madrid Noir* is a virtual reality project I am directing with the folks at No Ghost, a VR/XR studio in London, and will be out in late 2018. The design approach doesn't change much from a conventional production. We are looking at the project as if we were doing an animated short, so the visual language and appeal are going to be treated the same way. The one difference from a conventional 2D film is that you don't have control over the camera. In VR, the viewer is in a 360-degree world, so can choose to look at whatever they want from any angle. In other words, it is a director's nightmare.

Inevitably, there are going to be some compromises, since we can't frame the character the way we want. In a 2D film, you can trick a pose or push the silhouettes for one shot, but in VR there are no such things as shots, so you have to find ways to make the characters easy to read so they stand out from the background. We were very aware that we had to make the characters extremely readable from a distance so that people wouldn't get confused in the 3D space.

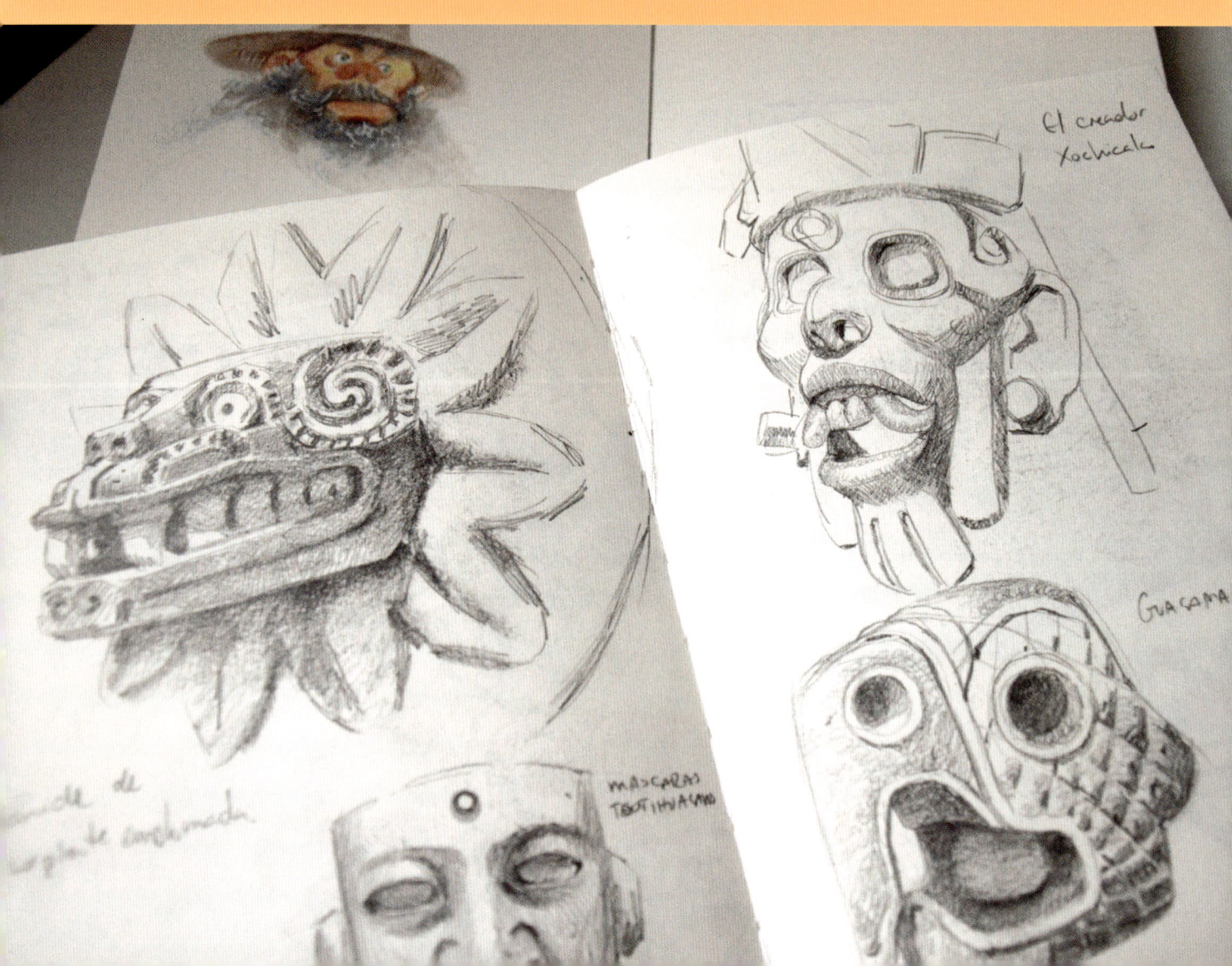

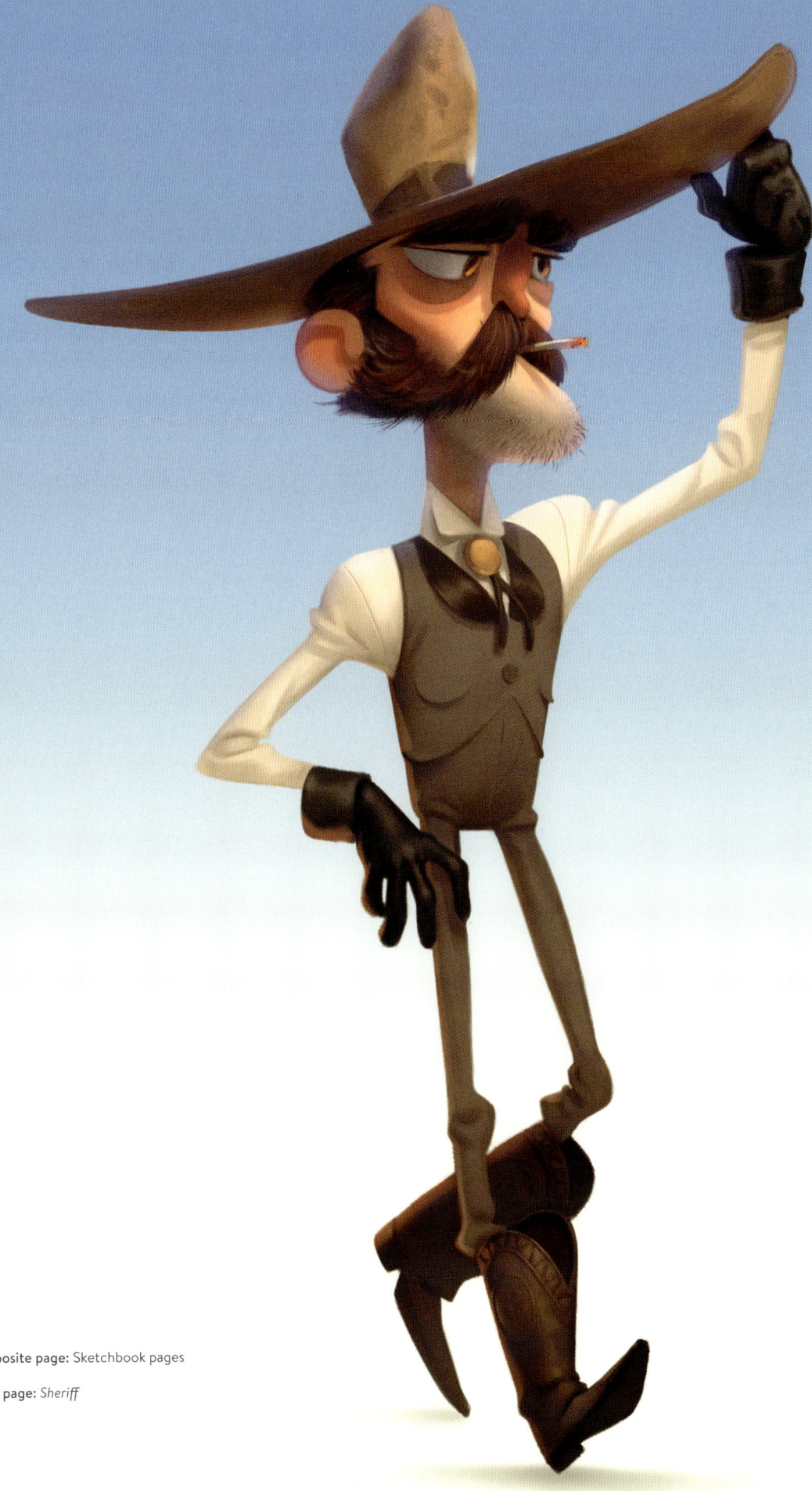

Opposite page: Sketchbook pages

This page: *Sheriff*

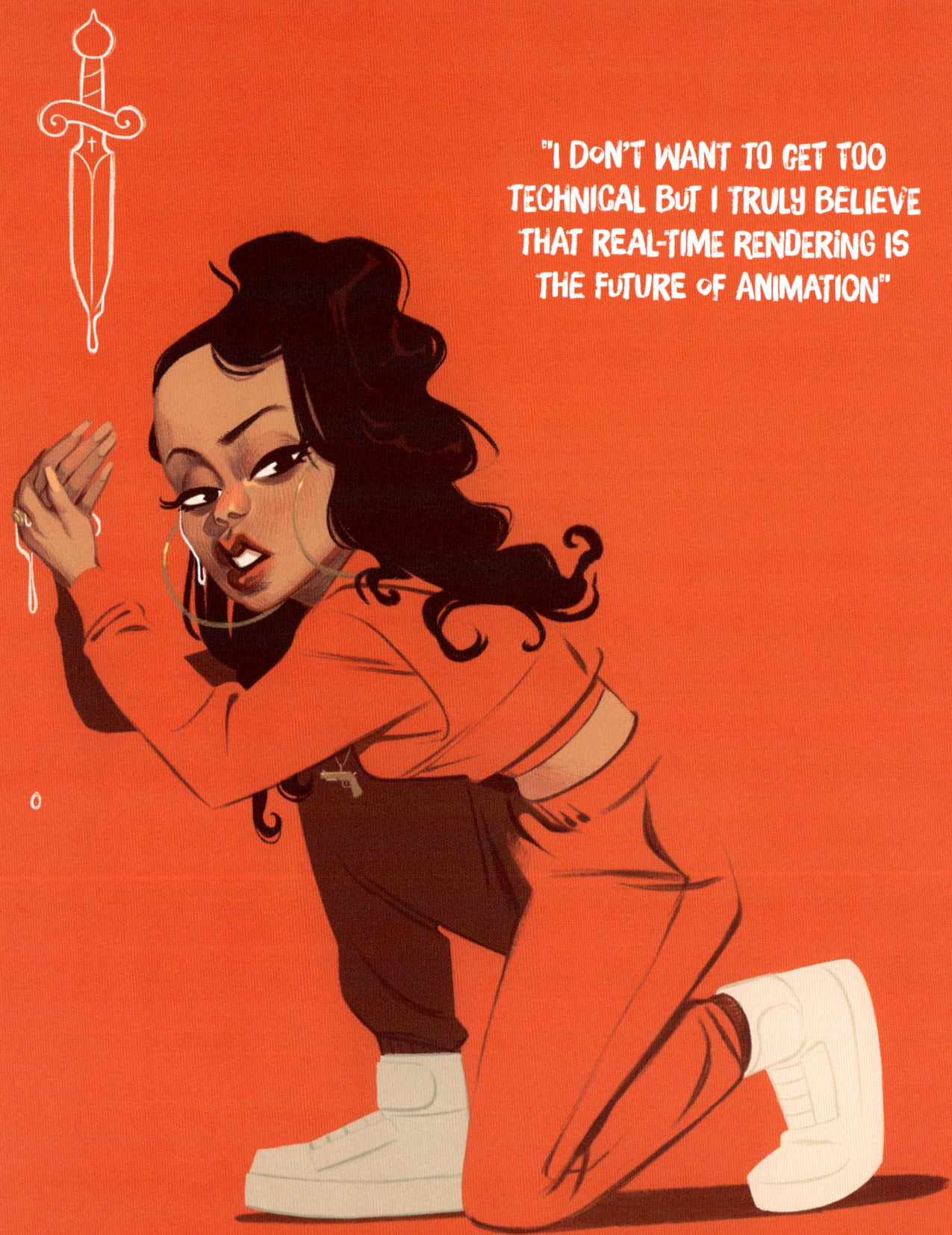

"I DON'T WANT TO GET TOO TECHNICAL BUT I TRULY BELIEVE THAT REAL-TIME RENDERING IS THE FUTURE OF ANIMATION"

This page: *Rosalia*, another example of the artist's love of drawing musicians

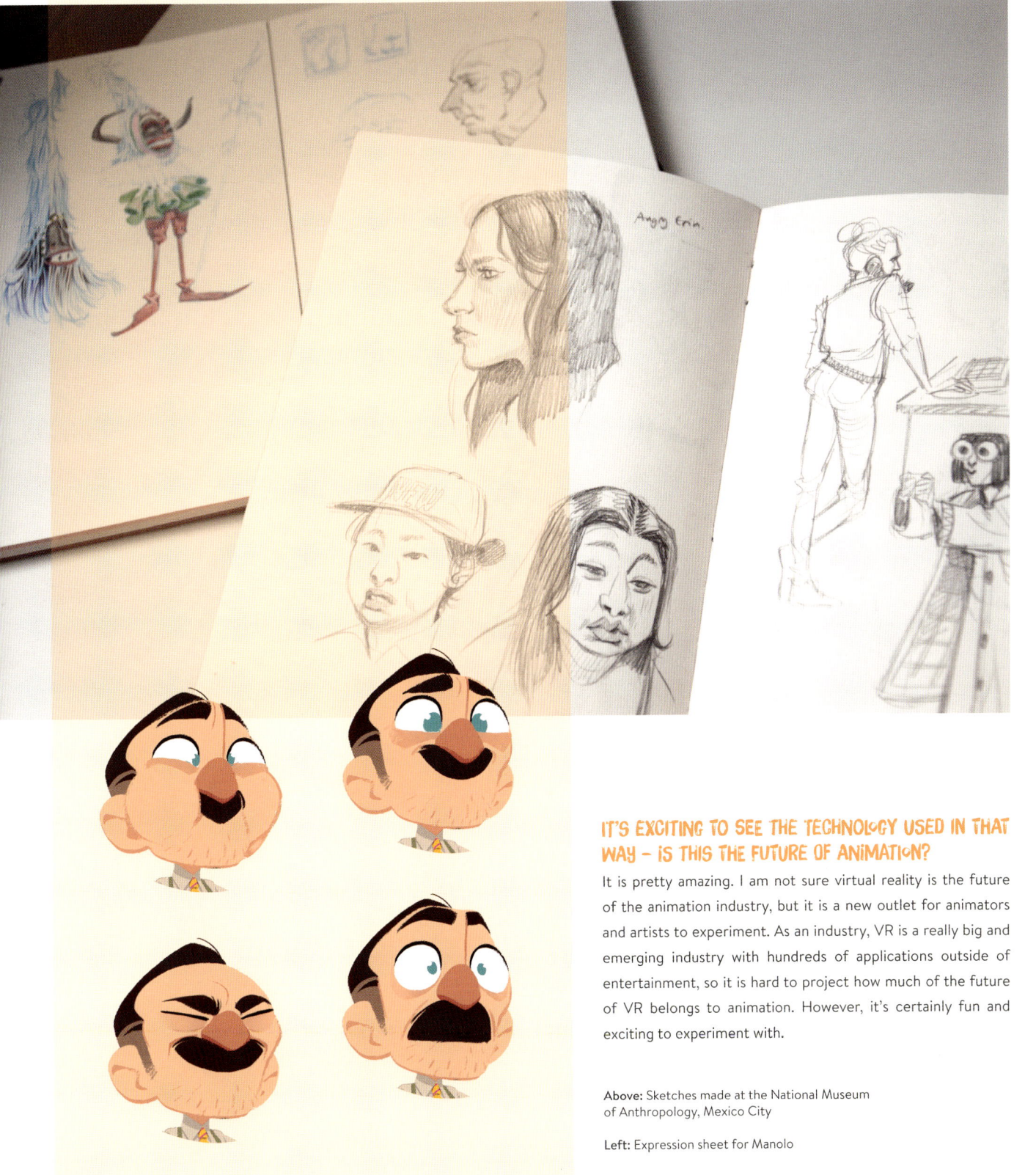

IT'S EXCITING TO SEE THE TECHNOLOGY USED IN THAT WAY – IS THIS THE FUTURE OF ANIMATION?

It is pretty amazing. I am not sure virtual reality is the future of the animation industry, but it is a new outlet for animators and artists to experiment. As an industry, VR is a really big and emerging industry with hundreds of applications outside of entertainment, so it is hard to project how much of the future of VR belongs to animation. However, it's certainly fun and exciting to experiment with.

Above: Sketches made at the National Museum of Anthropology, Mexico City

Left: Expression sheet for Manolo

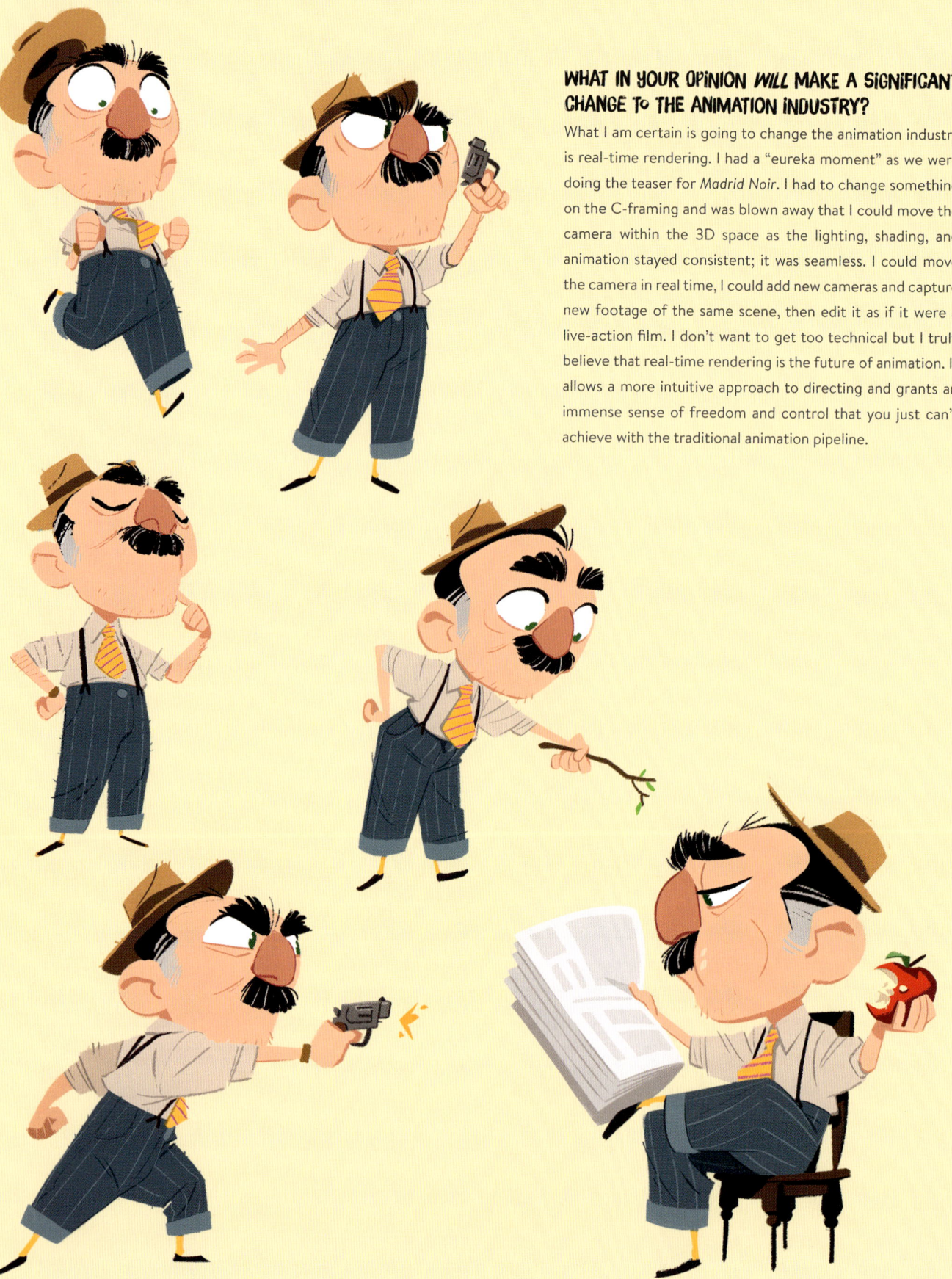

WHAT IN YOUR OPINION *WILL* MAKE A SIGNIFICANT CHANGE TO THE ANIMATION INDUSTRY?

What I am certain is going to change the animation industry is real-time rendering. I had a "eureka moment" as we were doing the teaser for *Madrid Noir*. I had to change something on the C-framing and was blown away that I could move the camera within the 3D space as the lighting, shading, and animation stayed consistent; it was seamless. I could move the camera in real time, I could add new cameras and capture new footage of the same scene, then edit it as if it were a live-action film. I don't want to get too technical but I truly believe that real-time rendering is the future of animation. It allows a more intuitive approach to directing and grants an immense sense of freedom and control that you just can't achieve with the traditional animation pipeline.

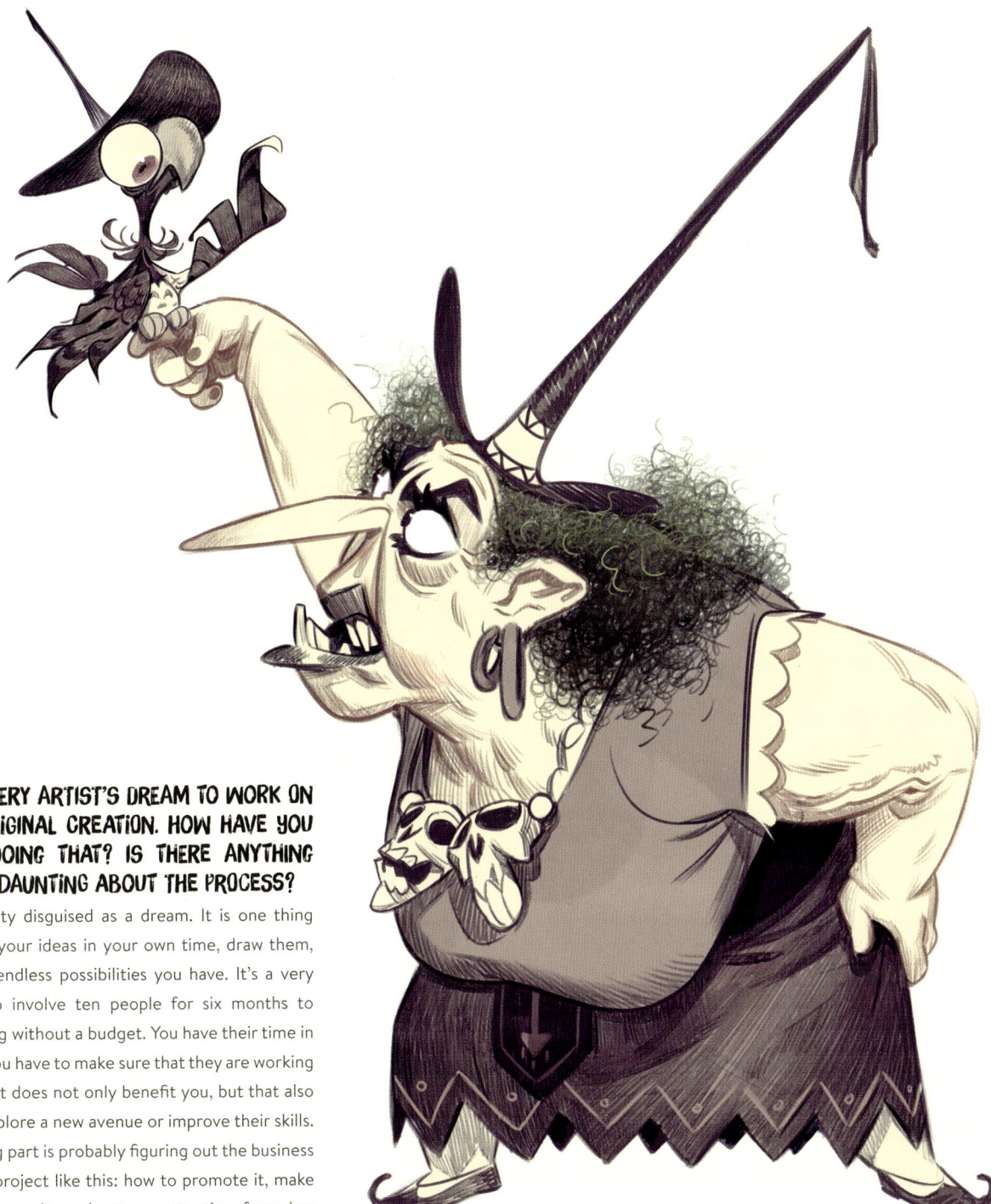

IT MUST BE EVERY ARTIST'S DREAM TO WORK ON THEIR OWN ORIGINAL CREATION. HOW HAVE YOU GONE ABOUT DOING THAT? IS THERE ANYTHING PARTICULARLY DAUNTING ABOUT THE PROCESS?

It is a responsibility disguised as a dream. It is one thing to come up with your ideas in your own time, draw them, and imagine the endless possibilities you have. It's a very different thing to involve ten people for six months to develop something without a budget. You have their time in your hands, and you have to make sure that they are working for something that does not only benefit you, but that also allows them to explore a new avenue or improve their skills. The most daunting part is probably figuring out the business side of making a project like this: how to promote it, make sure that people see it, and attract attention from key players in the industry.

Other than that, I do love it. It is fun to develop this project, and to see people's reactions to something that is so personal is very humbling. At the end of the day, we just want to keep doing what we love and are excited about.

Opposite page: Poses for Manolo

Above: *A Parrot With an Attitude*

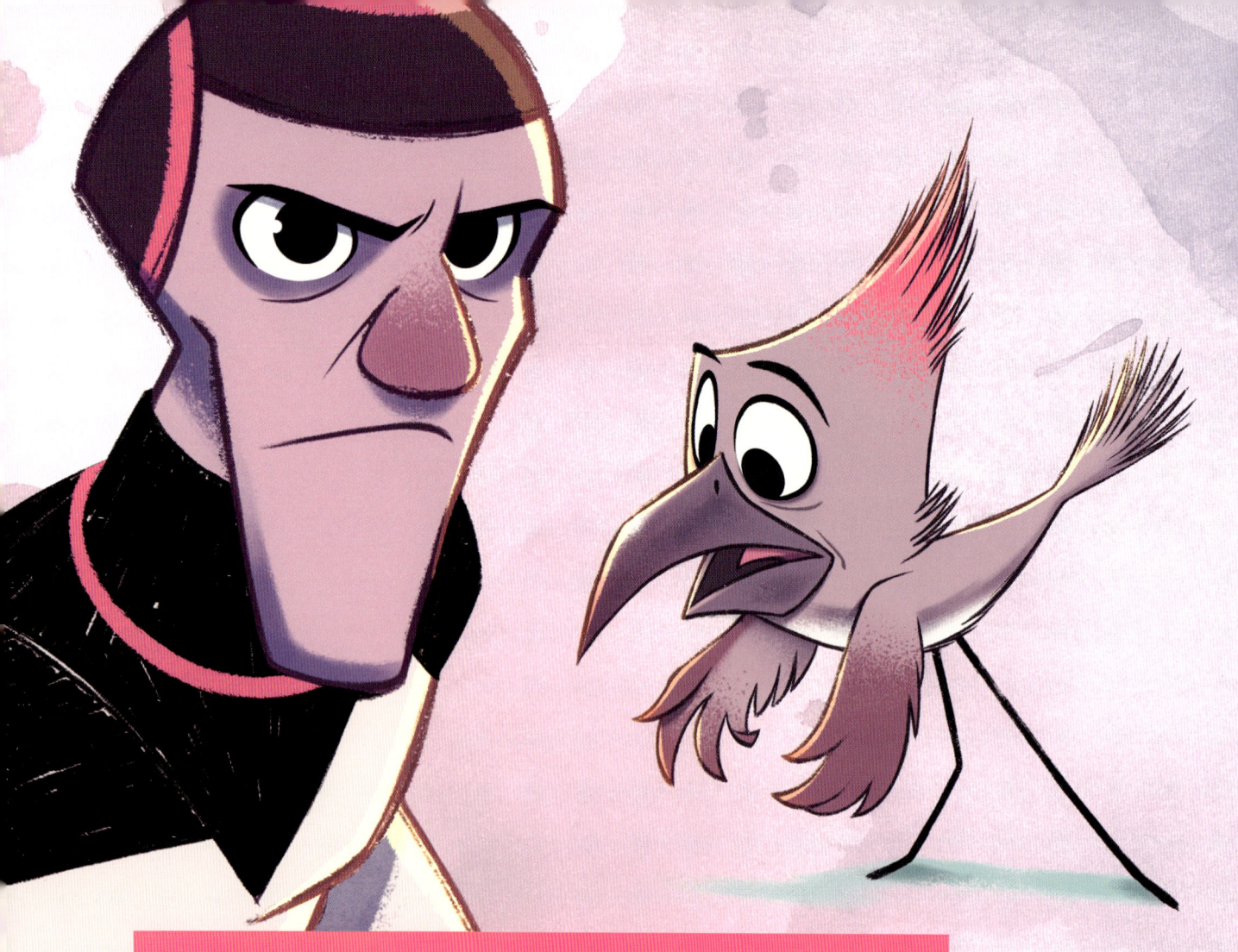

TRANSFORMING A CHARACTER

LUIS GADEA

For this exercise we will play with the idea of a character that can transform into a bird; much like Madam Mim from Disney's *The Sword in the Stone* who transforms into a rhinoceros, dragon, cat, and many other forms while maintaining a clear sense of character. I love how they played with those transformations in the film. A bird is a big change from a human character so it is a good choice for this demonstration, however the principles in this article can be applied to almost any variety of transformation. You could adapt your character from one species of animal to another or turn a sea creature into a human character, and so on. There are so many options to explore and have fun with. In this article, I will start with a ready-made character design and show the process of translating the character into a new physical form.

ASSESS THE ORIGINAL

To ensure the identity of a character is carried through to a new form variation it is very important to analyze all the traits of the original character that make their identity recognizable. What makes the character distinct and how can they be shown in a new form? I have a confident and adventurous man, a space explorer, as the original character so I look for ways to show confidence or adventure in a bird.

INTENSE EYES

It is important to translate the eyes and this intense look into the new character. Always keep the eyes as similar as possible in your transformations as they communicate your design ideas to the viewer.

EXPRESSIVE HANDS

This character has very expressive hands, so they need to translate into expressive wings. Using wings to act like hands is common in old cartoons and movies so it should work well for this project.

DETAILED TORSO

The focus of attention in the original character is on the upper body where there is much more detail. The new design will also need to draw the viewer's eye to the upper body so it is important to also keep this aspect now in the bird.

LONG LEGS

It is key to keep the same feeling as the original character design has. I intend to do this by making the character's legs completely black and extended as they are here. It is an easy area to translate into the bird design as bird legs are often portrayed as long, black lines.

This page: The original character is a confident space explorer

RESEARCH THE NEW FORM

Search for references to get a better understanding of the creature your character is going to turn into. One important thing I want to ensure is that the face is very interesting, so I look for head shapes and head feathers that will help with that. Beaks are the other key aspect I investigate as the shapes can be very expressive and will help when the original character's expressions are translated onto the bird. I want the beak to have a nice simple shape that is clear to read.

Research the different types of body birds have but focus your attention on the shapes, not on the details. Explore how to simplify the shapes to eventually get to a very simple solution. As human characters often gesture with their hands, pay particular attention to researching wings. The character needs to transform from hands to wings so I search for real bird wings that can create multiple gestures. It is important for this design to know how wings work.

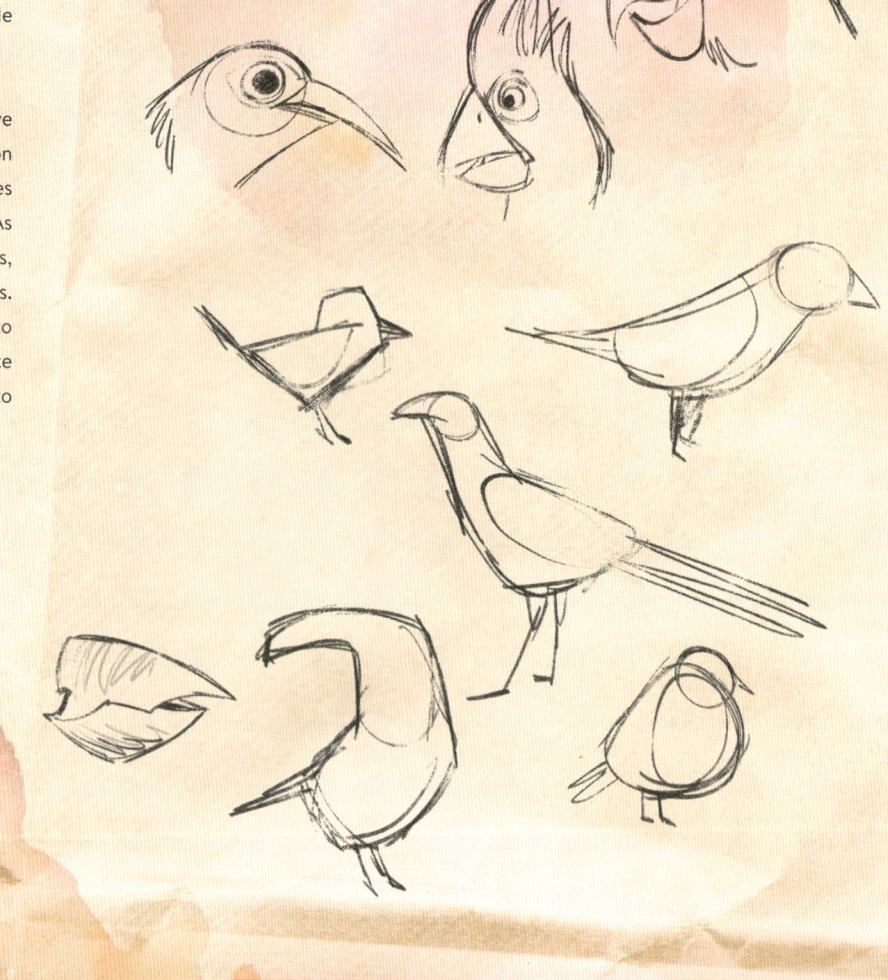

This page: Use sketches to explore variations in the bird form while researching

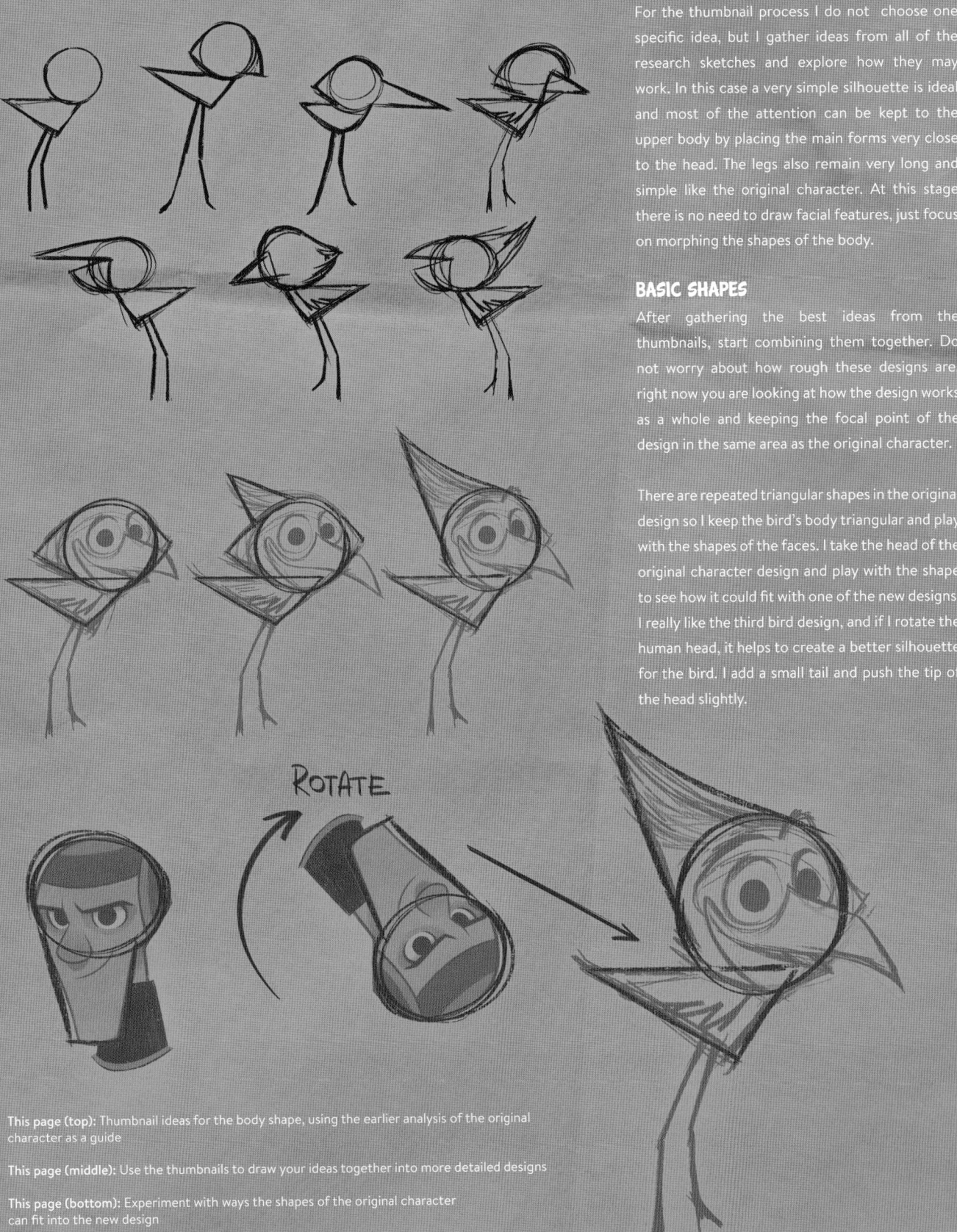

THUMBNAILS

For the thumbnail process I do not choose one specific idea, but I gather ideas from all of the research sketches and explore how they may work. In this case a very simple silhouette is ideal and most of the attention can be kept to the upper body by placing the main forms very close to the head. The legs also remain very long and simple like the original character. At this stage there is no need to draw facial features, just focus on morphing the shapes of the body.

BASIC SHAPES

After gathering the best ideas from the thumbnails, start combining them together. Do not worry about how rough these designs are, right now you are looking at how the design works as a whole and keeping the focal point of the design in the same area as the original character.

There are repeated triangular shapes in the original design so I keep the bird's body triangular and play with the shapes of the faces. I take the head of the original character design and play with the shape to see how it could fit with one of the new designs. I really like the third bird design, and if I rotate the human head, it helps to create a better silhouette for the bird. I add a small tail and push the tip of the head slightly.

ROTATE

This page (top): Thumbnail ideas for the body shape, using the earlier analysis of the original character as a guide

This page (middle): Use the thumbnails to draw your ideas together into more detailed designs

This page (bottom): Experiment with ways the shapes of the original character can fit into the new design

ADD DETAILS

This is the final stage of developing the character's new shape and general form. The essential details are now settled and the design just needs tweaks. I increase the quantity and size of the tail feathers because the smaller version feels too slight and shy for this character conversion. If you do not know how to improve the design, try flipping the image over. It can give you a new perspective which helps ensure that the design works from side to side. I clean the design up a little so that it is ready for the next stage, selecting a color palette.

POSING

Poses are a great opportunity to make a new animal character feel like the original design. Keeping the energy and positive personality of the space explorer is very important here. I also want to show expression in the character's eyes and beak which helps support the posing. In the pose on the left the character is very positive with an open expression; the wings transition from regular wings to hands made of feathers. The pose on the right is inquisitive and slightly crouched, as he inspects an apple; this bird is always curious. I play with the beak to see how it would work on the shapes when tilted down.

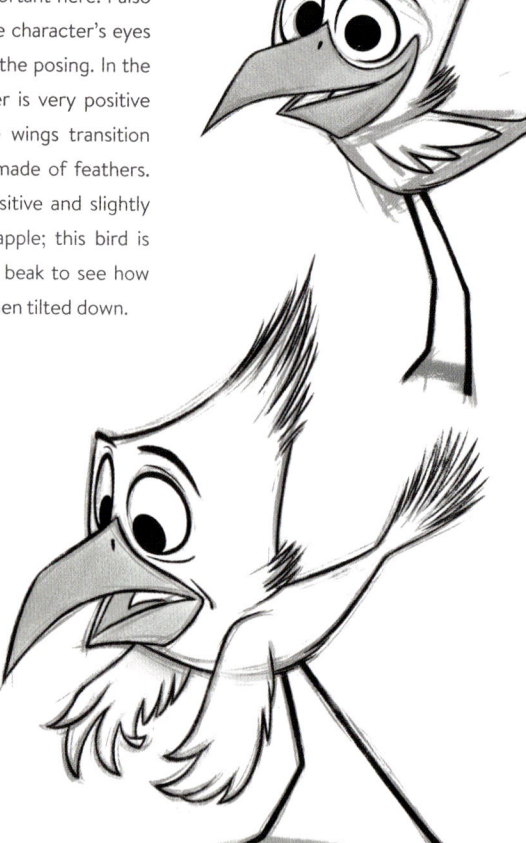

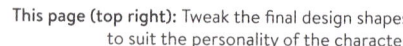

This page (top right): Tweak the final design shapes to suit the personality of the character

This page (bottom right and left): An open pose shows positivity, while replicating the original character's pose shows curiosity

IDEAS TRASH CAN

As I combine different design ideas together to create the finished forms, I try out a few variations. In this sketch I take a version of the bird that has a small beak and a much wider head shape. I try combining it with the small head feathers to see how these suit the personality I am aiming for but it is not successful. I definitely like the other version so I leave this design and continue with a design that has bolder shapes.

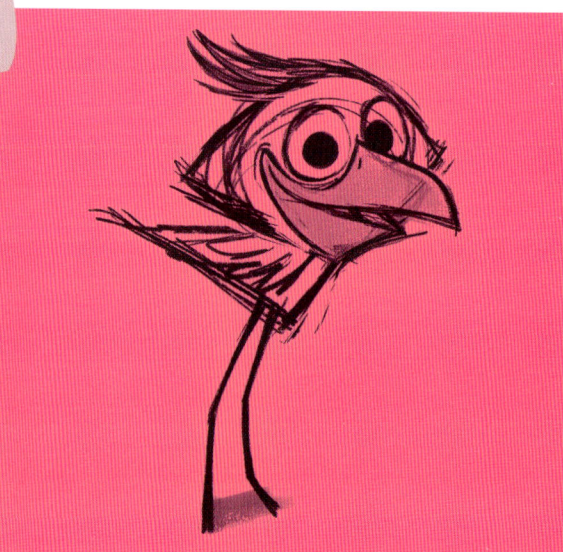

FEATHERS

CHEST

LEGS

DETAILS

BEAK

SHADOW ON MULTIPLY

EYES

LINE OF EYEBROWS

VALUES AND COLOR

I want to keep this character very similar in color and values to the original so I take the pink, white, and purple colors from the original and apply them to the bird. I want the values to be subtle on this character so I reduce the contrast, but keep the white hues on the character's chest, as in the original design, and the brighter pink hues on the details.

REVIEW THE DESIGN

Reviewing the final design, I think this pose works well because it shows the curious side of the character's personality and is in keeping with the original human design. I keep the dark beak, as this is like the original character's dark nose, and his very expressive eyes. The thin black legs are two silhouettes and also very similar to the original design. As a final detail I add an apple to give a size relationship scale that is useful if the project develops further.

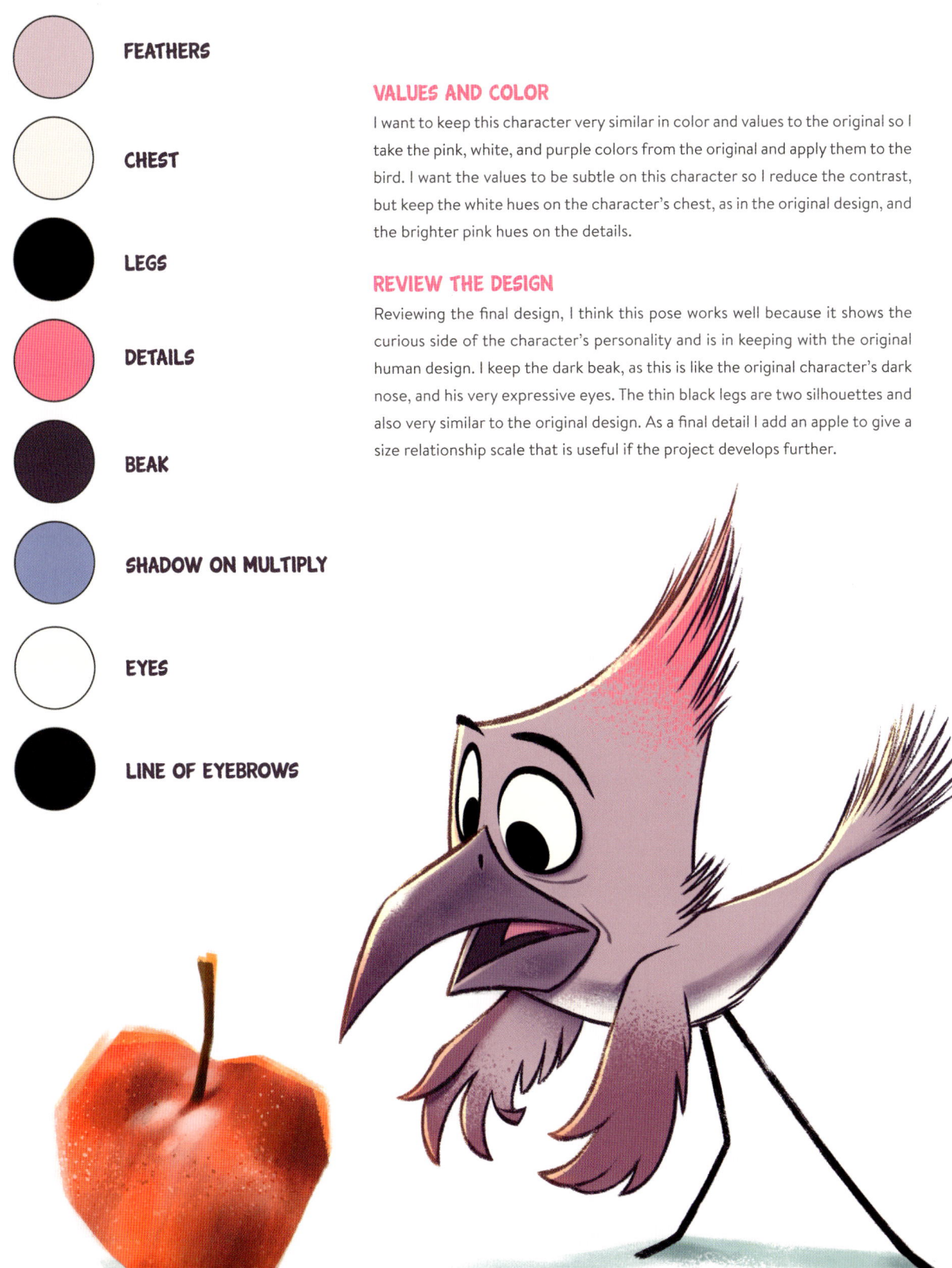

Top: Maintaining the color palette of the original design helps to identify them as the same character

Bottom: An apple gives a sense of scale to the final design

MEET THE ARTIST
FLORIANE MARCHIX

Like many children, Floriane Marchix was fascinated by the animated films she watched, and as a result of her love for animation she attended Gobelins School of Visual Arts and launched a career as an animator. Her career took an unexpected turn however into visual development which, by happy accident, she found suited her perfectly. Since becoming a visual development artist, she has worked for studios such as DreamWorks Animation and Aardman Animation on exciting feature films. Here, Floriane explains the ins-and-outs of a visual developer's role, shares her experiences working for top film companies, and reveals the approach she used to capture the emotion in a short series about her relationship with her daughter.

"COLOR HAS A HUGE STORYTELLING POWER. IT CAN EXPRESS SO MANY DIFFERENT THINGS; EMOTIONS, CONTRADICTIONS, AND THE MEANING OF SEQUENCES"

I have always been fascinated by the field of animation. After trying to become an animator, I realized by a happy coincidence that visual development was perfect for me, and am now a visual development artist.

With a mix of luck and hard work I worked first in the video game industry and now full-time for DreamWorks. I occasionally do freelance work for other studios. Proudly originating from France, I now live in Los Angeles, USA, where I try as best I can to balance my busy family life and my work. Like many people I guess!

In a film production, a visual development artist develops everything that will appear on the screen at a very early stage in the production process. We work immediately after, or at the same time as, the story artists. The story artists create the story and make an animated storyboard of the film. The visual developers will then take the storyboard and try to create the entire environment around it. A fun storyboard sequence drawn entirely with stick figures, for example, needs to be designed, and that is what the visual developers take care of.

As a visual developer you have to question what the characters will look like, what the environment around them shall be, and what is the best way to show this information? What could make the environment unique? You take all these elements and design everything piece-by-piece starting with the big parts and then tightening up the design little by little, until you reach the details.

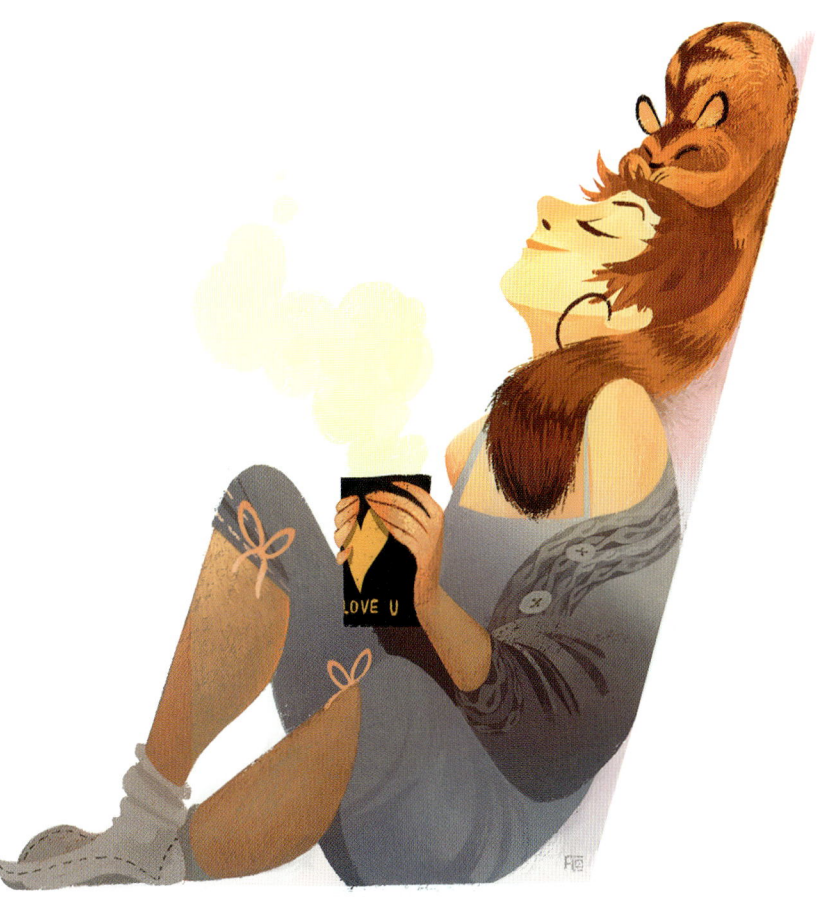

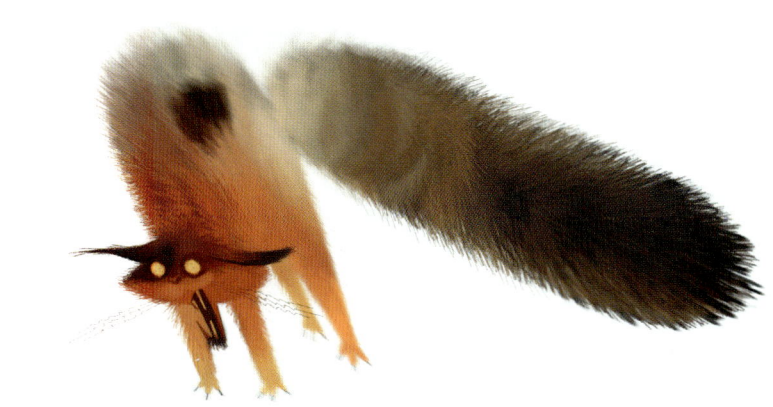

Opposite page: *Undersea mystery*

This page: *Wild Morning*

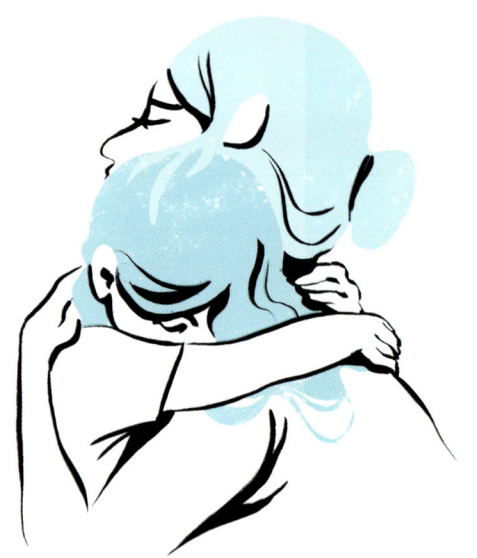

SPECIAL PROJECT
Drawing on Relationships

The series *Mother/Daughter relationship* was really a pretext for drawing the relationship I have with my daughter on an everyday basis. I wanted to crystallize these little moments of our life and capture that strong, emotional bond; the illustrations are like a photo album in a way. To create the images I used a relatively refined line and limited the amount of detail because I did not have much time to devote to them. I had to focus on the essential parts; depending on what you are trying to tell in your drawings, the focus points that are put forward in an illustration can vary greatly.

For this series, I just tried to represent the core of an anecdote. I wanted to take the essence of a reading night, for example, exploring what had marked me the most about it, such as a moment of laughing out loud, the way my daughter was sitting, or a look we exchanged. I took that point as a starting point and arranged everything else around it. I tried to avoid putting too many details where they are not needed. Drawing characters without faces can sometimes be more touching because their attitudes and poses can communicate the emotion in subtle ways.

This page: Illustrations from the *Mother/Daughter relationship* series showing moments between Floriane and her daughter

Opposite page: Floriane's workspace

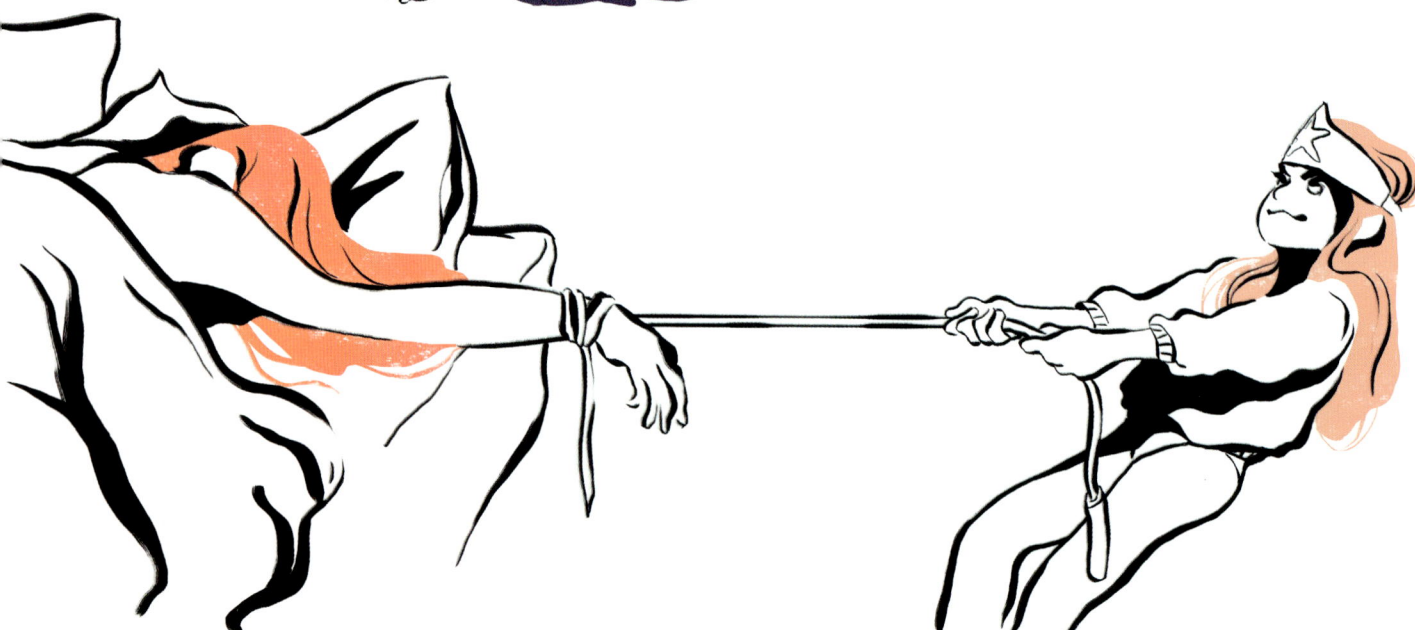

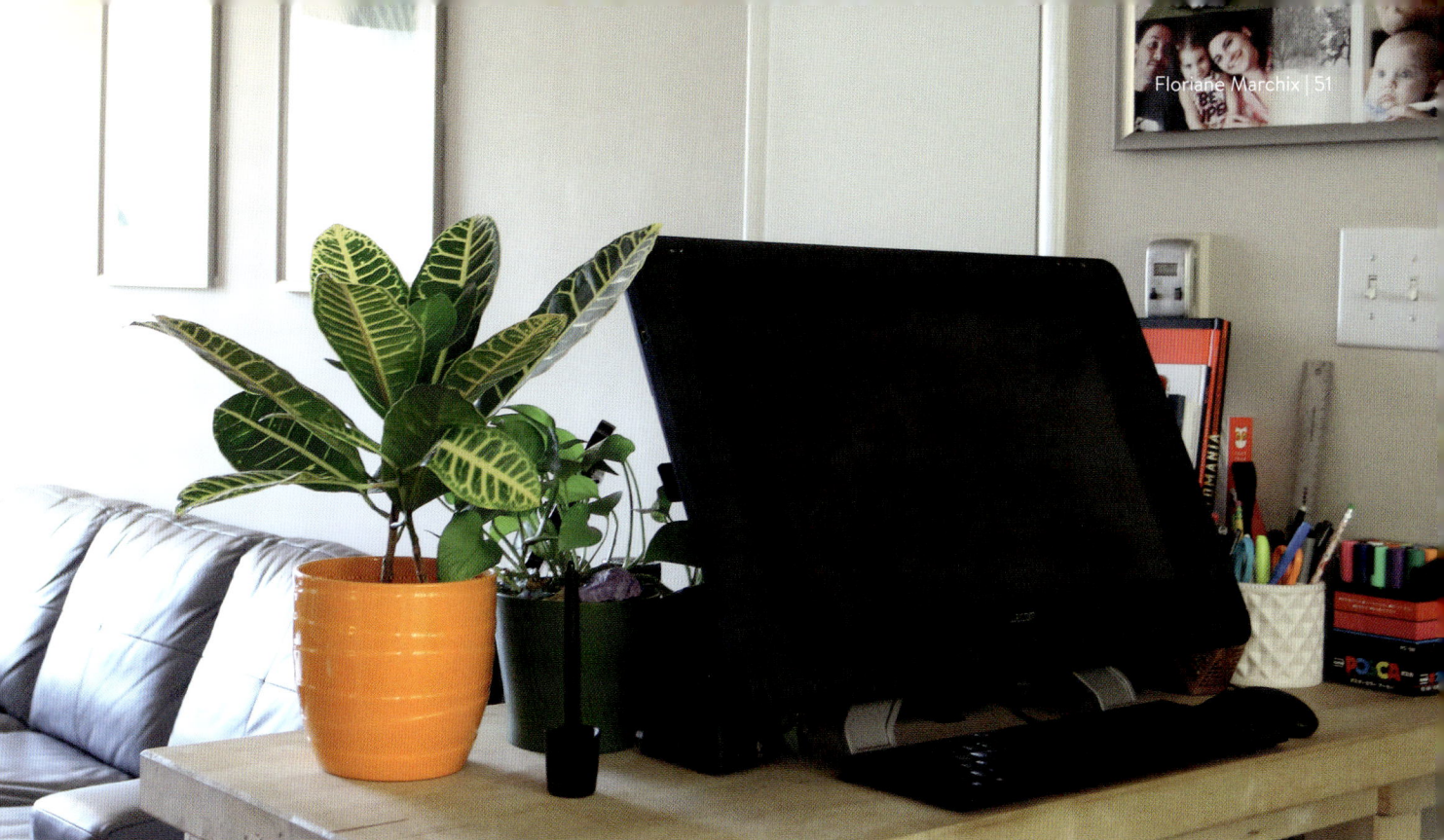

For example, you start working from the basic idea of a big manor on top of a snowy mountain and your work is done when you finish designing the door handles. You create pages and pages of sketches and paintings to explain a particular sequence as well as you can.

Everything you do needs to support the story and say something about the character; who they are, where they have been, the events that have occurred. You also need to think about the best lighting and color choice for the sequence. It sounds overwhelming at first; however, if you stay methodical, everything is fine! After the visual development, all your work goes to other departments for modeling, layout, surfacing, lighting, and so on.

HIGH-PROFILE STUDIOS

When I started my career, I never imagined that working for studios such as Aardman and DreamWorks would happen to me. It is amazing to work for the studio that made me dream as a kid and, it is interesting for me now, to see how these big studios work from the inside. It is still surprising. DreamWorks is a huge "film machine" yet every production is unique.

Sometimes a production is extremely well orchestrated and runs so smoothly that it is difficult to realize there are so many people involved in the project. Sometimes, the production is extremely complex and it cannot go that smoothly or progress quickly. With every project comes something unexpected; both good and bad surprises.

As I work at the beginning of the production chain, it is always rewarding to see my work grow and go from colleague to colleague until the final result. I am surrounded by passionate and extremely talented people, so it is interesting to see how my work is transcribed, reinterpreted, and improved by all the different departments. Even though the production time on these large projects is prolonged and it can often take years to see the final result; it's worth it!

TAKING ON CHALLENGES

At my level, a fairly recurrent issue is that the writing of a film production's storyline and script are often done at the same time the graphic development of the film is taking place. So sometimes whole environments or characters, on which you may have worked for several months, can disappear from the production because a script is rewritten. There is nothing you can really do about this; it is part of the production development process and you just have to adapt to the production needs.

Even if the change is for the good of the film, it can sometimes feel painful to see a lot of hard work going to waste. The hardest case of this is when a show you have worked on is cancelled entirely. It is not uncommon and is experienced by a lot of people in the industry but it is always very painful as you can put years of work into something that never becomes real. As the work you have done on the cancelled project is studio property (just like the work you do for a completed project) you often cannot even show the work. It can be quite traumatic and sometimes you have to go through true periods of mourning, in a way, for your lost work.

THE HIGHLIGHTS

I have a great freedom, especially in my choice of work. For most of the time, I do not find it stressful. Different people have their own individual pace which. I find that this is an important point to consider when tempering your passion.

Every day I have the opportunity to tell stories through illustrations and paintings. I do my best to build imaginary worlds that are as coherent and natural as possible so viewers can project their ideas onto them easily. I love the fact that a small idea that sprouted from my mind can grow into something so much bigger; whether it is an environment design, a choice of color atmosphere, or a furniture design. I find that it is always rewarding to spot my work in a project that has involved so many people, even if I am the only person to recognize my mushroom design in sequence 134!

USING COLOR SCRIPTS

The color script is a visual guide to the color choices of a sequence and it is a step that happens rather late in production. Sometimes it can be such an important part of the process that the whole project gravitates around it. It is a huge help for the lighting department, who will light the film, or it can just be useful information for yourself if you are working alone on a project.

Usually once the film's characters and environments have been designed, you start to think about what the color arrangement of the entire movie will be. This helps define the moods, color, and the lighting of the film. Color has a huge storytelling power. It can express so many different things; emotions, contradictions, and the meaning of sequences. For these reasons, it is so important to find the best color choices for your story. You could have a general idea of the colors from the start, but having a sequential visual decoupage, will help you resolve a lot of questions. The process can be extremely experimental and you will re-do it frequently before being satisfied.

EXPLORING COLORS

Color is about experimentation. I always work on very small thumbnails and in general, I start with color proposals that are relatively classic.

This spread: *Red through the woods*

Opposite page: *Summer swim*

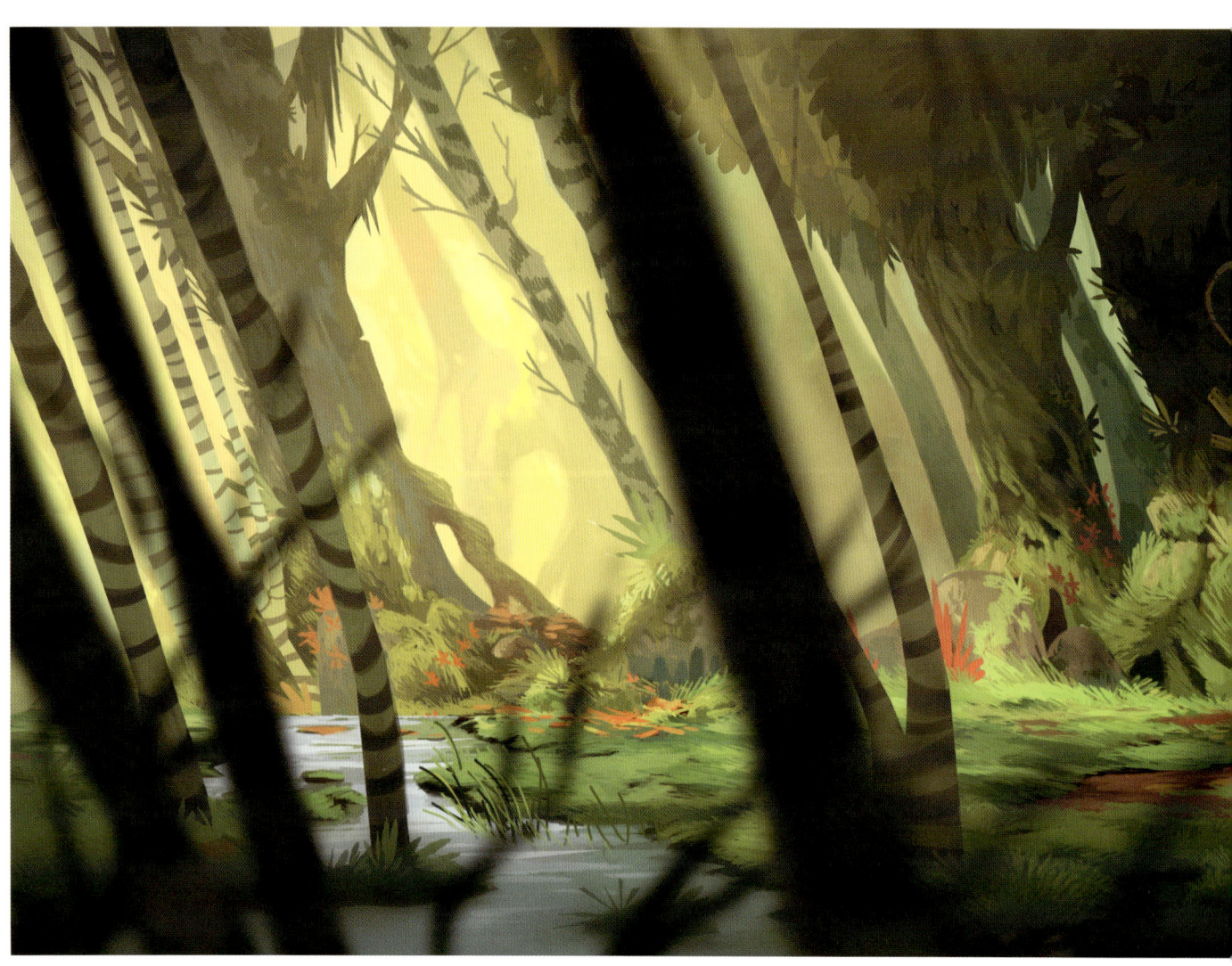

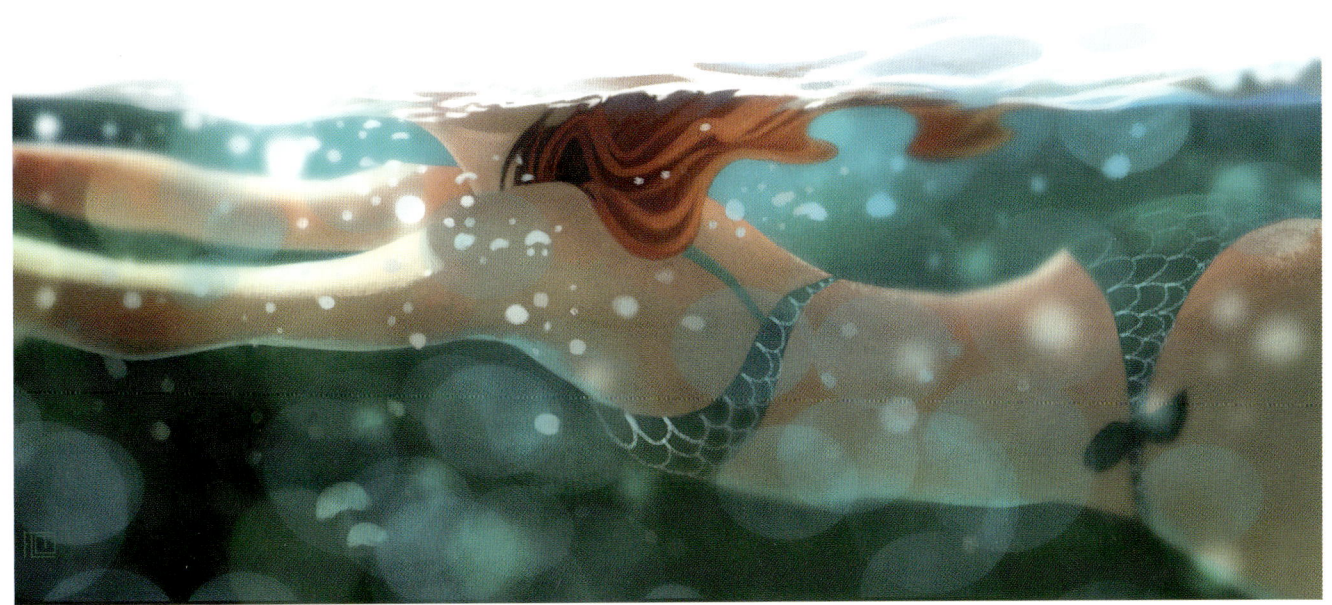

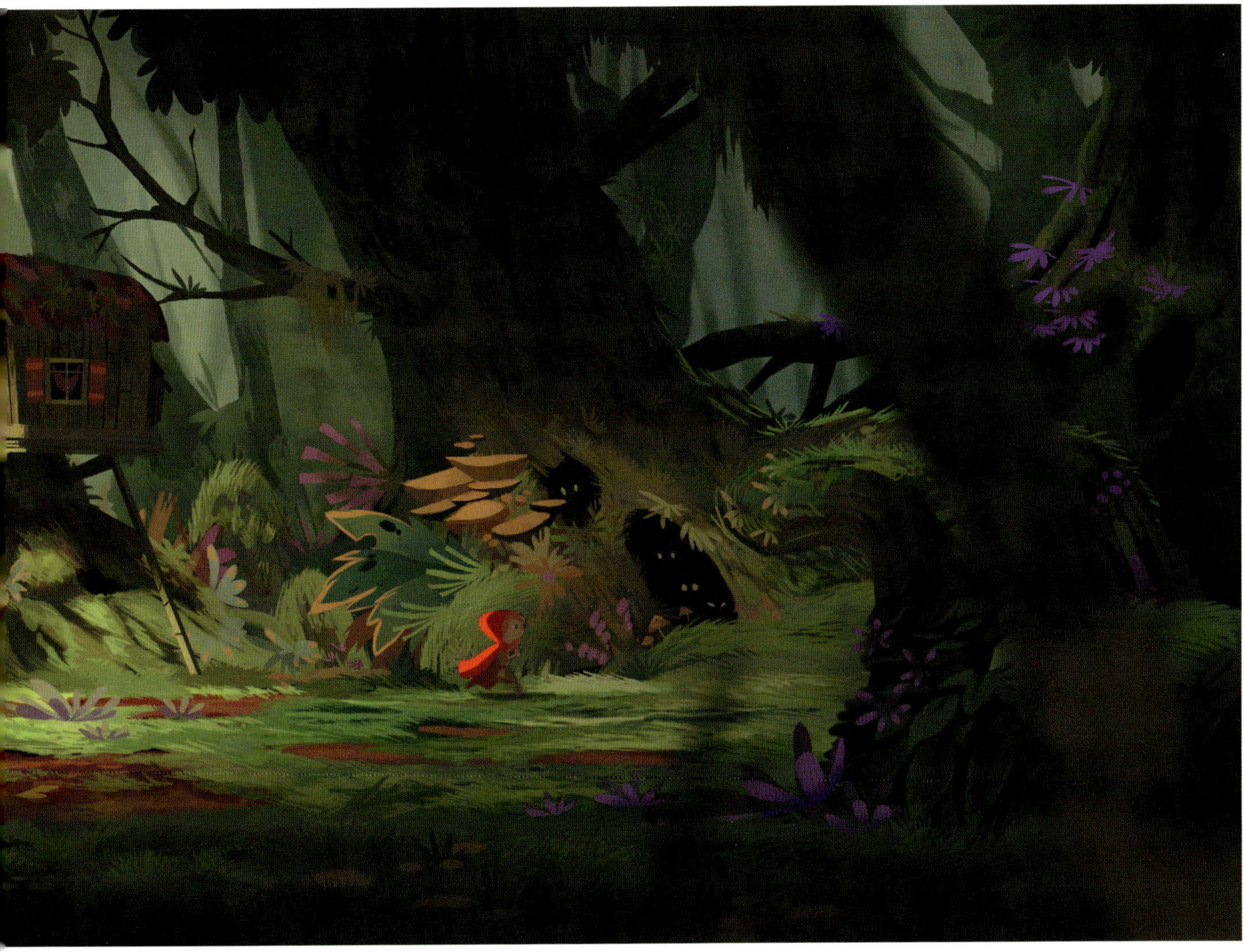

Then I move to something more unusual. I try to vary the colors from one thumbnail to another while working with the minimum of details. I might create one with strong contrasts, one with subtle tonal variation, and one with saturated colors. My aim is to emphasize the character or the situation with the best color choice possible. There isn't much method in my process, just a lot of different color tests.

VISUAL DEVELOPMENT CAREERS

Be passionate. This is an area I love working in and is a field that is spreading thanks to new technology. The arrival of VR (virtual reality) recently has created new opportunities and there are always new apps, TV series, films, video games, and advertising. People consume more and more images every day so a passion for creating exciting images is a must.

Working as a visual developer is an extremely diversified field so if you are trying to break into this field do not specialize too much. Sometimes having a very precise style can be tricky. It is great to be known and paid for doing a particular type of work which you love to do, but it could also turn into a trap. You might end up doing the same thing over and over again as it is all you are known for.

My advice is to be a chameleon-like artist, adapting your style as needed but with some of your own personal style on the side. In order to move from film to film, in a big studio, where you are required to constantly change styles, you have to have a good sense of adaptation. You should not be frightened by the idea of changing your style, so challenge yourself and be curious with your work.

> "MY AIM IS TO EMPHASIZE THE CHARACTER OR THE SITUATION WITH THE BEST COLOR CHOICE POSSIBLE"

This page: *Wind*

Opposite page: *Bye-bye my friend*

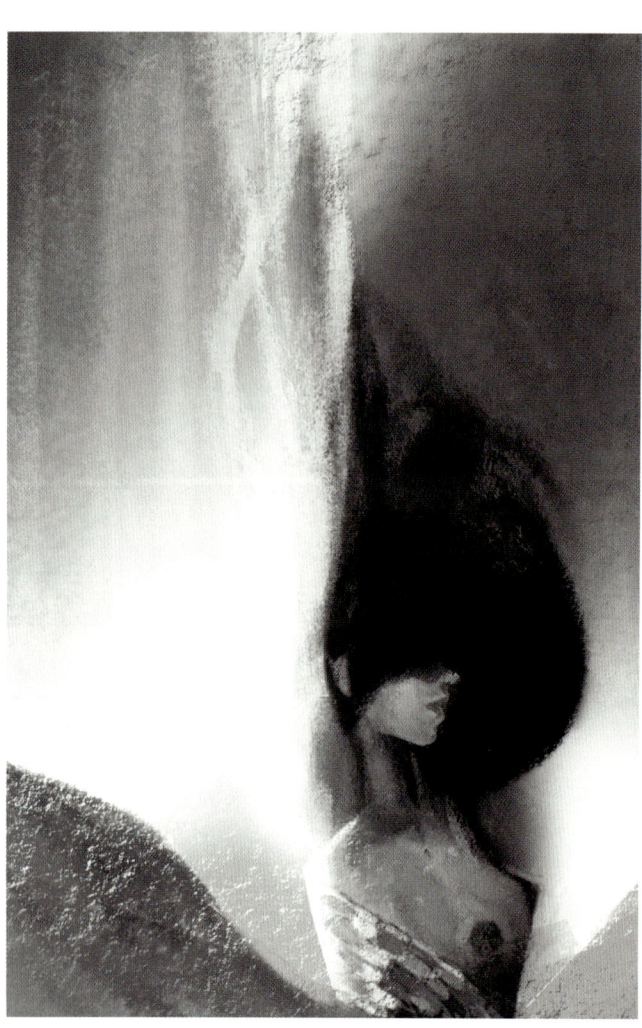

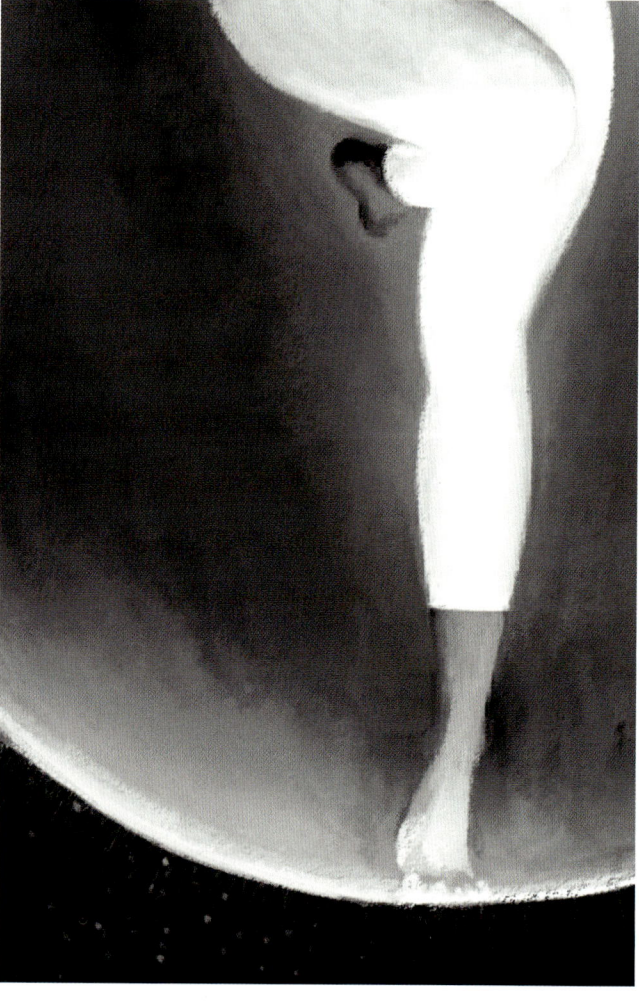

"I AM SURROUNDED BY PASSIONATE AND EXTREMELY TALENTED PEOPLE, SO IT IS INTERESTING TO SEE HOW MY WORK IS TRANSCRIBED, REINTERPRETED, AND IMPROVED BY ALL THE DIFFERENT DEPARTMENTS"

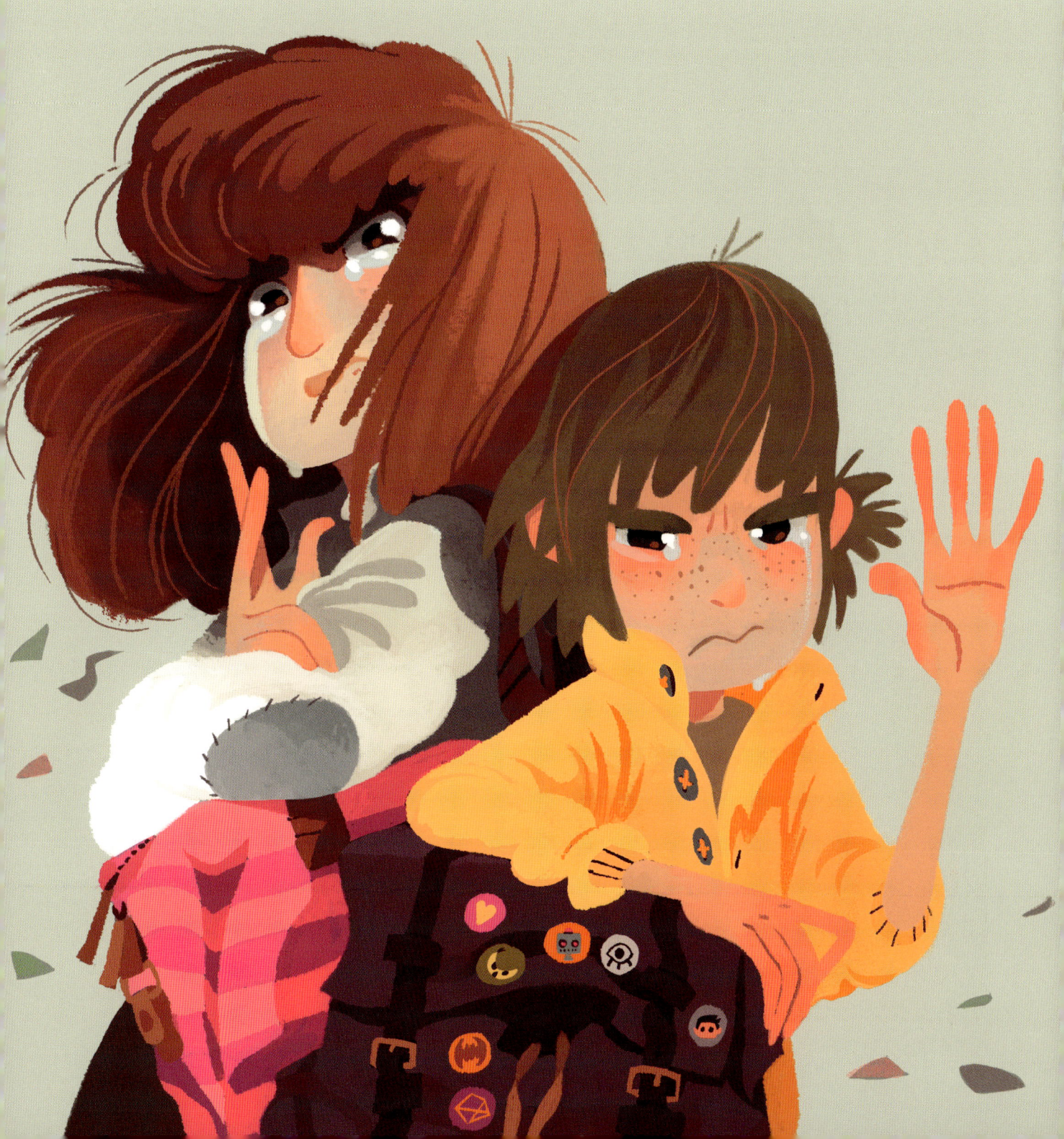

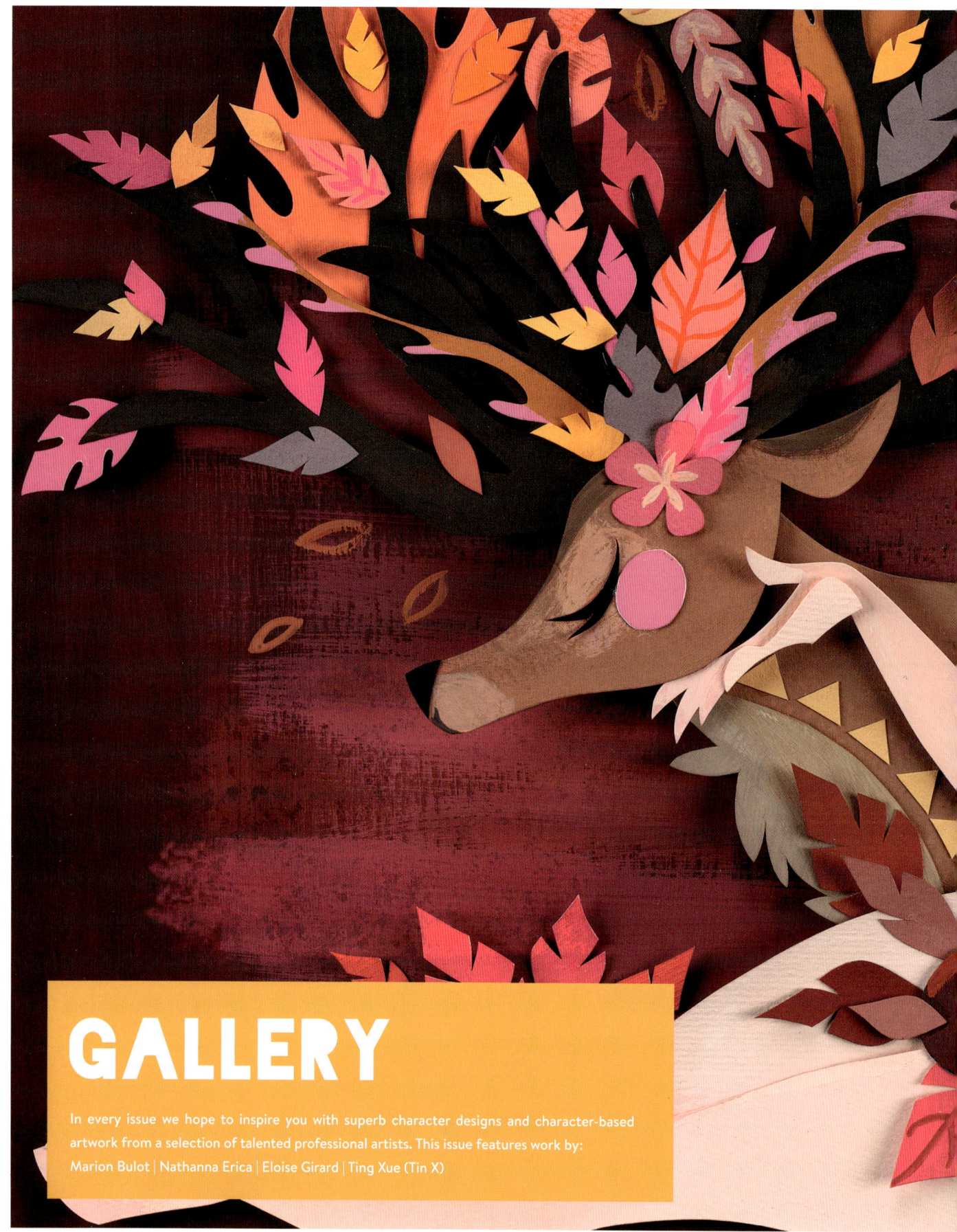

GALLERY

In every issue we hope to inspire you with superb character designs and character-based artwork from a selection of talented professional artists. This issue features work by:

Marion Bulot | Nathanna Erica | Eloise Girard | Ting Xue (Tin X)

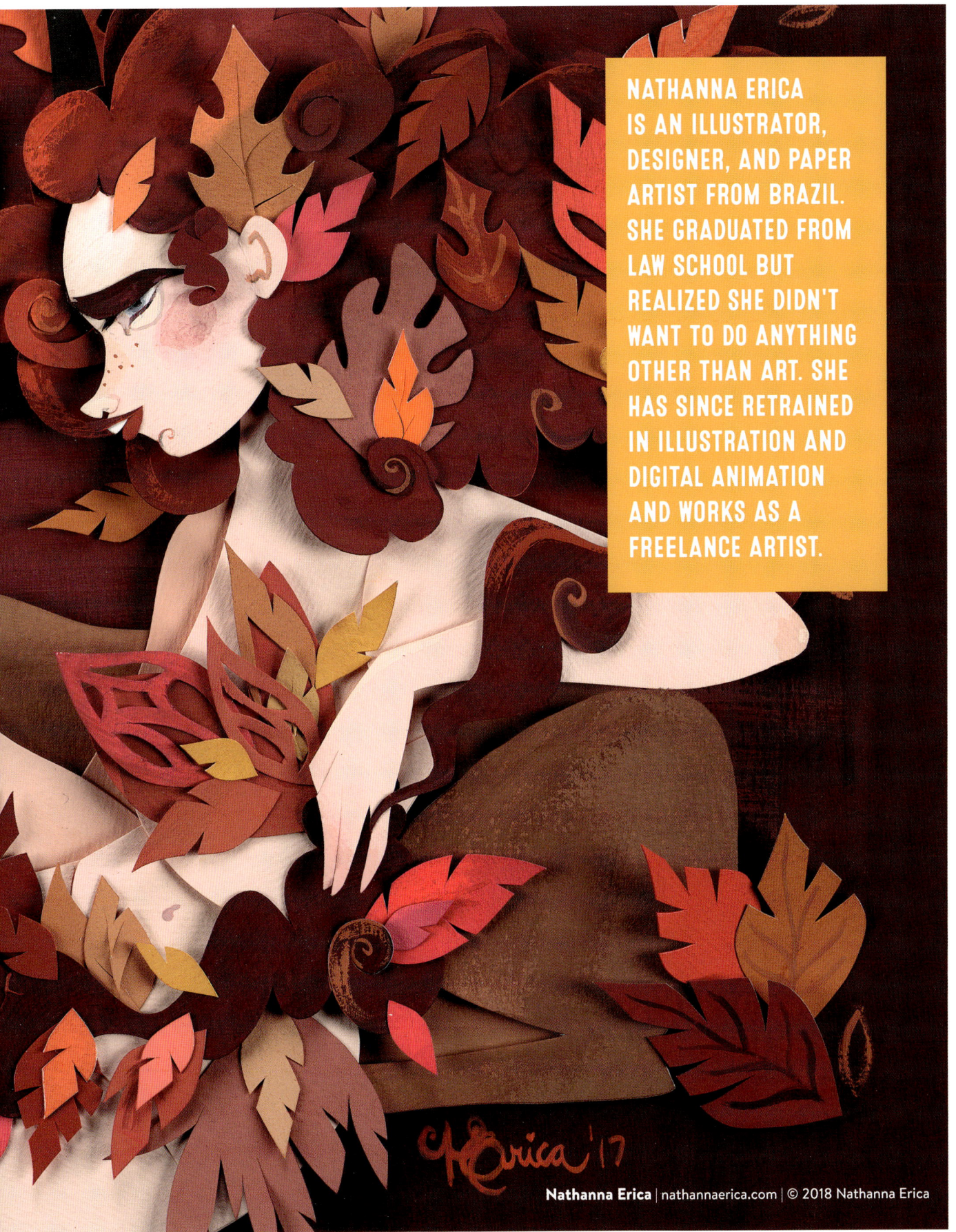

NATHANNA ERICA
IS AN ILLUSTRATOR,
DESIGNER, AND PAPER
ARTIST FROM BRAZIL.
SHE GRADUATED FROM
LAW SCHOOL BUT
REALIZED SHE DIDN'T
WANT TO DO ANYTHING
OTHER THAN ART. SHE
HAS SINCE RETRAINED
IN ILLUSTRATION AND
DIGITAL ANIMATION
AND WORKS AS A
FREELANCE ARTIST.

Nathanna Erica | nathannaerica.com | © 2018 Nathanna Erica

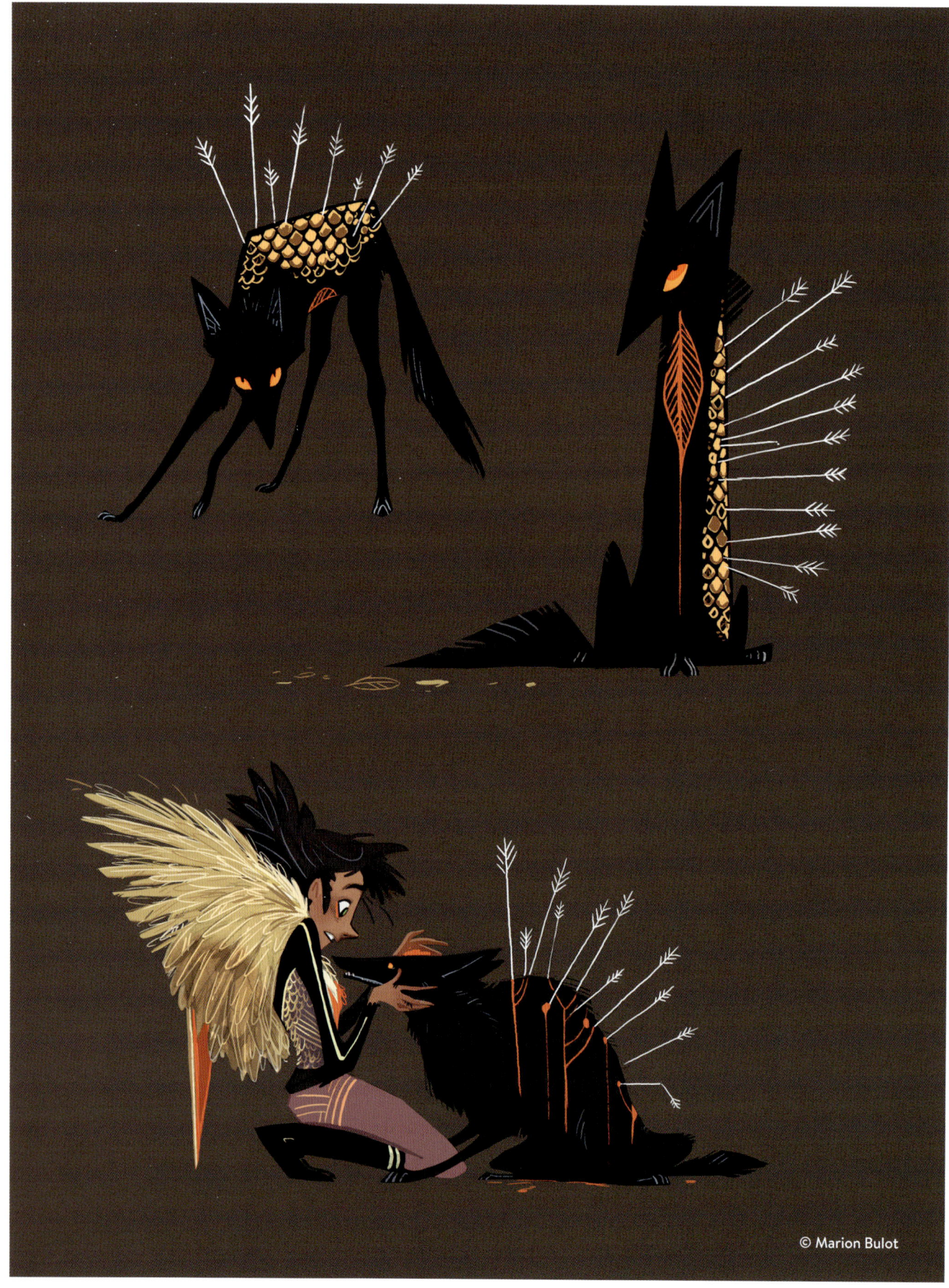

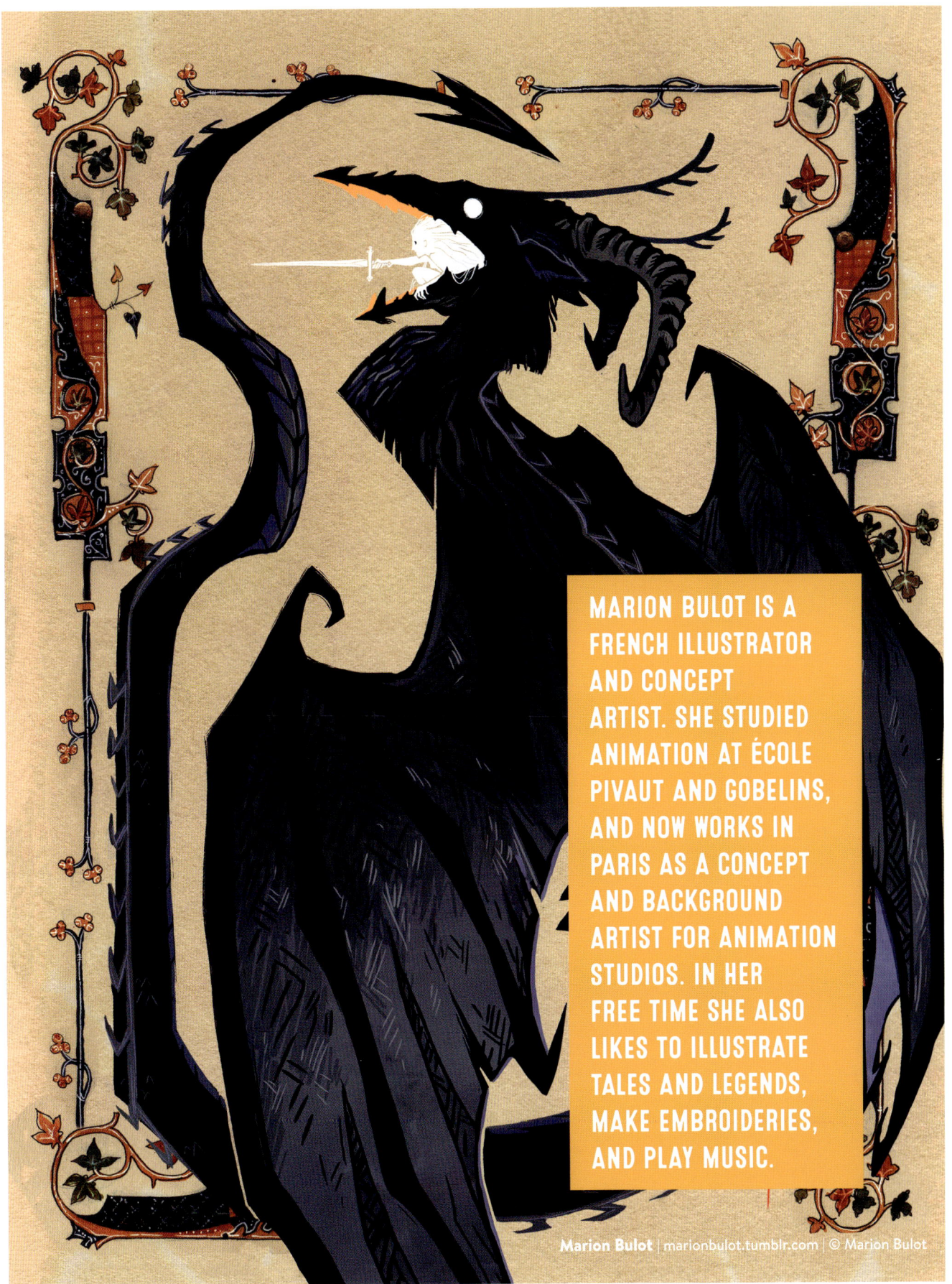

MARION BULOT IS A FRENCH ILLUSTRATOR AND CONCEPT ARTIST. SHE STUDIED ANIMATION AT ÉCOLE PIVAUT AND GOBELINS, AND NOW WORKS IN PARIS AS A CONCEPT AND BACKGROUND ARTIST FOR ANIMATION STUDIOS. IN HER FREE TIME SHE ALSO LIKES TO ILLUSTRATE TALES AND LEGENDS, MAKE EMBROIDERIES, AND PLAY MUSIC.

Marion Bulot | marionbulot.tumblr.com | © Marion Bulot

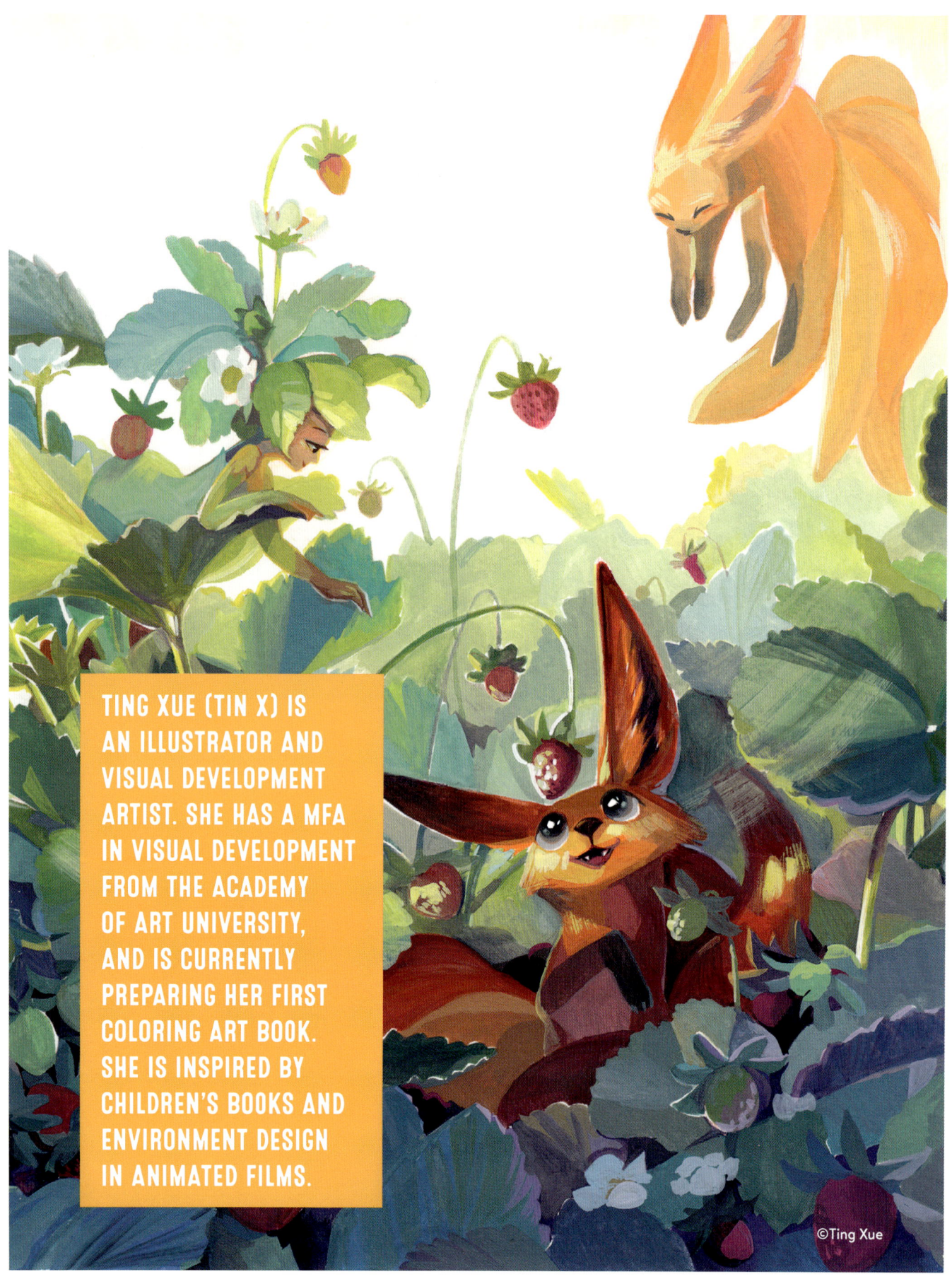

TING XUE (TIN X) IS AN ILLUSTRATOR AND VISUAL DEVELOPMENT ARTIST. SHE HAS A MFA IN VISUAL DEVELOPMENT FROM THE ACADEMY OF ART UNIVERSITY, AND IS CURRENTLY PREPARING HER FIRST COLORING ART BOOK. SHE IS INSPIRED BY CHILDREN'S BOOKS AND ENVIRONMENT DESIGN IN ANIMATED FILMS.

©Ting Xue

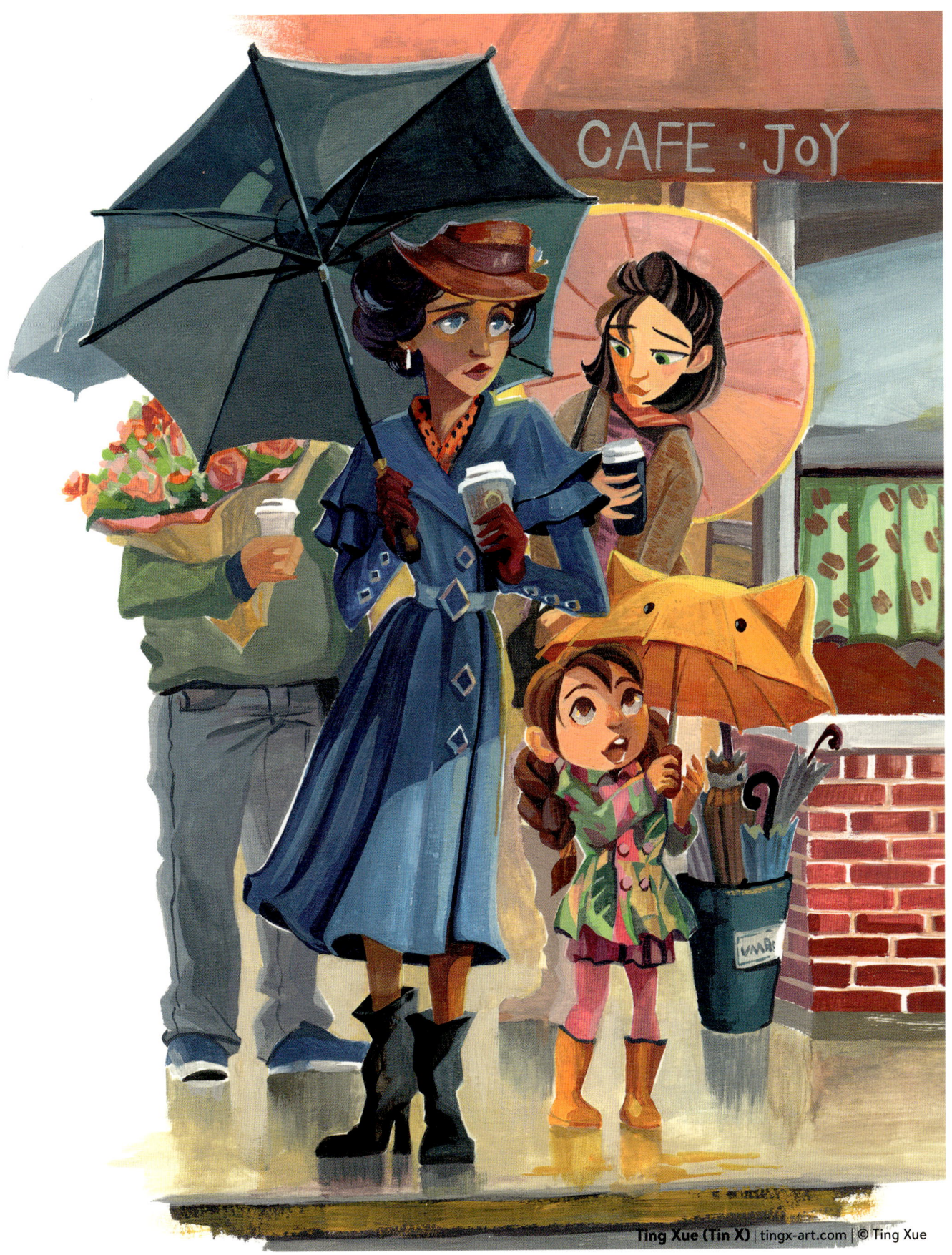

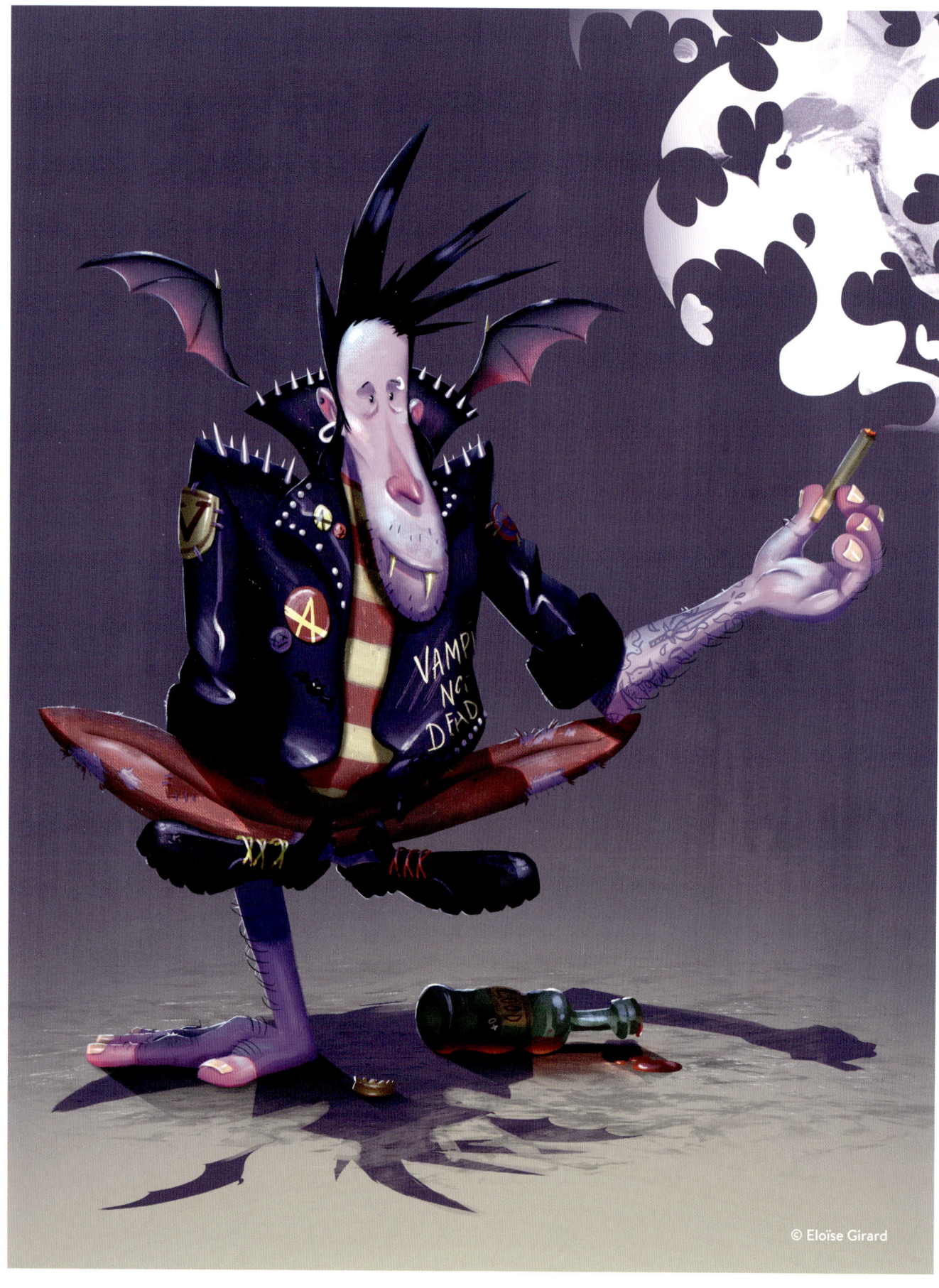

© Eloïse Girard

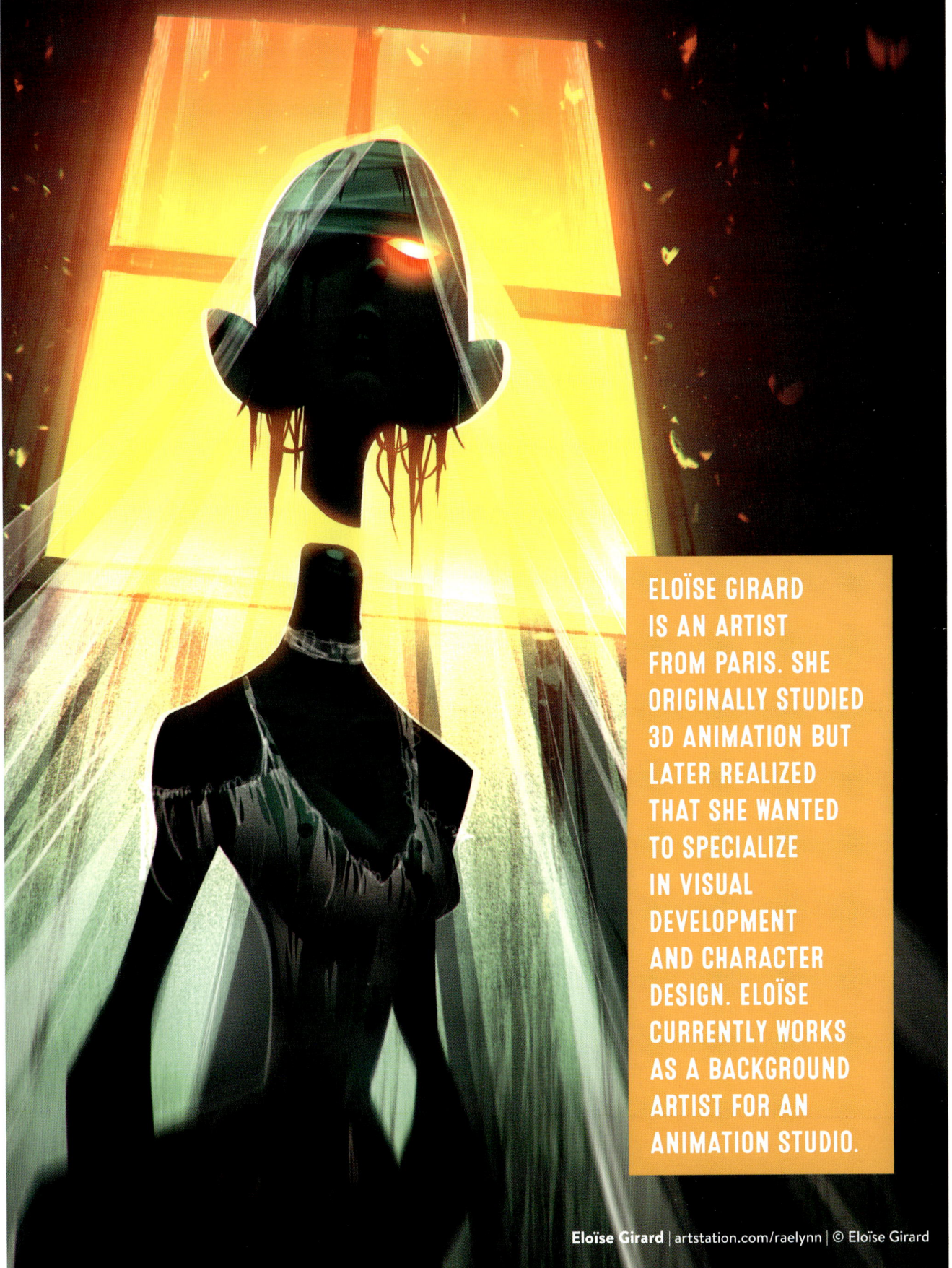

ELOÏSE GIRARD
IS AN ARTIST
FROM PARIS. SHE
ORIGINALLY STUDIED
3D ANIMATION BUT
LATER REALIZED
THAT SHE WANTED
TO SPECIALIZE
IN VISUAL
DEVELOPMENT
AND CHARACTER
DESIGN. ELOÏSE
CURRENTLY WORKS
AS A BACKGROUND
ARTIST FOR AN
ANIMATION STUDIO.

Eloïse Girard | artstation.com/raelynn | © Eloïse Girard

OPEN AND CLOSED POSES

Victoria Kosheleva

When you design a character, both their personality and mood must be easily readable through pose. Even a very impressive character can appear uninteresting when presented in the wrong pose. How can you use pose to make a character seem alive and dynamic, and encourage the viewer to feel compassion for them?

An understanding of the psychology of poses and gestures will help you draw a character in any mood. A character's mood can change regardless of personality type. A good character can be angry, and an evil character can demonstrate kindness, mood that can be illustrated through pose. Briefly put, there are two kinds of pose: open and closed.

OPEN POSES

The character turns towards the viewer with no physical barrier between them. In open poses, the character's arms are uncrossed and their palms stay open. With this openness, the viewer feels that the character is ready to communicate.

CLOSED POSES

In contrast, in closed pose the character turns away from the viewer, or crosses their arms or legs. This is a protective stance which indicates that the character does not want to communicate.

Here are my top tips to make your character appear more alive and interesting.

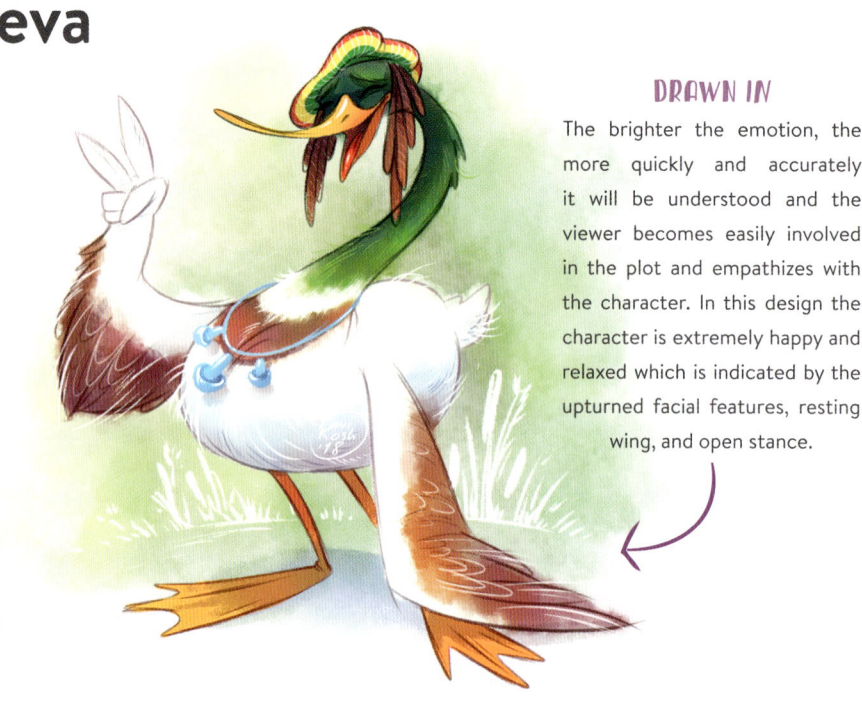

DRAWN IN

The brighter the emotion, the more quickly and accurately it will be understood and the viewer becomes easily involved in the plot and empathizes with the character. In this design the character is extremely happy and relaxed which is indicated by the upturned facial features, resting wing, and open stance.

SURPRISE!

A fully open pose instantly involves the viewers with what is happening. The pose and gesture must emphasize any movement within the composition. In this case, the bear's open pose and expressive gesture suggests sudden motion, while the face communicates the character's surprise in the action.

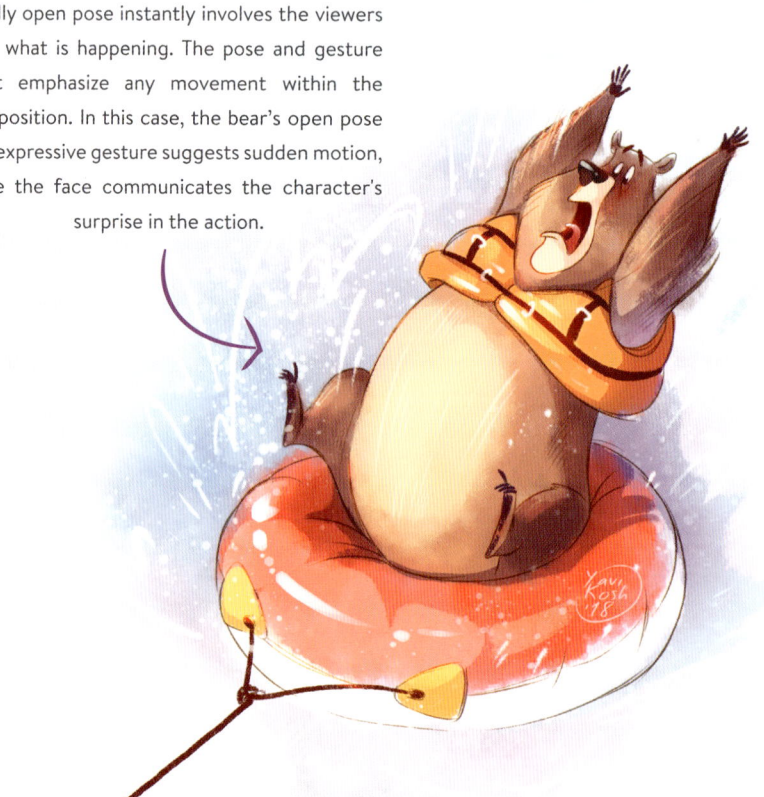

OPENING SOON...

Closed poses do not have to be a sign of negative emotion, and can be a temporary state. The fox's pose, hugging his tail, shows that the character is keen or excited, and is only momentarily unavailable. The facial expression supports this assumption and adds a more dynamic feel to the action.

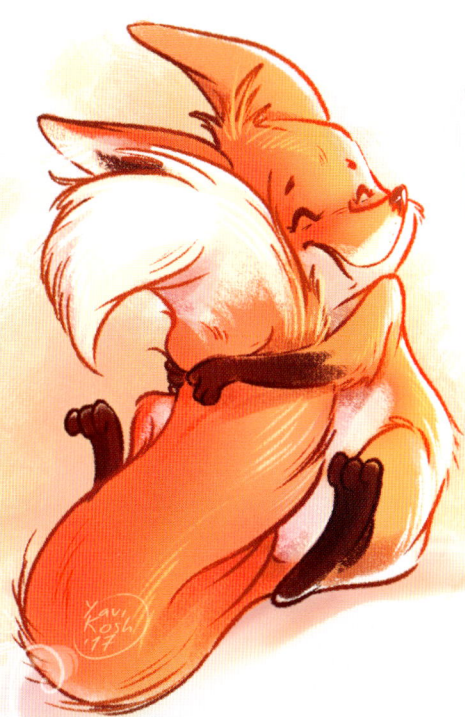

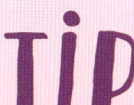

TIP

When commissioned to create a character, always consider the context in which it will be used. A happy, positive, or playful context suggests a hero who exhibits welcoming open poses and uplifting gestures. Where the context is serious, somber, or downbeat, closed poses will help you to create a character that belongs within that story. Ask the client about the context of your commission and how your character interacts within it. This will save time and nerves for both of you.

OPEN AND CLOSED?

Play with variations of the gestures by combining them. This squirrel's pose is coquettish, posing for the viewer with her head turned to us, but with a half-closed pose. She appears to be hiding something from us. This combination of open and closed gestures in a single pose adds mystery and intrigues the viewer.

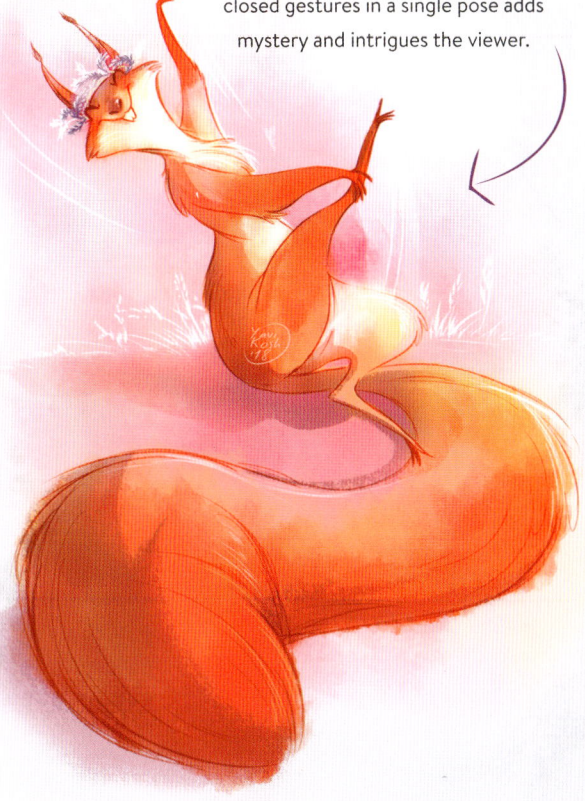

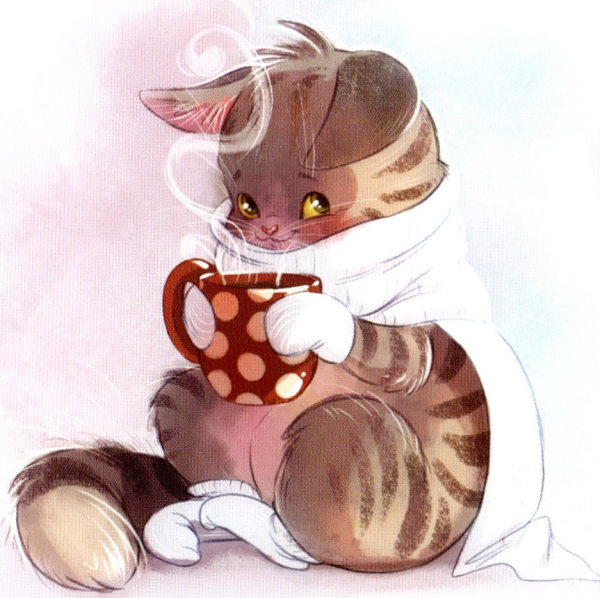

PERSONAL SPACE

Use closed poses when a character is lost in thought, is wrapped-up in their own world, or is in an uncooperative mood. This kitten is clearly happy, yet the pose is closed. Gathered into a ball and closed off from the viewer, he is using the mug as a barrier. It is clear that the character is enjoying the coziness and warmth, but is happy to be on their own.

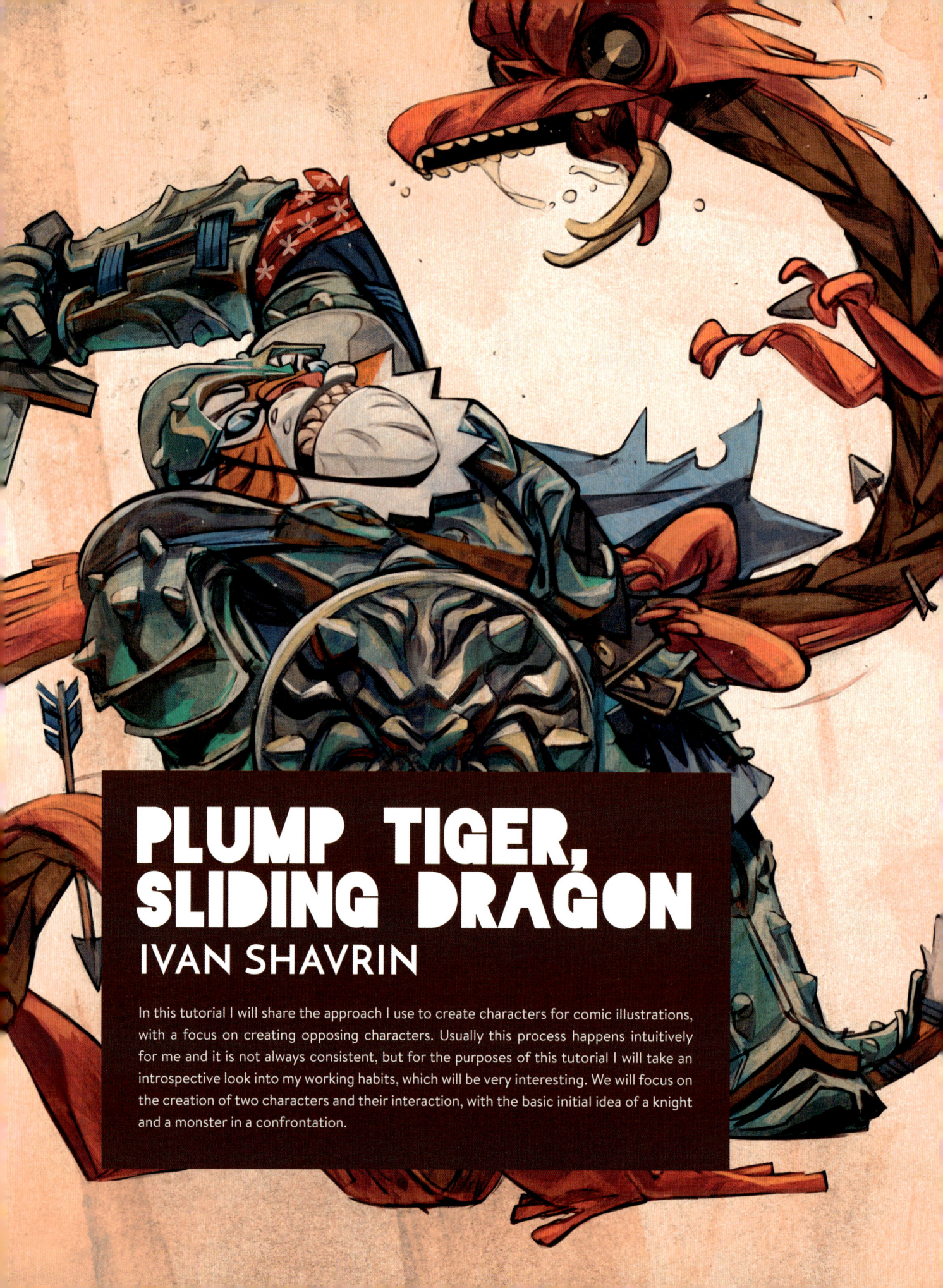

PLUMP TIGER, SLIDING DRAGON

IVAN SHAVRIN

In this tutorial I will share the approach I use to create characters for comic illustrations, with a focus on creating opposing characters. Usually this process happens intuitively for me and it is not always consistent, but for the purposes of this tutorial I will take an introspective look into my working habits, which will be very interesting. We will focus on the creation of two characters and their interaction, with the basic initial idea of a knight and a monster in a confrontation.

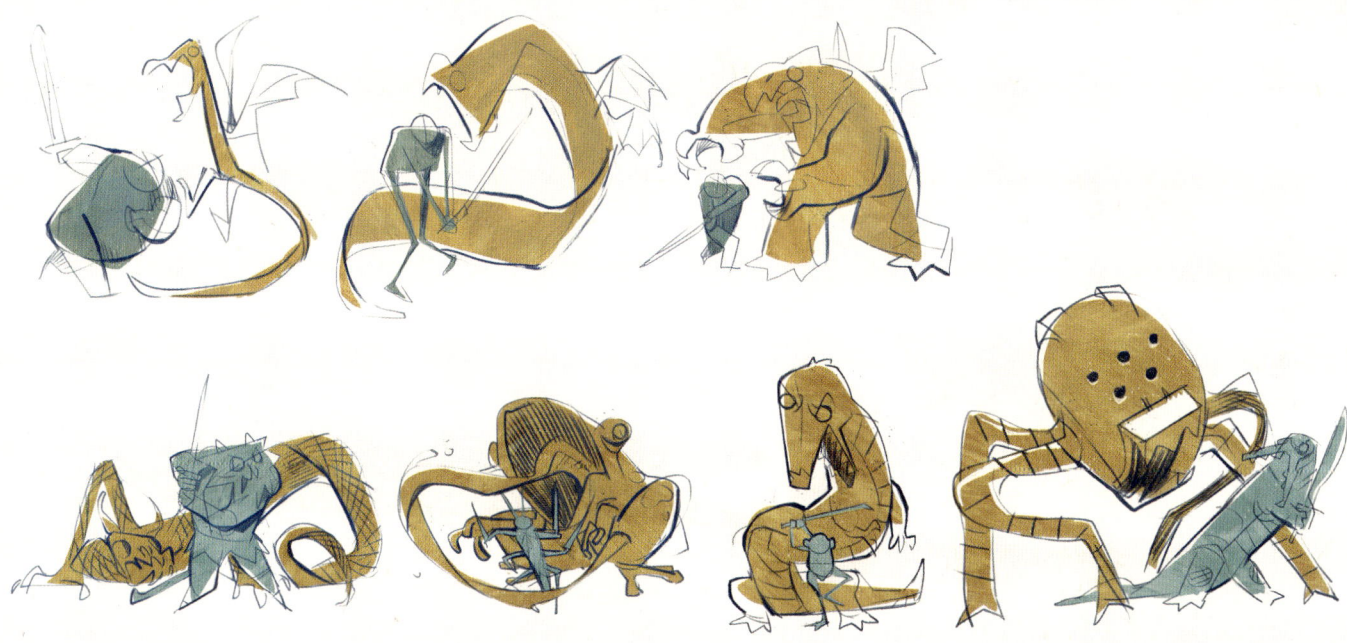

SKETCHES

Having chosen a topic, in this case opposing characters, you need to understand how to make characters which, regardless of their interaction, will be interesting to look at in one comic frame. Loosely sketch out ideas for your characters, choosing several different poses and shapes. Usually the first sketches are understandable only to you, but that is fine for the purpose we are using them for here.

Think first about the volumes and dimensions of your characters and how they can contrast. Thin and thick, small and large, or many other contrasting forms are frequently used in cartoons and animations. Any contrast creates a tension between the character forms and generates energy in a composition. Remember that in a confrontation scene such as this, the viewer will intuitively empathize more with a smaller character who is not afraid and gives a rebuff to a larger opponent.

MATERIALITY

The texture and materiality of the characters is very important and can also be used to create contrast. Introduce ideas for the materiality of characters early in the sketch ideation phase.

Thinking about these character's textures and how they could contrast, it immediately occurs

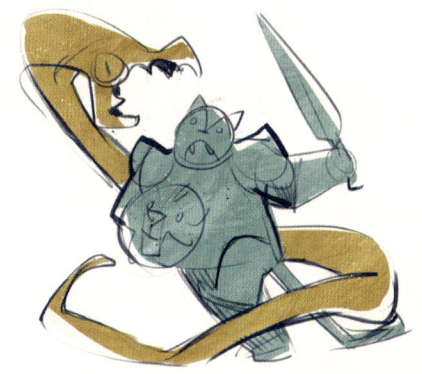

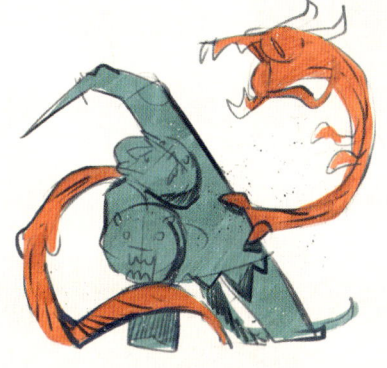

to me to make a representative of the furry feline world who fights with some scaly dragon. I imagine a tiger character who is a knight and defender of the "Meow-Fur" kingdom fighting a serpentine dragon. I consider other contrasting models, such as a grasshopper and frog, a frog and a crocodile, a crocodile and a huge robot, but I like the opposition of feline and reptile here.

COLOR

Consider now how you can use color to create contrast. Colors should reflect the attitude of the characters, and during their interaction it should be possible to understand where each character is and what he does without effort. In this case, the interaction is a battle. When

we first look at the characters it must be immediately understood that one is a hero, and the other is his evil enemy.

Blue and red are a win-win option for opposing characters as they are both strong colors but they are not very original. I decided to keep working with these colors however, trying to use more complex shades to make the choice more interesting.

Above, top: Create rough sketches focusing on broad contrasts in shape between the characters

Above, middle: Explore possible combinations of characters concentrating on their materiality

Above, bottom: Try opposing color options to see which works best for the roles each character plays

DESIGNING THE PLUMP TIGER

Analyze the work you have done so far and choose a sketch that you want to continue working with. In this step we will proceed to creating a more scrupulous design which will give a better understanding of the character and his story.

A rectangular, clumsy, but intricate design is what I need for the warrior. I try to add a comic, doomed look to the facial features by spreading the ears and eyes. As this character is a knight he will need armor and a helmet that should be tight against his head, a tie under the massive chin emphasizes his jaw and of course there will need to be armor over the tail as this is a tiger.

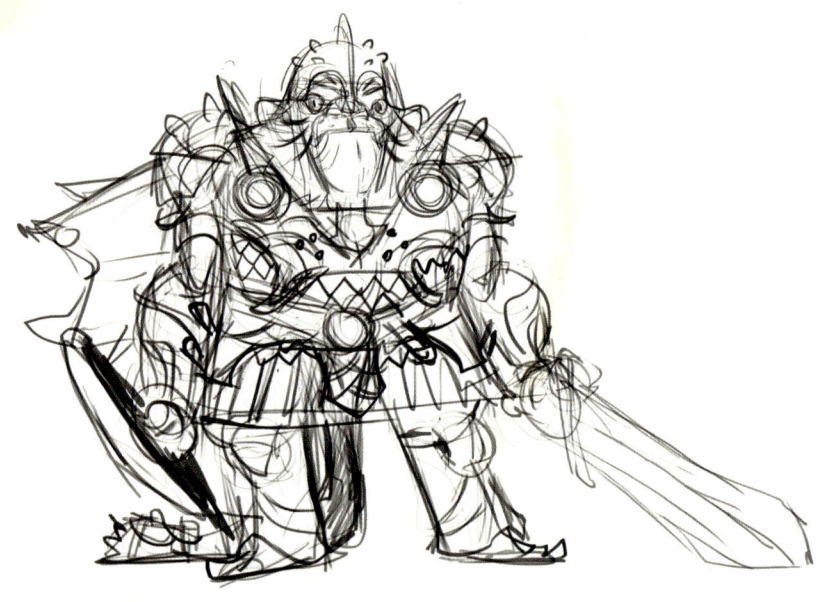

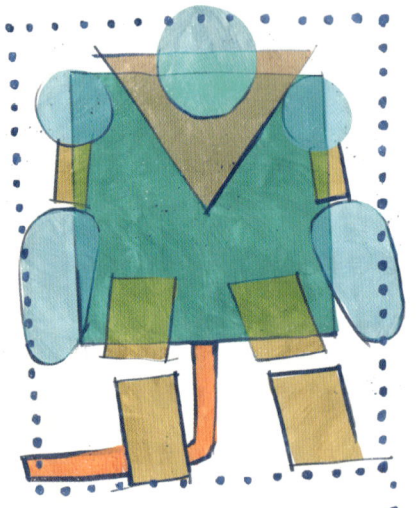

DETAILS CREATE A STORY

A good character design tells a story about the character's origin, just by looking at it, and therefore you should pay attention to every detail you add that could help to tell a story. This hero's armor is broadly constructed of mixed geometric shapes such as triangles, spheres, and spirals. I make contiguous lines and duplicate elements throughout the design, so that the forms look complete.

Looking at the armor construction in more detail, I add spirals, curves, repeating lines, and angular cones. These shapes add interest to design and create a sense of dynamism which implies the character's energy as an action hero.

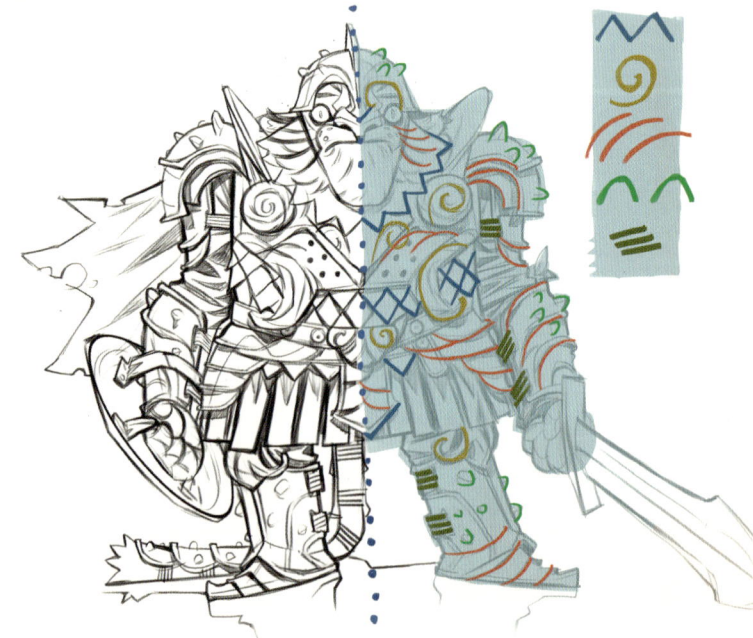

Top: Focusing on one character, develop a definite idea for how the character will look

Above right: Strong geometric shapes help to give the character's form a feeling of completeness

Above left: Spirals, cones, and repeated lines give the armor variety and a sense of movement

Right: A ripped cloak and cumbersome sword show that the character is an experienced warrior

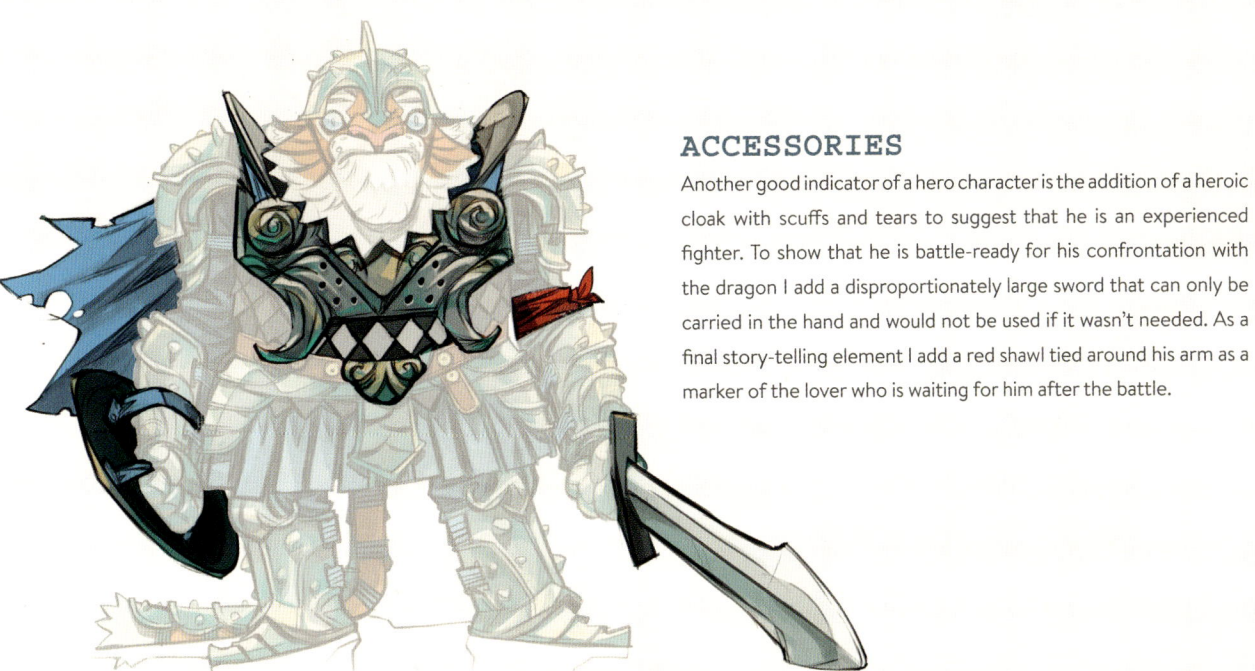

ACCESSORIES

Another good indicator of a hero character is the addition of a heroic cloak with scuffs and tears to suggest that he is an experienced fighter. To show that he is battle-ready for his confrontation with the dragon I add a disproportionately large sword that can only be carried in the hand and would not be used if it wasn't needed. As a final story-telling element I add a red shawl tied around his arm as a marker of the lover who is waiting for him after the battle.

TEXTURE

After the detailed design has been refined, I paint the character making the outline a dark brown which is not as jarring as a solid black outline. When the clean line art and colors are complete I add one of my favorite textures which gives the design a more material book-like effect. A textured finish helps to add movement to the design as it encourages the viewer's eye to keep moving around the page.

Now I have a voluminous, but appealing, tiger in authentic armor which supports the story that he is a protector of a cat kingdom. His expression shows he is a little scared and there is no sharp mind behind his glance, but we know he is loved because of the red shawl from his love who is waiting for him at home.

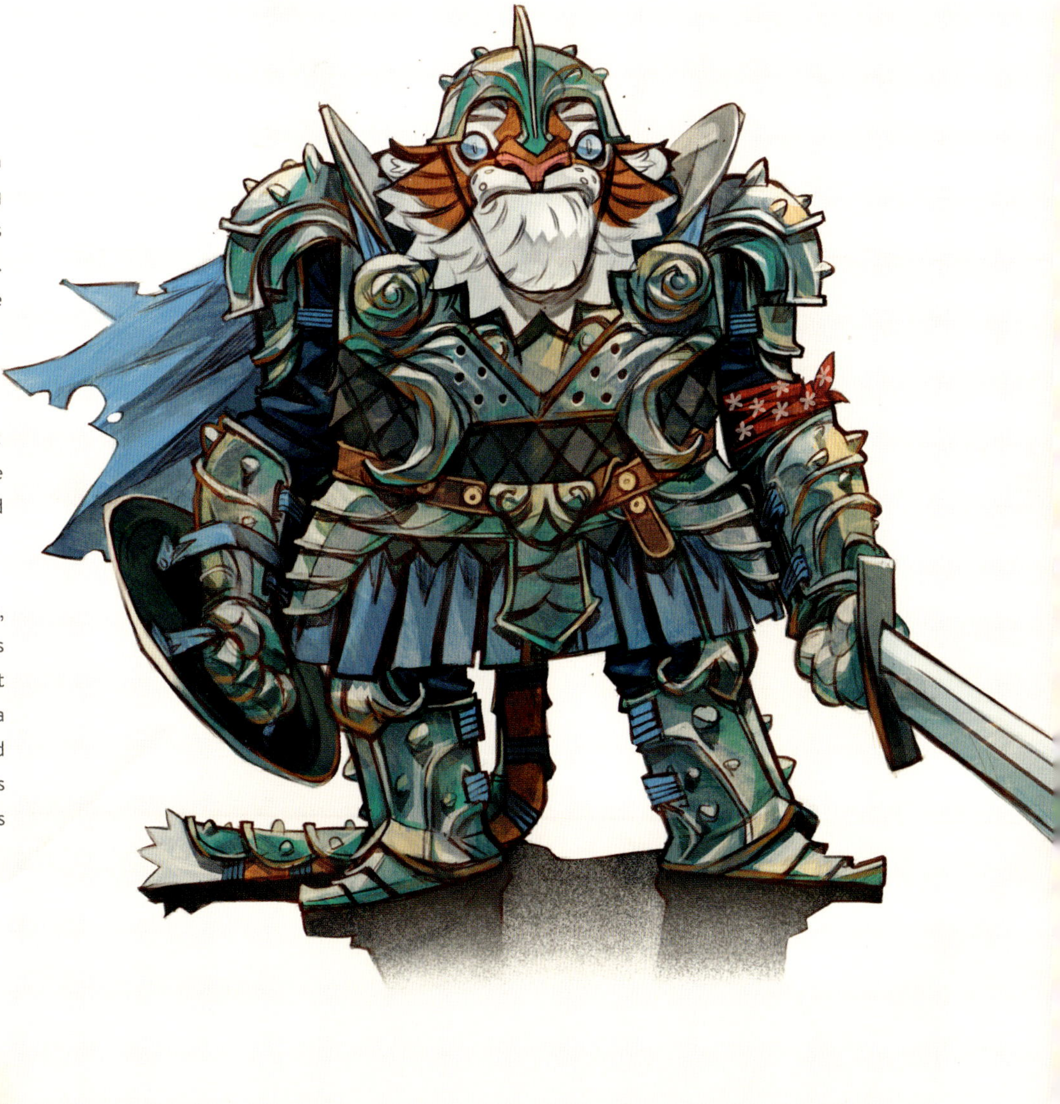

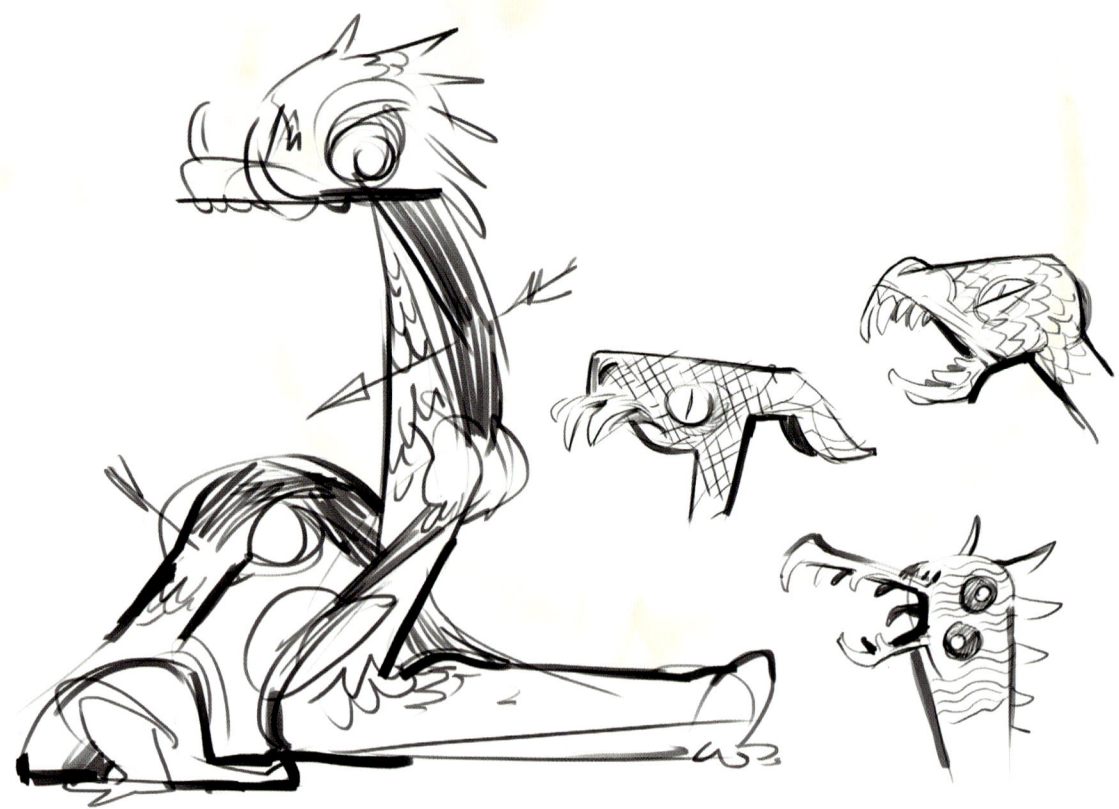

DESIGNING THE
SLIDING DRAGON

Now begin to consider the hero character's opponent. It is easier now to design the enemy as you can work with contrasts to the design you have already created. This character is an elongated red snake-like dragon. To make the basic shape of the design more complex I give the dragon very short legs and add arrows embedded in his flesh. These additions will help to make a more interesting interaction with his opponent.

Work on the design of the head, exploring several different options. Since we are creating two opposing characters, the designs should have markedly different shapes and there should not be a problem with getting stuck in a single style.

Above: The design of the knight's opponent, the dragon, can be long and slim to create contrast

Right: The elongated shape naturally lends itself to interesting twists and contortions

Opposite page: Adding a texture to the final rendering helps to give the design a greater sense of movement

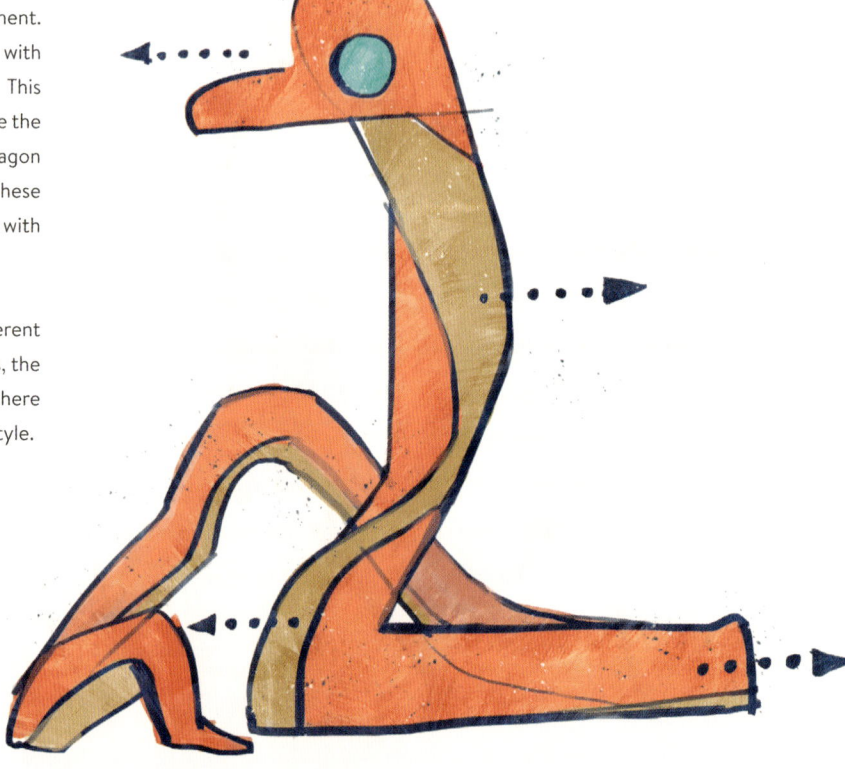

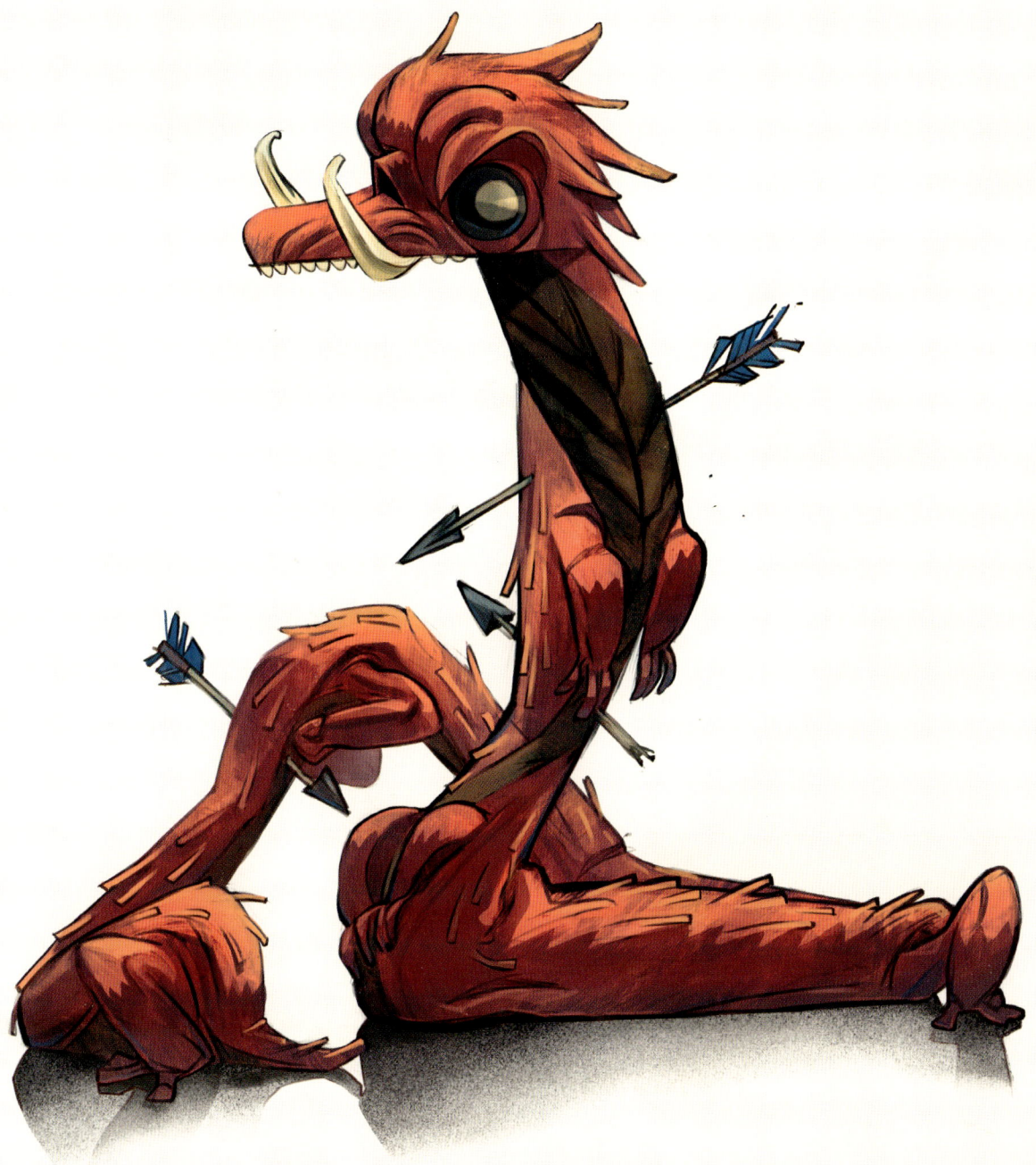

One of the key advantages of this dragon's elongated form is that you can easily make the pose feel dynamic, even when the dragon is in a static position. The body can be constantly twisting and unfolding, moving the lines of his body around the frame to create variety. Even a simple sitting pose can be made interesting by having the head facing in one direction while the body is directed in the opposite and then curved back around again.

THE DRAGON'S STORY

What about the opponent's story? To the arrows I add blue plumage which has already been defined as the classic color of the army of the knight's kingdom. From this it can be assumed that this is not the dragon's first battle with our hairy hero. That he is unfazed by the arrows also shows that he is a very strong opponent. When I clean and render the design, I use the same principles as I did for the knight, using a dark brown line instead of black and adding a texture for movement. Using the same finish on both characters will help unify them when they are put in a frame together, making the battle scene more cohesive.

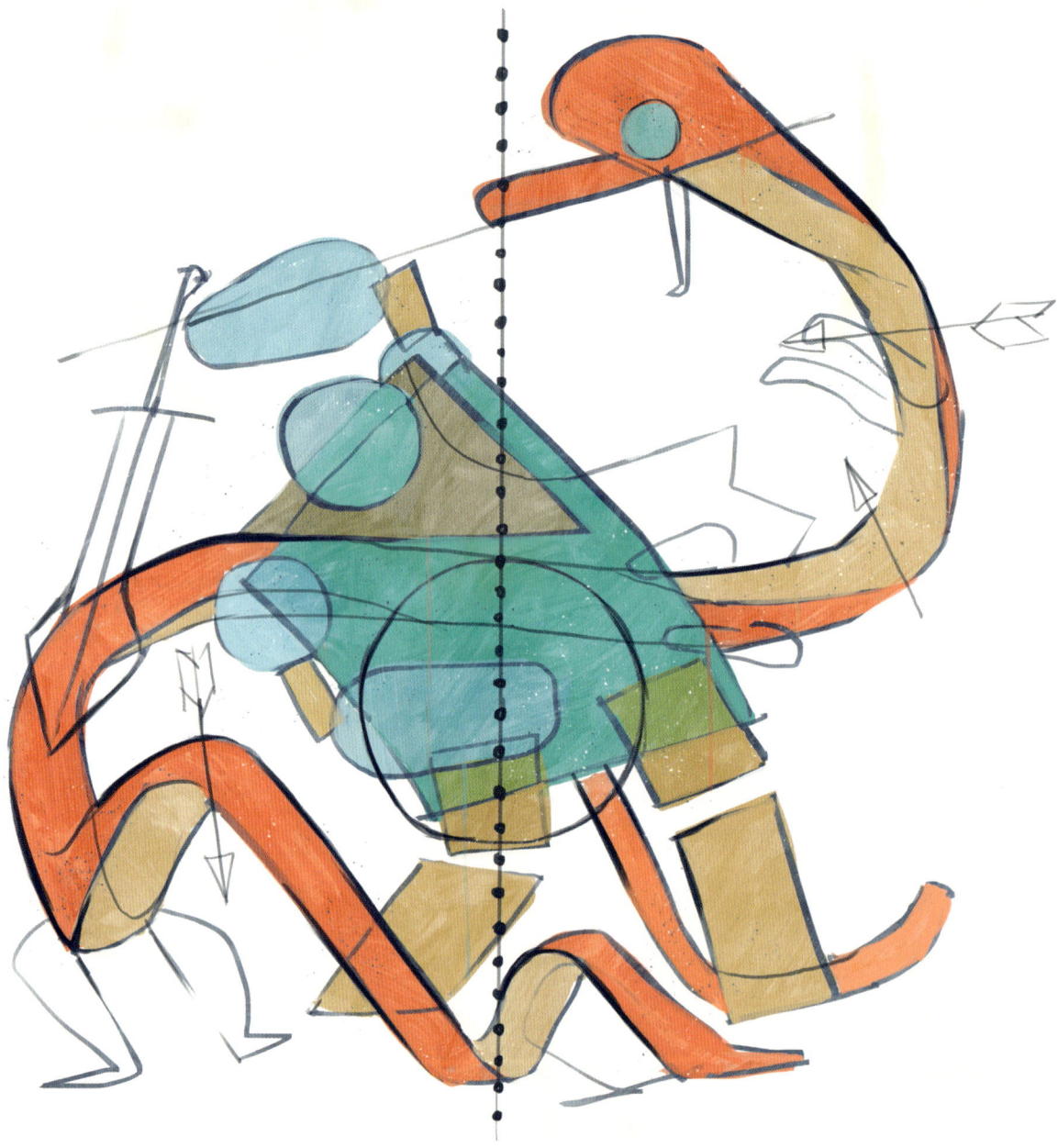

THE BATTLE SCENE

Having gone through all these design refinement stages, you can go back to sketching the two designs together again. The process now should be relatively simple, especially if you use basic shapes to help with the posing of the characters. As the blocky knight will be fighting off the elongated dragon in every direction, the battle can be reduced to a massive rectangle which will be in tension with a wriggling, aggressive line.

Take the shape outlines and pose them. Find adjacent lines and symmetrical opposites in the knight and then use the twisting shape of the dragon to wrap and loop around the knight. Since you are working out the poses with the basic shape it is easy to foresee where there might be any possible problems in the composition of the picture, such as too much or too little space between specific parts of the characters. It is much easier to correct these at this stage than later on. This will ultimately result in a dynamic, memorable fight.

Top: Adding blue to the arrows shows that the dragon has been in many battles with the knight's army

Left: Designing the pose composition using the character's basic shapes makes the process easier and helps you to spot any flaws in the poses

Opposite page: The final design shows a dynamic battle scene and tells the story of a knight defending his kingdom from a twisted dragon

FINAL DESIGN

With the knight's shield positioned front-facing there is another opportunity to add a symbol of the cat kingdom. An ornate embellishment of a lion's head, matching the colors of the armor is very effective in this case.

Reviewing the designs, they have resulted in a balanced scene with a clear story and correlation between the characters. The hero and opponent correctly perform their roles and you can continue to fantasize about the tiger knights and lion king, who protect the "Meow-Fur" kingdom from all sorts of scaly monsters. It's an interesting scene that is aesthetically pleasing and imaginative.

"USING THE SAME FINISH ON BOTH CHARACTERS WILL HELP UNIFY THEM WHEN THEY ARE PUT IN A FRAME TOGETHER"

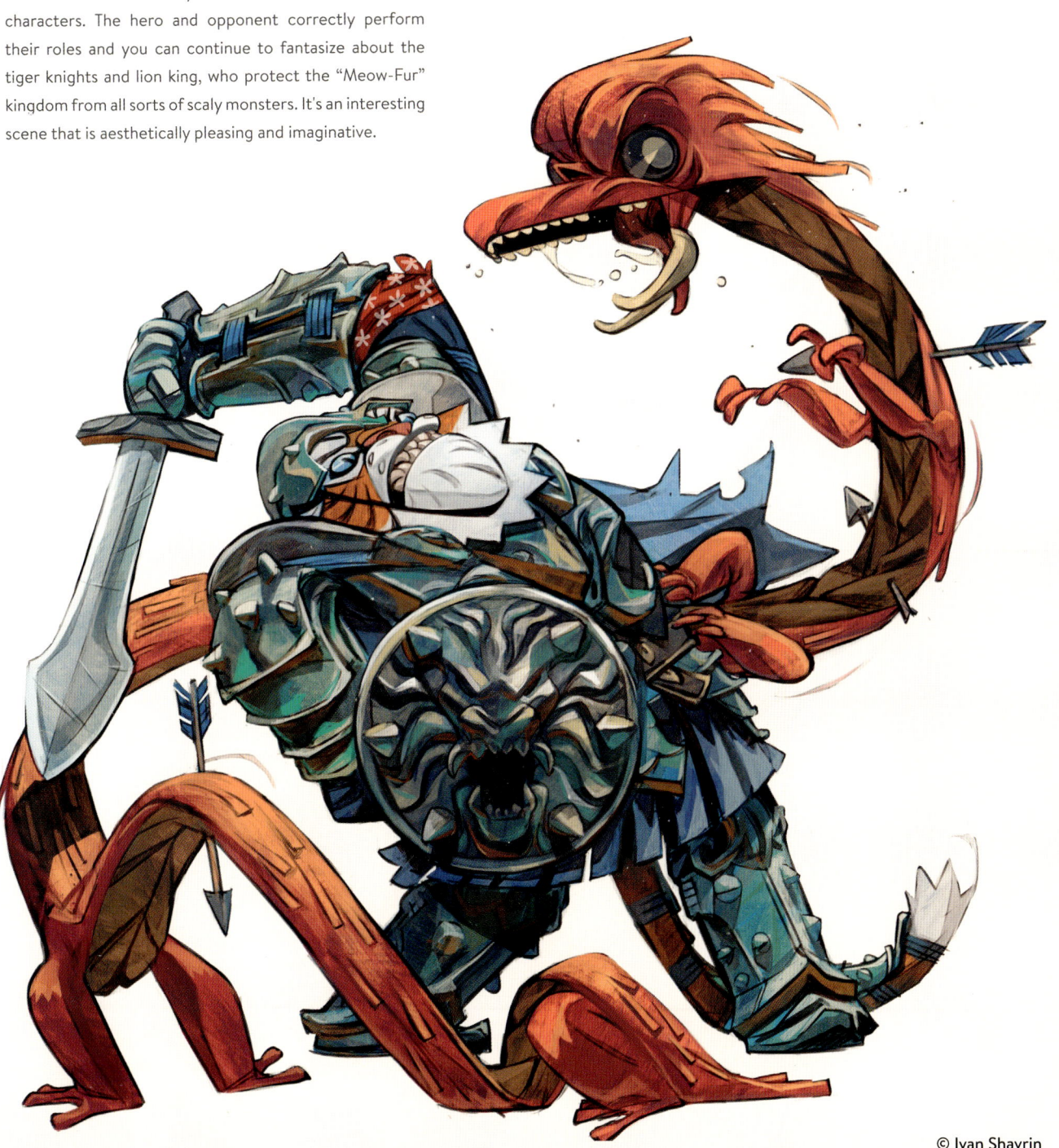

© Ivan Shavrin

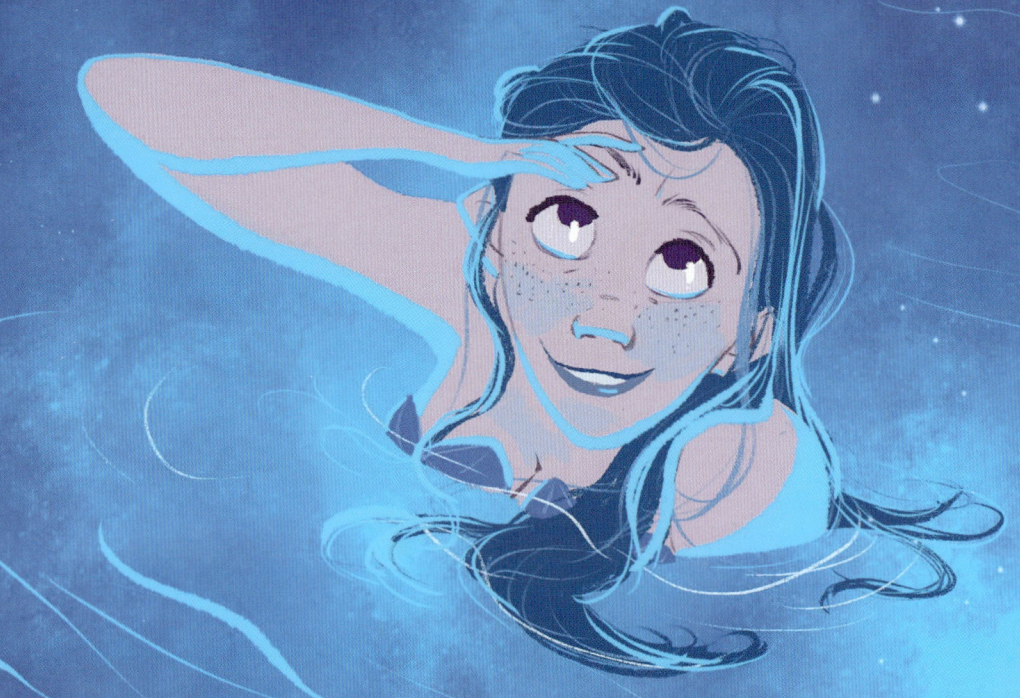

MEET THE ARTIST
AMANDA MACFARLANE

Amanda MacFarlane is a self-taught artist with a passion for creating spirited characters and concept art. Running her freelance business, The Animated Life, from home Amanda has worked on animation and character design projects for a number of impressive clients including Warner Bros. Animation and Elastic.tv. Her lively, imaginative works have also attracted a large online following and esteem from industry peers. In this issue, Amanda discusses her charismatic style, shares tips on how to become a successful character designer without formal training, and explains why designing a character feels like deciphering a mystery to her.

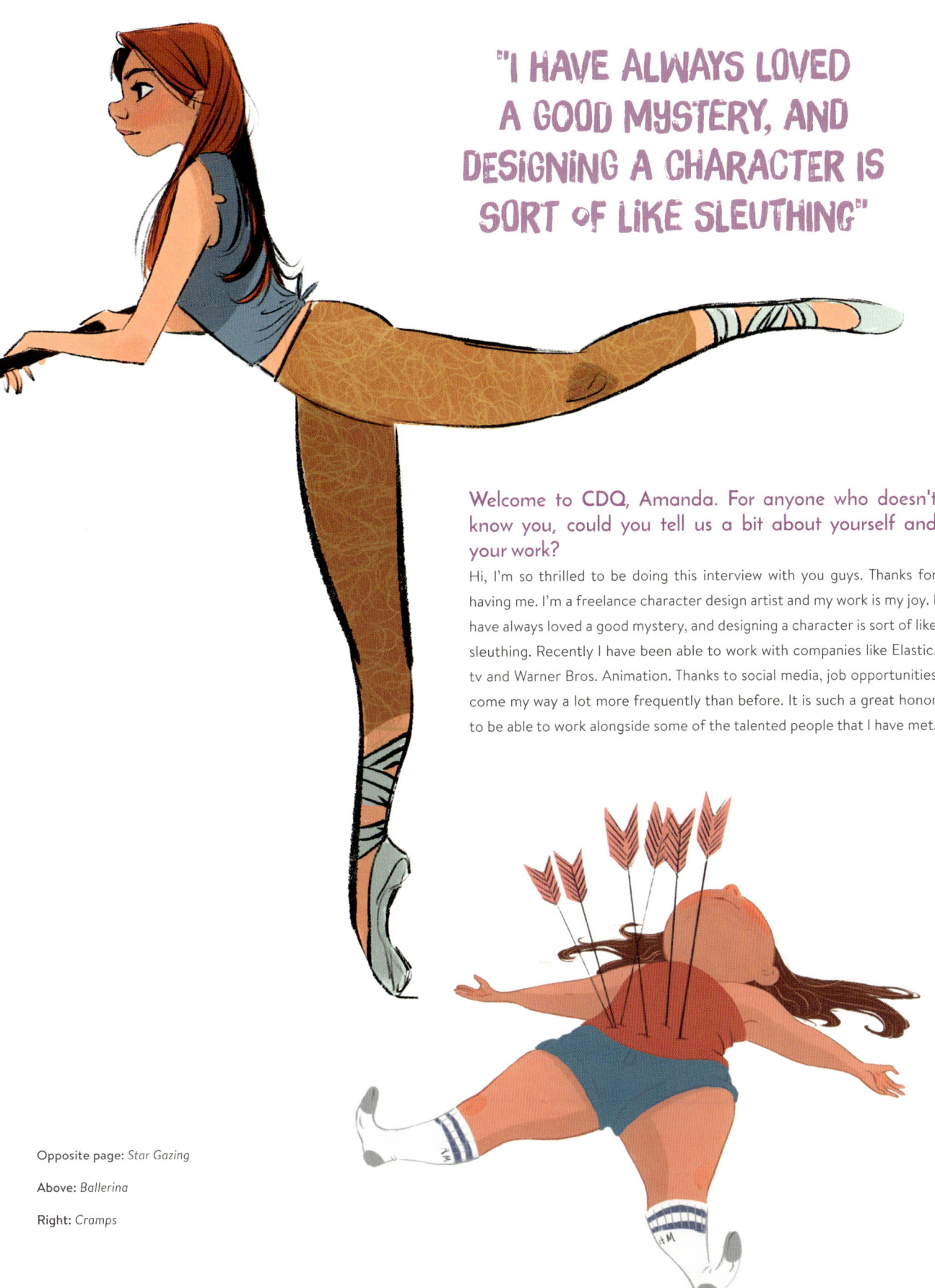

"I HAVE ALWAYS LOVED A GOOD MYSTERY, AND DESIGNING A CHARACTER IS SORT OF LIKE SLEUTHING"

Welcome to CDQ, Amanda. For anyone who doesn't know you, could you tell us a bit about yourself and your work?

Hi, I'm so thrilled to be doing this interview with you guys. Thanks for having me. I'm a freelance character design artist and my work is my joy. I have always loved a good mystery, and designing a character is sort of like sleuthing. Recently I have been able to work with companies like Elastic. tv and Warner Bros. Animation. Thanks to social media, job opportunities come my way a lot more frequently than before. It is such a great honor to be able to work alongside some of the talented people that I have met.

Opposite page: *Star Gazing*

Above: *Ballerina*

Right: *Cramps*

With so many opportunities, what is your approach to balancing different jobs?

I usually take on jobs one at a time. Being a mom to my three daughters takes center stage, so I try to keep the projects at a minimum. Currently I am working with Warner Bros. Animation on the upcoming film *S.C.O.O.B.* I can't go into detail about it, but I will say that it has been my first feature length animated film to work on, and I love it!

As you begin each assignment, do you have a particular approach to designing the character?

I wish I could tell you I have a secret plan that works every time, and that it is the key to all success, but in actuality I just draw until I get it right. My approach to drawing for a client is to try and get in their shoes and figure out where they want to go with the project. They are coming to me with expectations, hopes and dreams for the character, so I try my very best to make them come true.

I want to make the client happy and when they are happy with the design, I am too. So if my creativity is not working well enough I will take a small break, drink some coffee, sketch something for myself, and get back to the drawing board. Taking on someone else's vision is a challenge at times but it is rewarding to see yourself improve as an artist.

Opposite page: *Race is on*

This page: *Teenage Self Portrait*

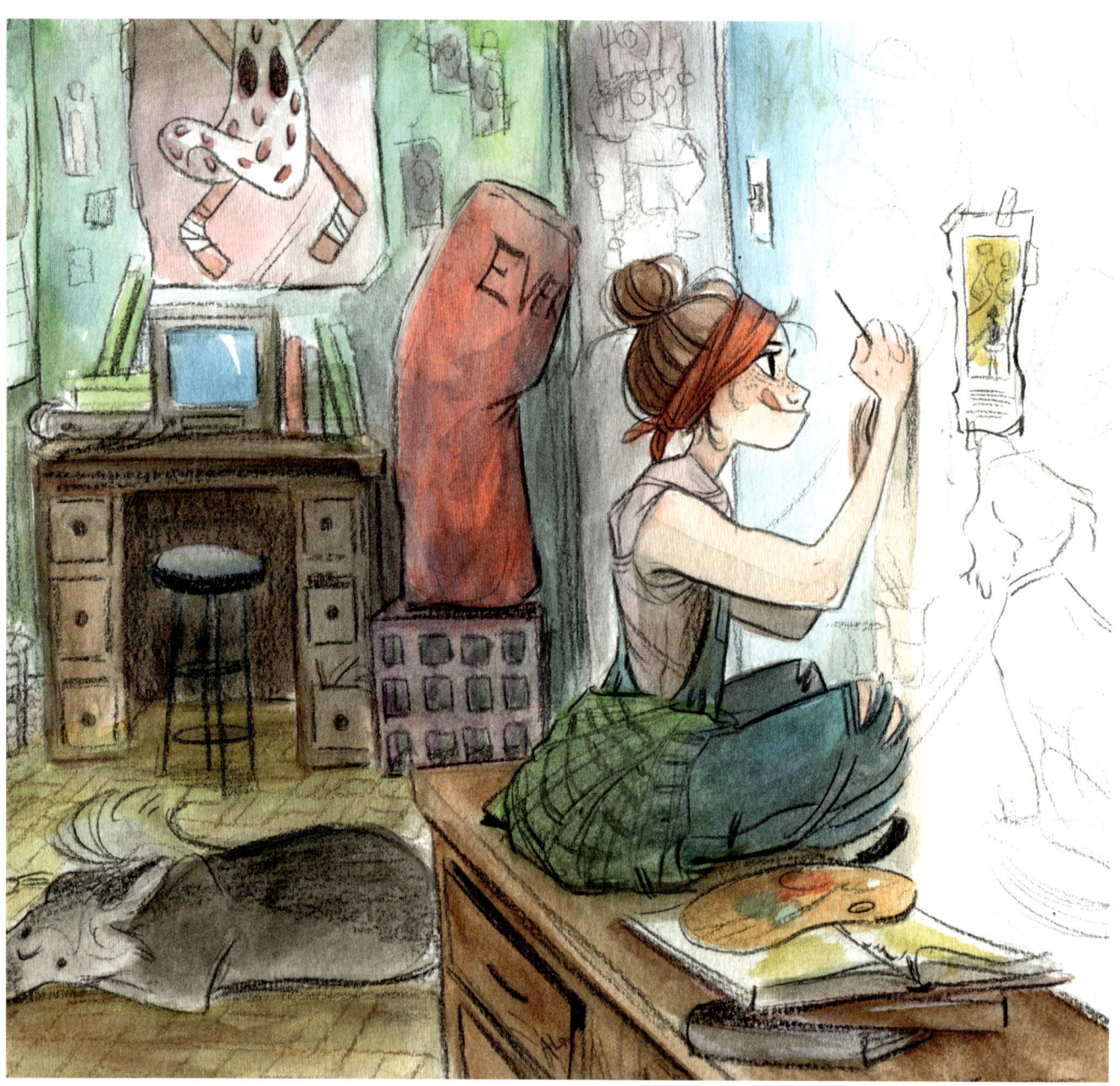

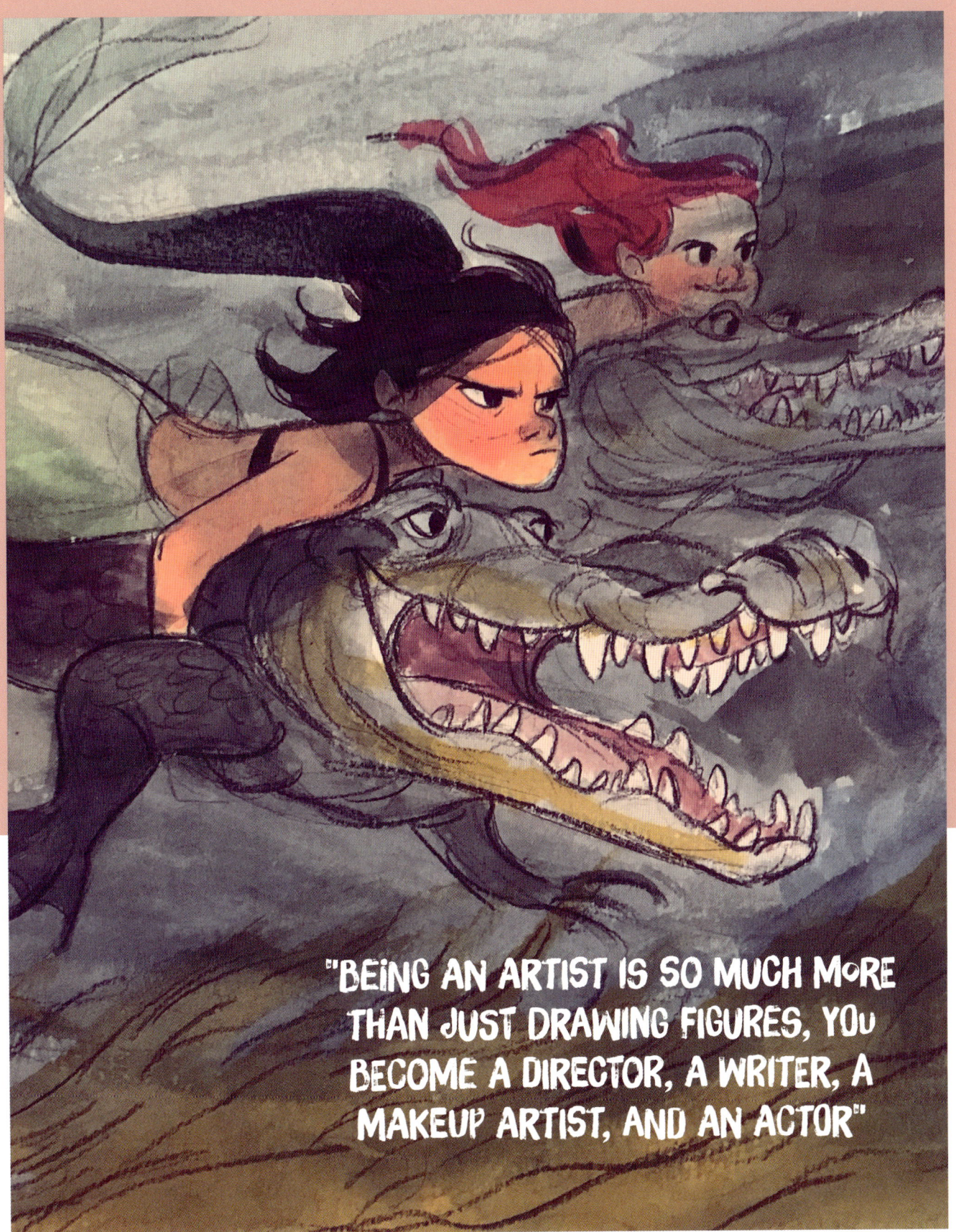

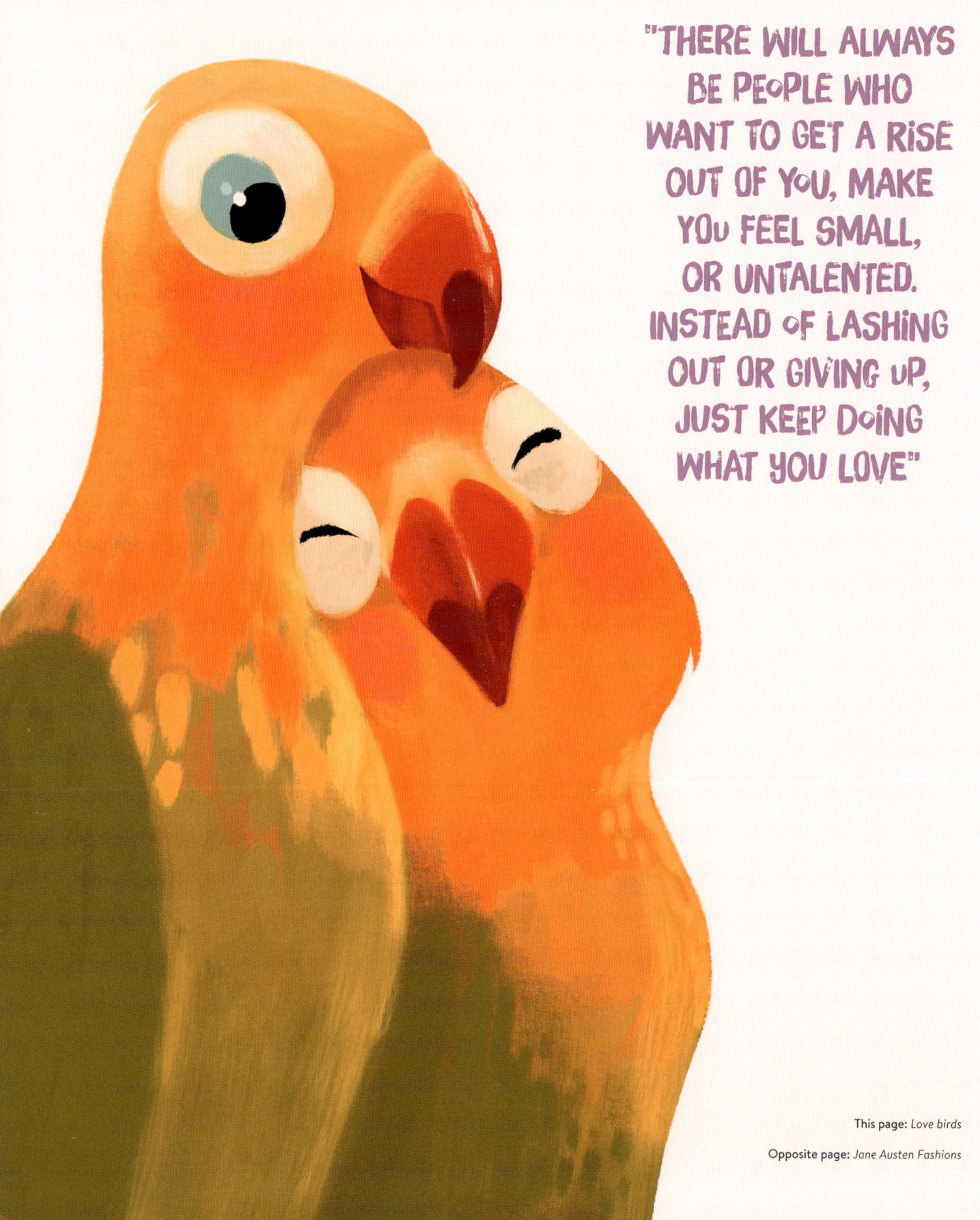

"THERE WILL ALWAYS BE PEOPLE WHO WANT TO GET A RISE OUT OF YOU, MAKE YOU FEEL SMALL, OR UNTALENTED. INSTEAD OF LASHING OUT OR GIVING UP, JUST KEEP DOING WHAT YOU LOVE"

This page: *Love birds*

Opposite page: *Jane Austen Fashions*

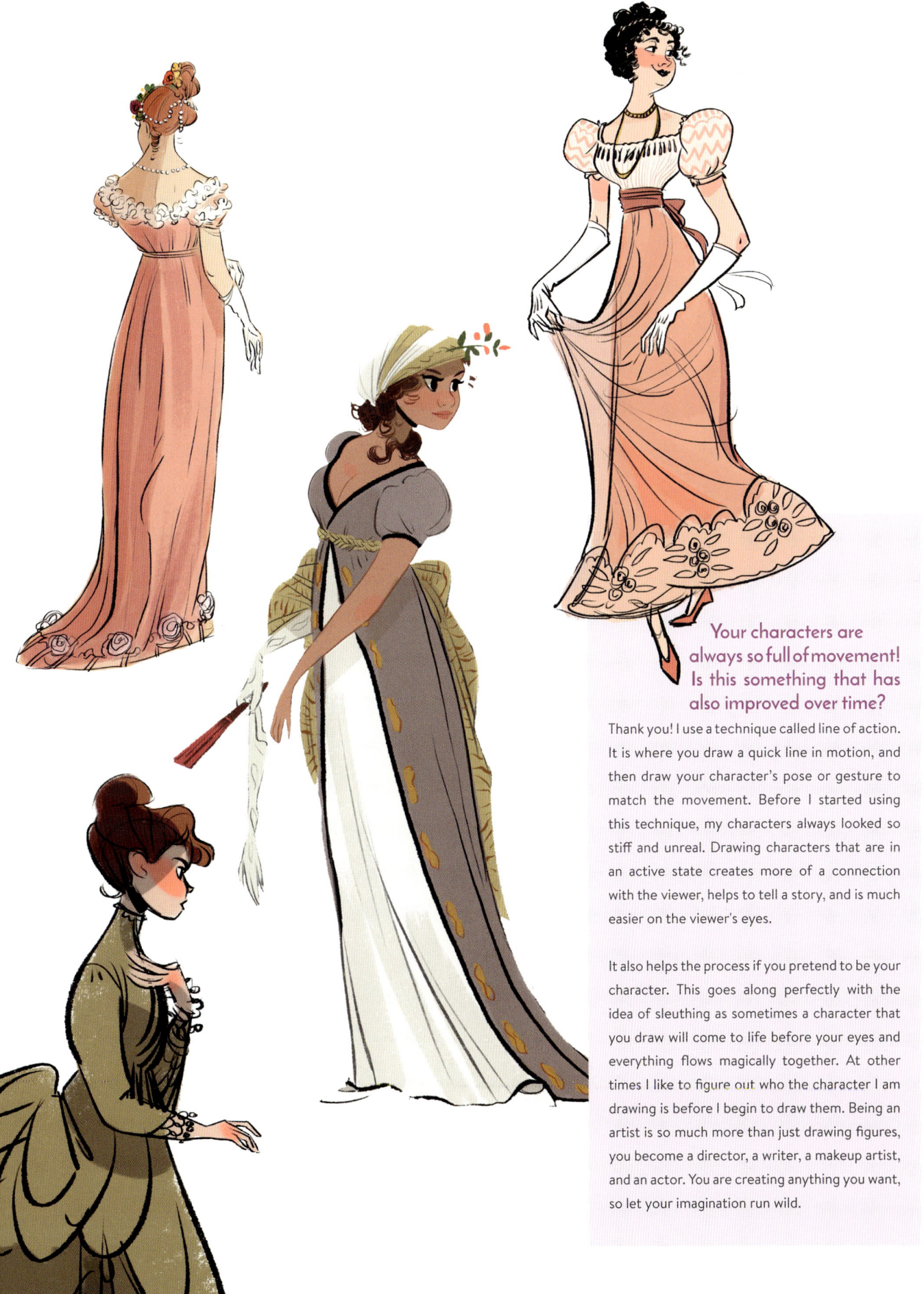

Your characters are always so full of movement! Is this something that has also improved over time?

Thank you! I use a technique called line of action. It is where you draw a quick line in motion, and then draw your character's pose or gesture to match the movement. Before I started using this technique, my characters always looked so stiff and unreal. Drawing characters that are in an active state creates more of a connection with the viewer, helps to tell a story, and is much easier on the viewer's eyes.

It also helps the process if you pretend to be your character. This goes along perfectly with the idea of sleuthing as sometimes a character that you draw will come to life before your eyes and everything flows magically together. At other times I like to figure out who the character I am drawing is before I begin to draw them. Being an artist is so much more than just drawing figures, you become a director, a writer, a makeup artist, and an actor. You are creating anything you want, so let your imagination run wild.

"CLASSIC ANIMATIONS LIKE 101 DALMATIANS, ROBIN HOOD, SLEEPING BEAUTY, AND I GUESS ANY WORN OUT VHS CARTOON THAT I HAD AS A KID, STILL PLAY A PART IN MY IMAGINATION PROCESS TODAY"

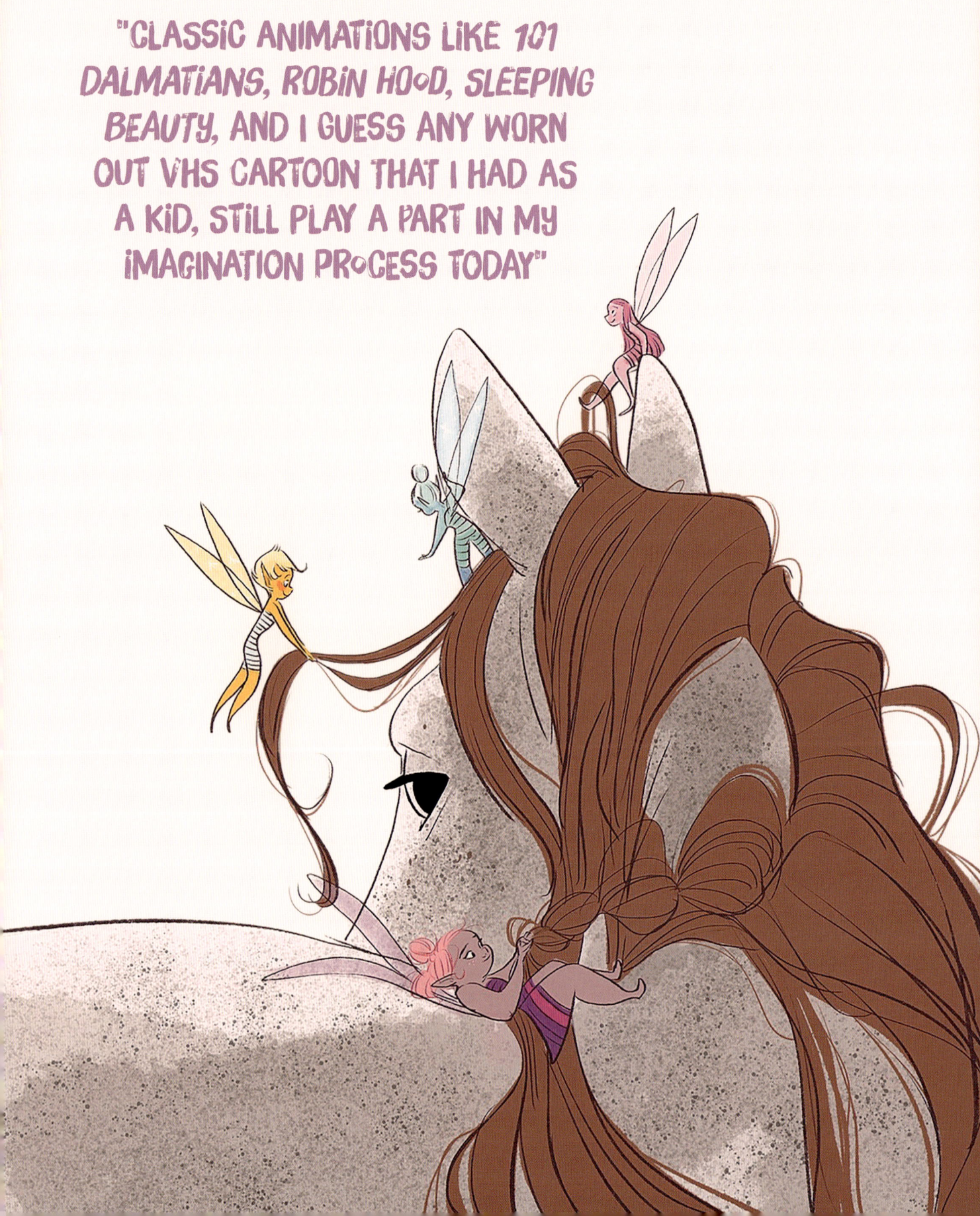

Do you have any tips for readers on staying positive when their work is given negative feedback?

I believe there is both negative feedback and helpful criticism. When the criticism comes from an educated source or a friend it is much easier to take and they encourage you to improve. When it comes from an unwanted source and they are bashing your work in front of others on social media or in person, it is very hard to take. We as artists are vulnerable because we bare our souls for the world to see and await its opinion. When our art is being attacked, it feels personal and cuts deeply. I have had a few of these moments and I stopped drawing for a while because I couldn't take the internet trolls, but then I remembered how much I loved drawing and how many other positive people had my back. There will always be people who want to get a rise out of you, make you feel small, or untalented. Instead of lashing out or giving up, just keep doing what you love. If you do not give up, you will grow and they will look like an idiot.

This page: *Hi There*

Opposite page: *Helping Out*

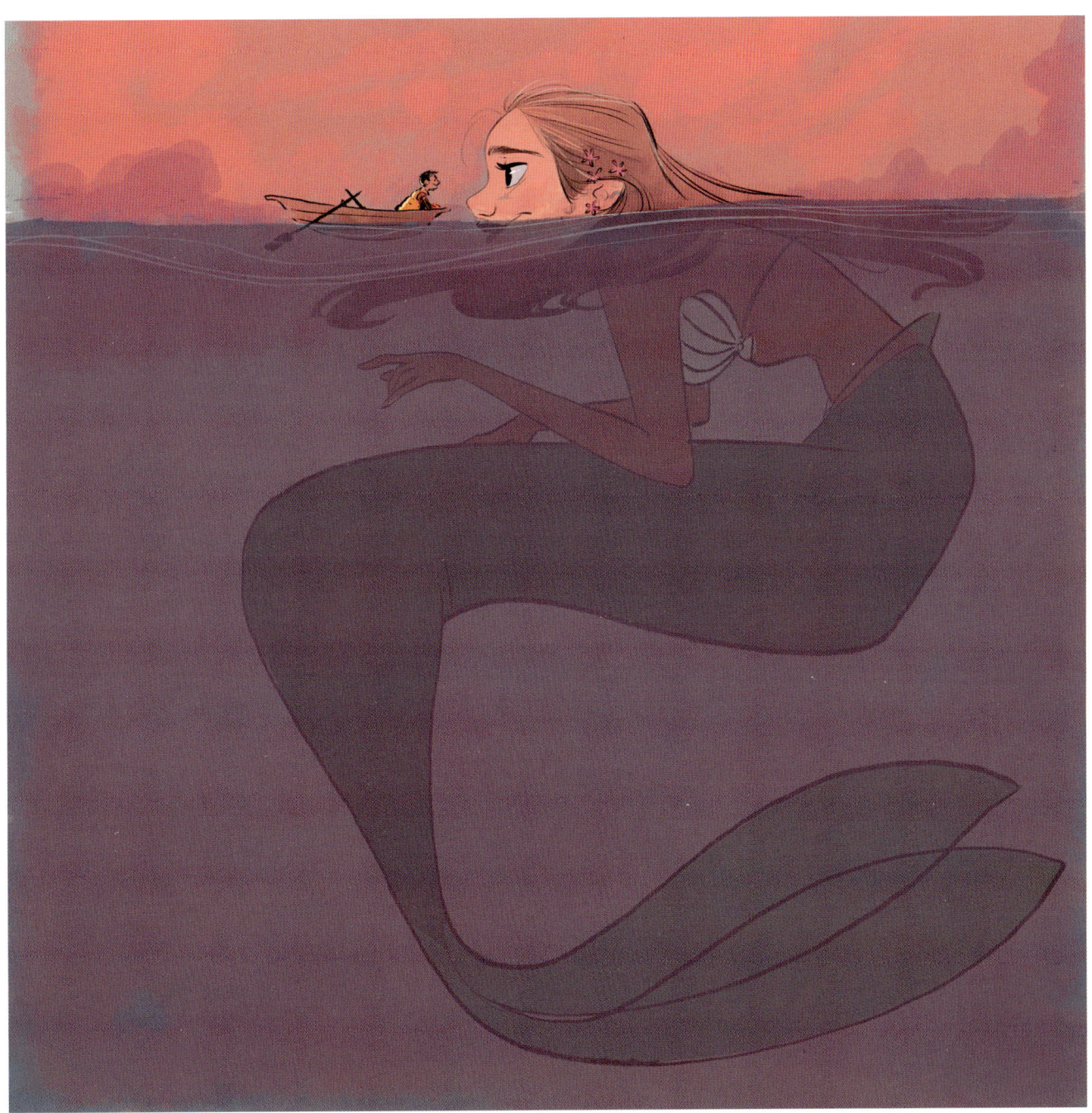

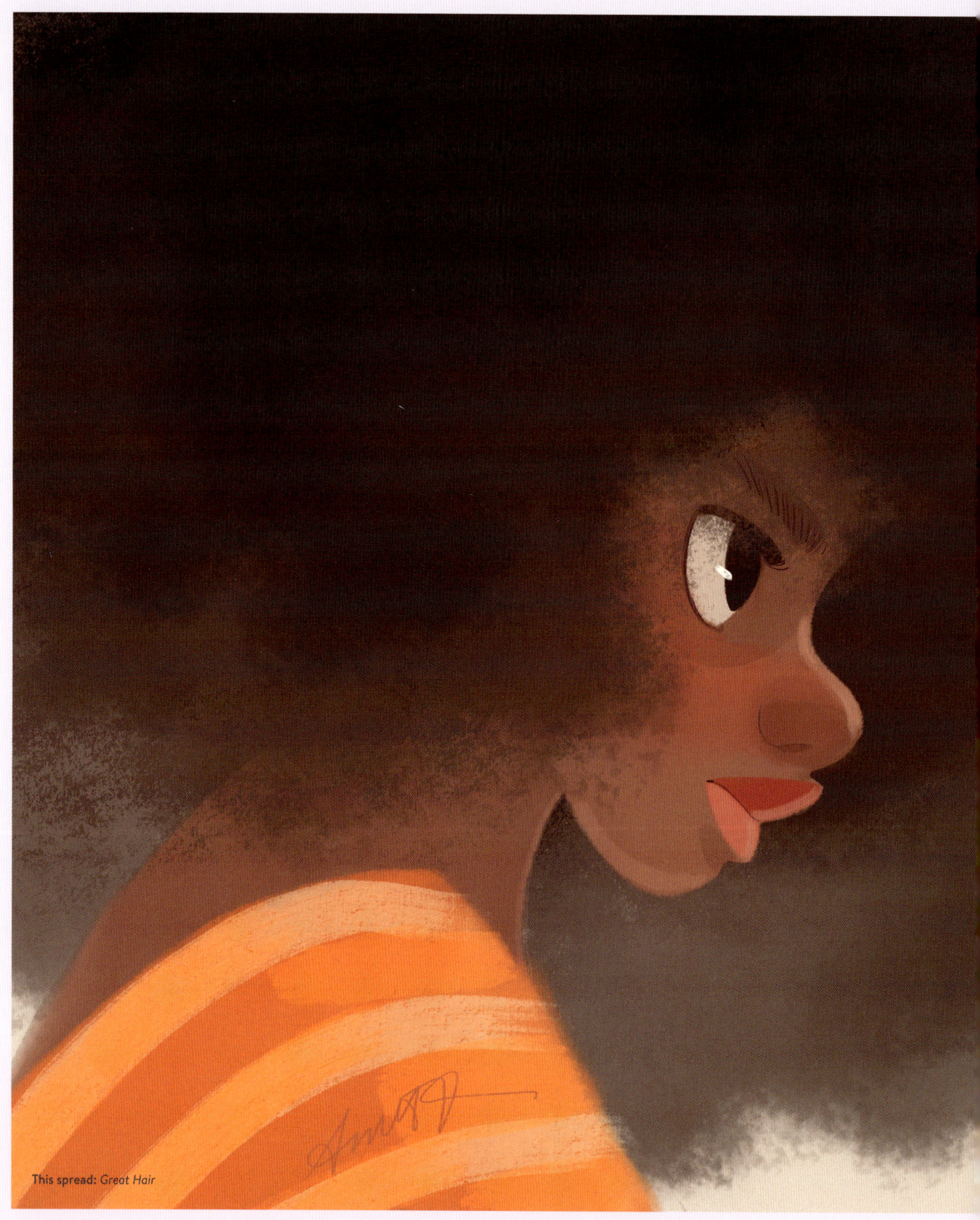

This spread: *Great Hair*

Despite any negativity, you have obviously stayed true to your style!

I don't think I can lose my style; I've tried but it keeps coming back so I guess I'm stuck with it! Every time I go to draw something realistic, my cartoon style slowly creeps onto the page and takes over. It has a mind of its own. When drawing for companies that want a different style than your own, it is a bit difficult to tone it down and retrain yourself. I'm optimistic that it gets easier over time.

Can you pinpoint any influences on your character design?

Many artists have influenced my style. I'm particularly fascinated by Norman Rockwell with his ability to tell a story in one picture, and all of Disney's "Nine Old Men," the animators who created the studio's most famous characters. Classic animations like *101 Dalmatians*, *Robin Hood*, *Sleeping Beauty*, and I guess any worn out VHS cartoon that I had as a kid, still play a part in my imagination process today. The current artists I am influenced by are greats like Cory Loftis and Glen Keane.

What were your experiences of setting up your Patreon account?

Patreon has been very helpful to me as an artist. The phrase "starving artist" is a real thing, and my Patrons have literally fed me and my family. I am still learning as I go with the site, but I will tell you that you meet a lot of fantastic people there. It can be a great place to share your work with people who really care about it! I think the only issue I had with running a Patreon account was managing my time at first. I started out making too many promises and thought I could keep up with all of them. I couldn't. If or when you create your own Patreon page, start out simple. It will save you a lot of stress.

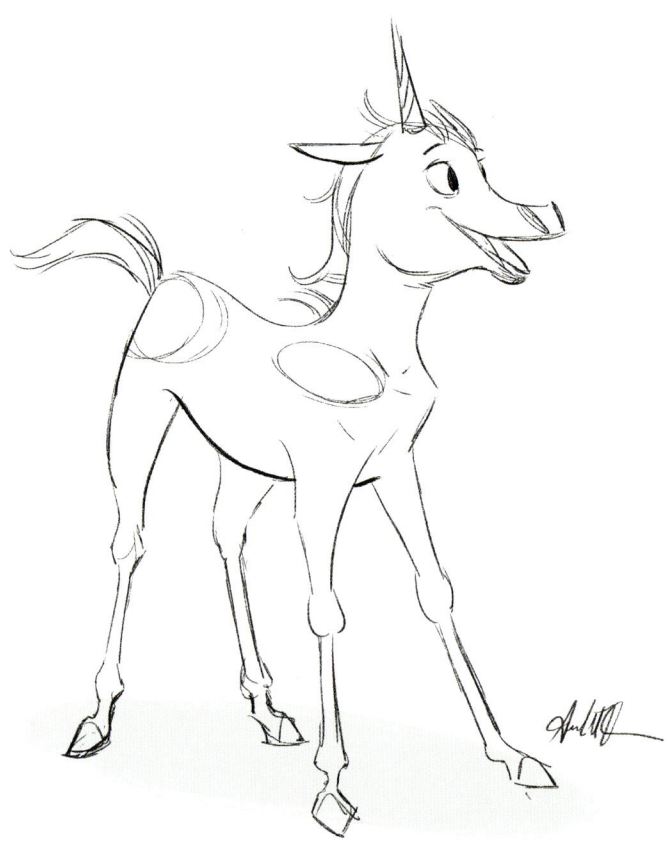

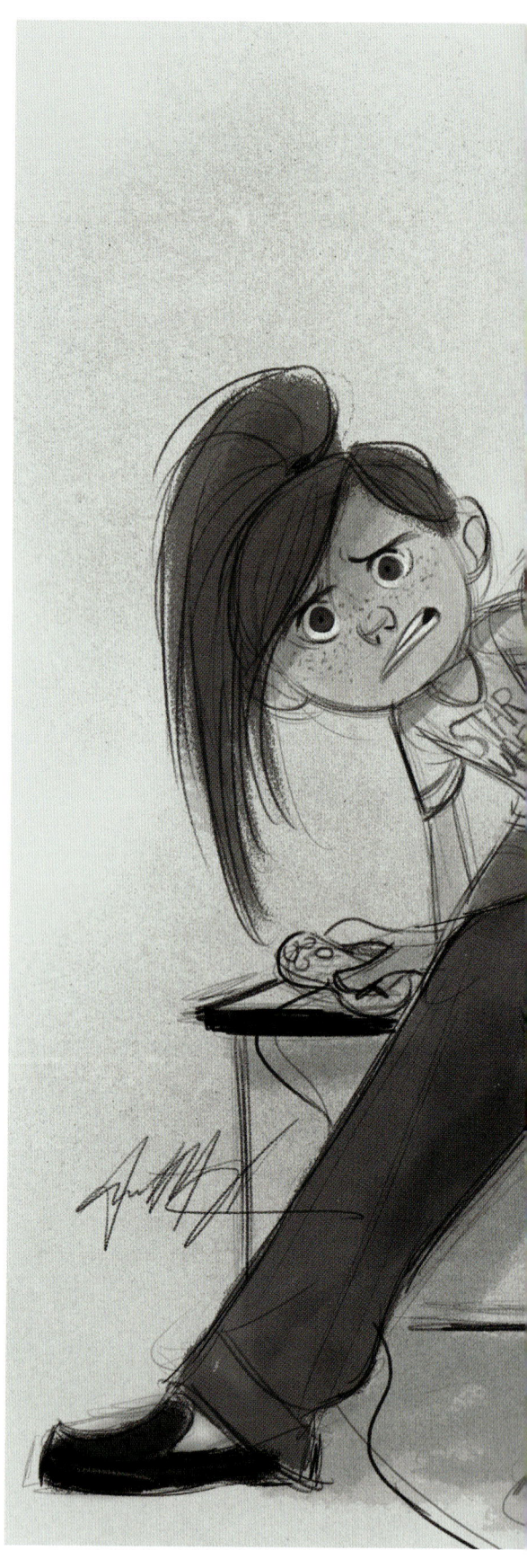

As a self-taught artist, what advice would you give to readers who want to become professional character designers without taking a formal education route?

If you do not have the opportunity to go to school for your art career, my top five tips would have to be the following:

• Find inspiration and draw at every chance you get to practice your skill.

• Get on social media, post often and ideally every day.

• You are your own agent. It is up to you to get your work out there for the world to see.

• Once clients find you, don't doubt yourself. They saw something in you, otherwise they wouldn't have contacted you.

• Charge by the hour. You do not have to be a starving artist.

Above: *Unicorn*

Opposite page: *Us*

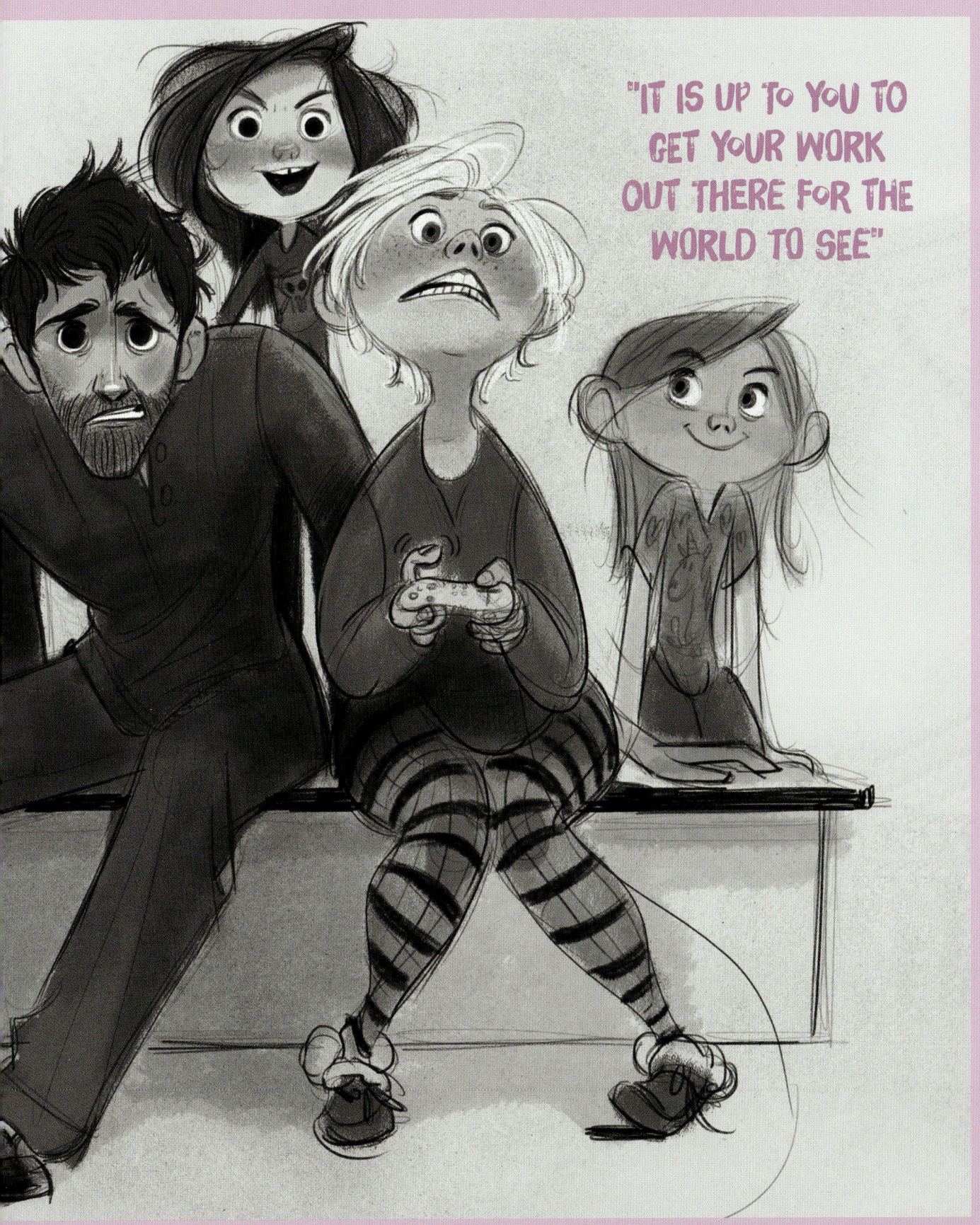

"IT IS UP TO YOU TO GET YOUR WORK OUT THERE FOR THE WORLD TO SEE"

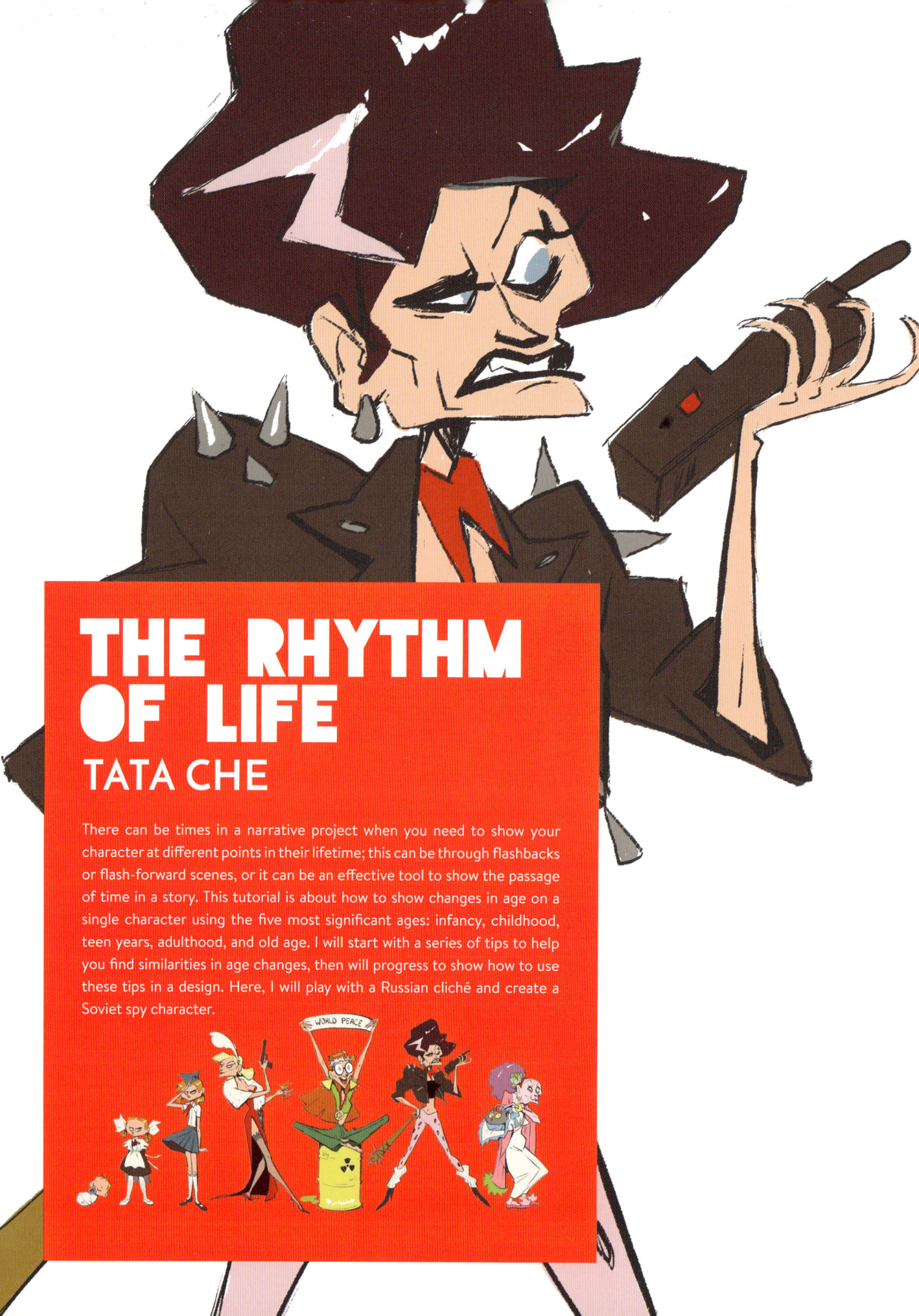

THE RHYTHM OF LIFE

TATA CHE

There can be times in a narrative project when you need to show your character at different points in their lifetime; this can be through flashbacks or flash-forward scenes, or it can be an effective tool to show the passage of time in a story. This tutorial is about how to show changes in age on a single character using the five most significant ages: infancy, childhood, teen years, adulthood, and old age. I will start with a series of tips to help you find similarities in age changes, then will progress to show how to use these tips in a design. Here, I will play with a Russian cliché and create a Soviet spy character.

CHECK POINTS

There are two ways in which to approach character evolution: consistent and contrasting. Consistent evolution is when your character evolves in a predictable and logical manner. For example: when you see a small fish you can imagine how it will look when it becomes bigger. Alternatively, contrasting evolution is unpredictable, such as the magical transformation of a caterpillar into a butterfly.

The evolution of a character can define the narrative and indicate their role as the main character. This evolution can take place in three different ways: physically, socially, or psychologically. A physical evolution can involve changes to the character's height, weight, and shape as well as their age. It can even be as simple a transition as a character loosing their hair. Social evolution can be marked by a lifestyle change or a new social role, such as a homeless orphan being taken in by a wealthy, loving family. A psychological evolution can be shown through a change in the character's mood or attitude, such as a rude or angry character becoming pleasant. An exciting part of working on a character that needs to evolve throughout a narrative is exploring the different ways you can achieve this with your design.

> "WHEN YOU SEE A SMALL FISH YOU CAN IMAGINE HOW IT WILL LOOK WHEN IT BECOMES BIGGER. ALTERNATIVELY, CONTRASTING EVOLUTION IS UNPREDICTABLE, SUCH AS THE MAGICAL TRANSFORMATION OF A CATERPILLAR INTO A BUTTERFLY"

CHARACTER EVOLUTION

CONSISTENT   CONTRAST

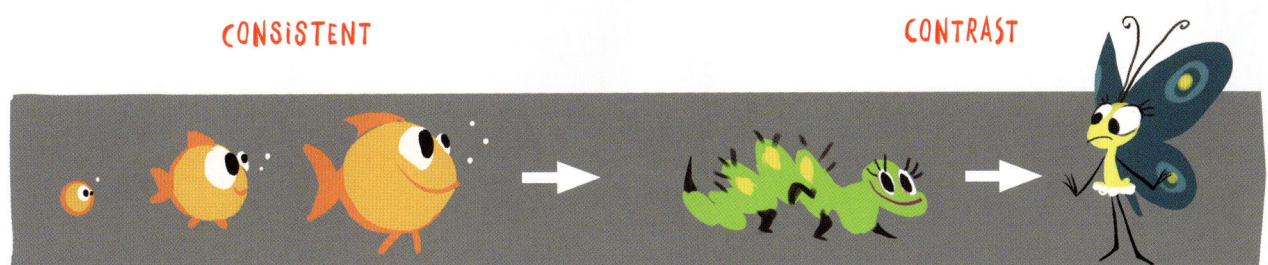

FORMS OF EVOLUTION

PHYSICAL   SOCIAL   PSYCHOLOGICAL

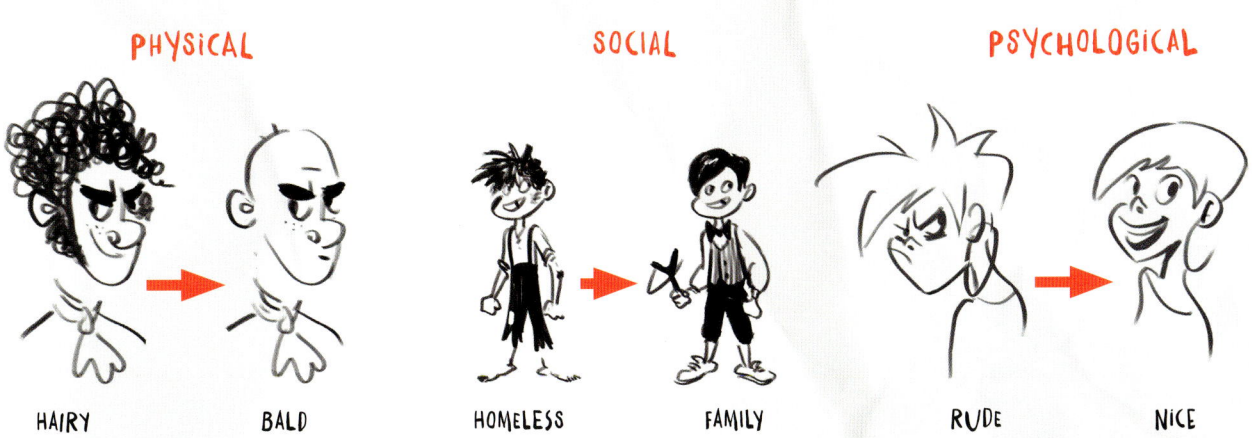

HAIRY   BALD   HOMELESS   FAMILY   RUDE   NICE

This page: A character can evolve consistently or in contrasting ways through physical, social, or psychological change

CHANGES THROUGH AGING

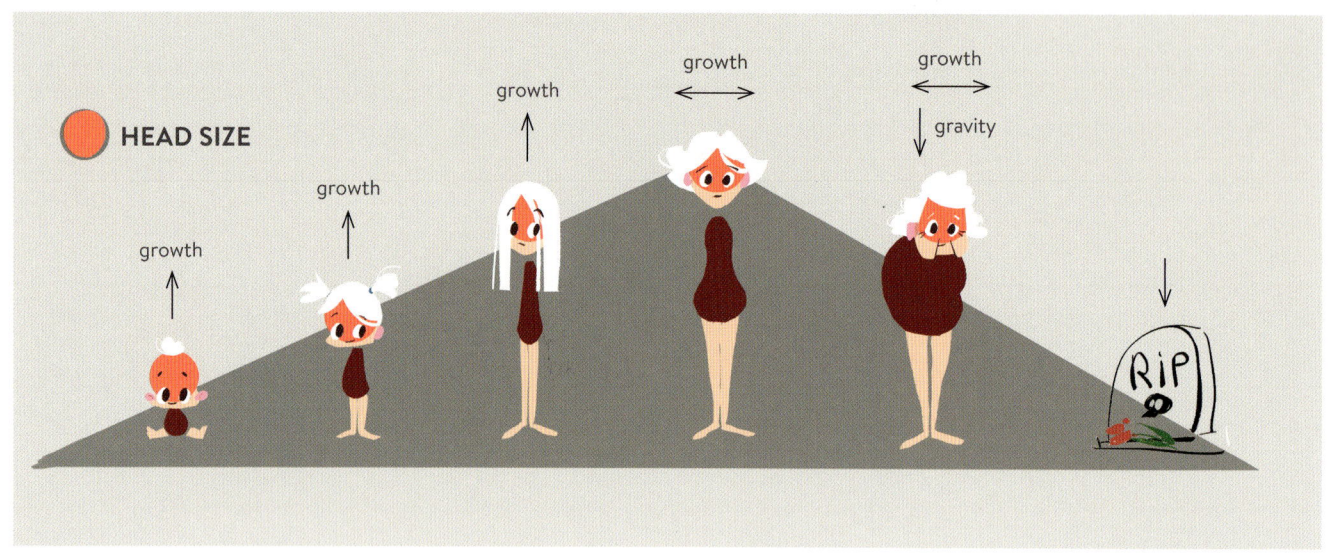

Above: This aging diagram shows how the general shapes of a person can change drastically over their lifetime

Below: A bent posture can be used to show age as well as mood

SPINE AND POSTURE

STRONG TIRED WEAK

THE AGING FIGURE

I want to start with an ageing diagram. This is an easy way to see general changes across a person's lifespan. The first thing to notice is how the head size is almost equal in all ages. Unless the style of your project calls for a change in head size it should generally stay the same in size no matter the age of the character. However, heads can look bigger at the expense of the jaw which can change significantly throughout life.

The gray triangle on the diagram above shows the overall direction of growth for one character through their life. People keep growing until they are around twenty-five years old, and when they stop growing their body shape is more affected by gravity, so as people age their form is pulled down to the ground. After twenty-five most people's metabolism will slow down, so characters can also put on weight in adulthood. A shorter, thicker frame is often used to depict an older person due to their slow metabolism and compressed body.

POSTURE

Sometimes the posture of a person is enough to tell their age. Posture can indicate other elements of a character, such as a sad or tired mood with rounded shoulders. This is typical for teenagers or office workers, but it is not a constant pose.

There are two ways to think about posture: mood and health. Mood posture is a temporary rounding or stretching depending on the character's feelings. Health posture is about a correct or incorrect posture and it is something people wear all the time. For example, old people often have weak spines, so their backs look round and the neck juts forward. This later form of posture is particularly useful when depicting aging characters as their posture can gradually deteriorate as they age. This technique can also be used on non-human characters, such as a plant character, which can be shown growing with a strong straight stem but slumps and crumples as the character grows old.

WEIGHT

Characters can be overweight or underweight at any age, but mostly it is noticeable in adulthood. The individual weight spread depends on the body type of the character but generally weight on a man's body will be most visible on the stomach, and on a woman weight will usually appear on the hips.

However, the stomach and hips are not the only areas to add weight to. Weight tends to build up across the whole body in the shape of a star; it spreads from the center of the body out to the limbs. On a very stylized design however, you can make design choices that deviate from normal human anatomy. Choose which parts of the body you want or need to increase.

As a person puts on weight, their body shape will generally still be visible. For example, the hourglass shape will retain those proportions. However past a certain point, the shape will be lost and become more generically rounded.

WRINKLES

Face mimicking is a non-verbal way of communication that starts from infancy. These expressions are used throughout life to demonstrate different emotions, and create short-term wrinkles in that moment. As we age our skin becomes less elastic, creating permanent wrinkles. Therefore you can define the dominant emotions of a character by the locations of their wrinkles.

For example, if a character smiles a lot during their life, his dominant wrinkles will be near the corners of the mouth and eyes, as when you smile your cheeks lift. Negative emotion results in wrinkles between the eyebrows.

Below: Weight is spread across the adult body in a star shape

Bottom: Wrinkles show expressions most commonly used by the character throughout their life

GENERAL WEIGHT GAIN

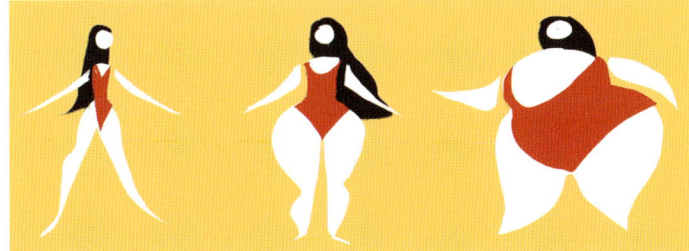

DIFFERENT BODY TYPES

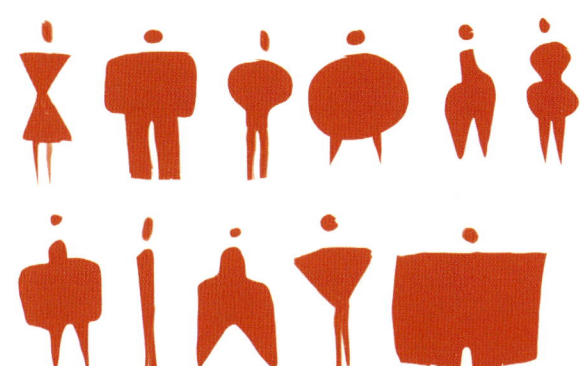

WRINKLE MAPS

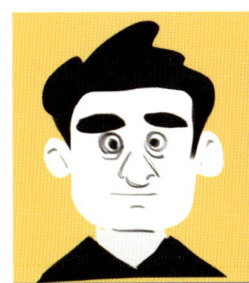 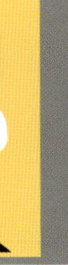

NEUTRAL	DEPRESSION	JOY	ANGER	AMAZEMENT

     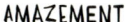

BABY CHARACTERS

CUTE PROPORTIONS

Now let's look at the other end of the aging timeline. One thing that is noticeable about babies is that they are cute! This is because their physical proportions are different to adults; their heads are disproportionately large for their bodies, they have big eyes, and rounded forms. Placing a baby's facial features lower on their face is an easy way to make them appear cute. These altered proportions can even be used in adult characters to make them look more appealing.

Babies also have no discernible neck and a small jaw because they do not have a full set of teeth yet. Baby hair is very fine and looks more like fluff. These subtle differences between babies and adults can be used to make any character appear cute, and should be kept in mind when presenting an existing adult character as a baby, for example in a flashback.

PHYSICAL EXPRESSION

You can play around with the poses and actions of babies a great deal as they are often exaggerated due to the flexibility of their fast growing bodies. Babies experience life physically, so they try everything, eat everything, and mirror adult acting. They express themselves without words, meaning the design should rely on strong gestures. Babies cannot live without care, which is why tactile contact is so important to them. These aspects give you many opportunities for experimenting with interesting poses, props, and interactions with other characters.

Furthermore, babies can understand basic emotions like joy and fear. They laugh and cry a lot so the shape of their mouths is important to setting the character's mood. Adding a few teeth can help suggest that the baby's small mouth is wide open, and adding dimples increases cuteness as it highlights the baby's chubby cheeks.

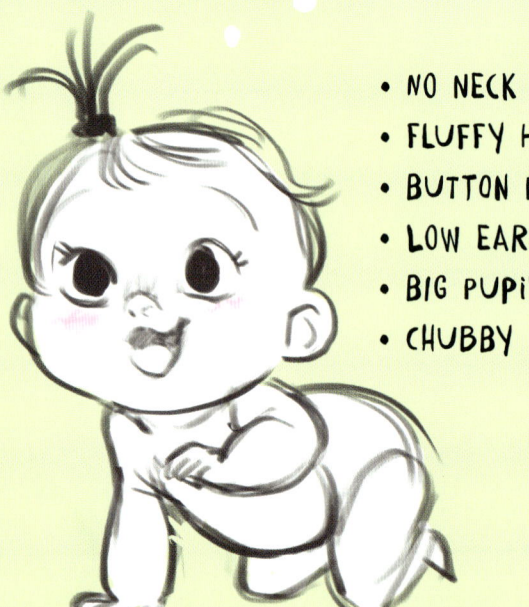

MILK AND MOM

- NO NECK
- FLUFFY HAIR
- BUTTON NOSE
- LOW EARS
- BIG PUPILS
- CHUBBY

SAME FACIAL PROPORTIONS FOR ALL BABIES

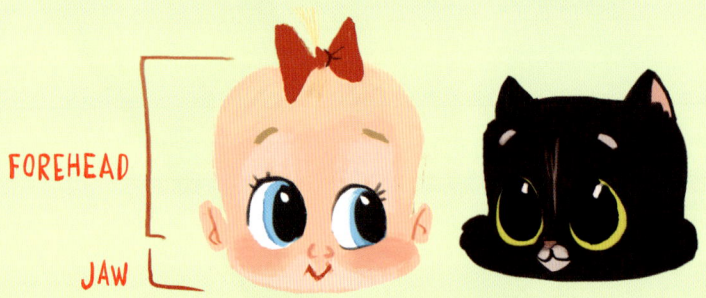

FOREHEAD

JAW

Top: Slight adjustments make babies different and cute compared to adults

Bottom: No matter which species the character is, the facial proportions of the young tend to be the same

CHILD CHARACTERS

FACE TRIANGLES

Children can be roughly grouped from the age they start to speak and run around until they are teenagers. They are still cute and naïve and share similar proportions with babies such as a small neck, rounded tummy, and a big forehead. In this period the nose still looks button-like and the facial features are located close together. This is very important to avoid making your child characters look like short adults. As we age, our features spread further apart and droop. If you loosely group the eyes, nose, and mouth of characters in a triangle you will see that the older a character is, the more elongated the triangle becomes.

CHILDLIKE DETAILS

Generally kids are very active, so they have scratches and bruises which can be added to your design. They have never ending energy which gives you lots of scope for fun scenes: coloring walls, shaving carpets, cutting grandfather's moustache, and so on. Children have no barrier between imagination and reality, so everything they imagine seems possible to them.

However, most children are not yet independent so family is important to them, as is making friends with other kids, animals, and imaginary friends too. Again, this gives you a lot of opportunities to make interesting scenes, and bring other characters into play.

Top: Children have great imaginations so you can create interesting scenes and side characters

Middle: Children's facial features are very close together. As they grow older the features begin to stretch down

Bottom: Extra energy and playfulness results in many additional physical details

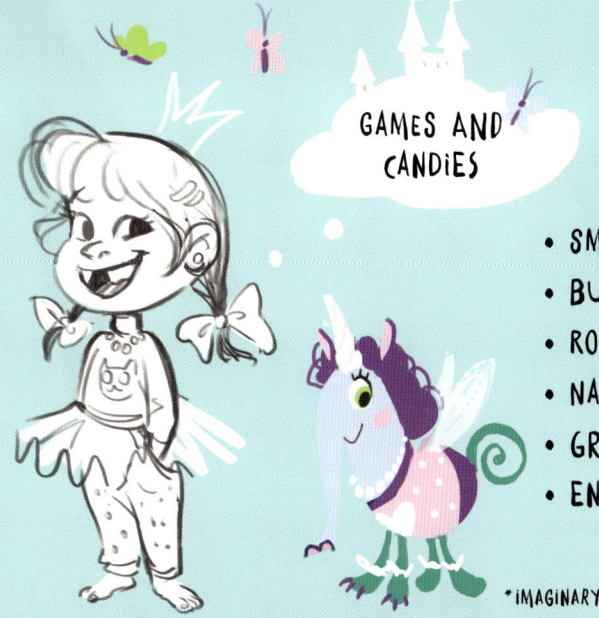

GAMES AND CANDIES

- SMALL NECK
- BUTTON NOSE
- ROUNDED TUMMY
- NAÏVE
- GREAT IMAGINATION
- ENERGETIC

*IMAGINARY FRIEND

FACE TRIANGLE

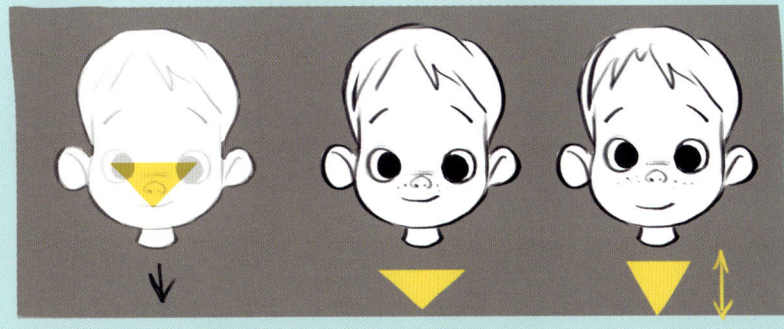

EYES AND MOUTH   YOUNGER   OLDER

ACTIVE LIFE STYLE

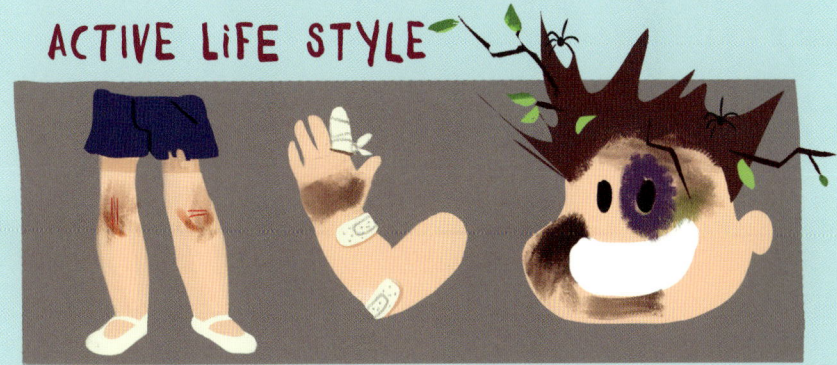

TEEN CHARACTERS

GROWTH SPURTS

It is a tough time of life to be between childhood and adulthood. Teen bodies grow unevenly so they often look clumsy and awkward with disproportionately big hands and feet. Their body and head proportions come closer to those of an adult and they now have a defined chin, neck, and nose. Many teens are skinnier than adults due to sudden growth spurts, and their posture is often slumped or hunched due to a bad mood.

DRAMA KINGS AND QUEENS

The physical changes of teen years also come with an emotional storm and in this period characters push themselves away from their parents and learn to be independent. This is a time of wild experimentation and freedom for the design. The more freedom your teen character has, the more complicated your design choices can be. You can give your character really interesting fashions, hairstyles, or braces; it may be suitable to give them piercings or tattoos. Teens are emotionally unstable and tend to act in an overly dramatic way. At the same time it is also necessary for them to be part of a society which is why they are interested in different subcultures.

Teens also have some very specific physical details, such as pimply skin from the sudden changes in their hormones, and patches of hair. You may want to add sweat stains or something to indicate a smell as your teen character gets to grips with the increase in sweat and the need to wash more regularly.

This page: Teen proportions are closer to those of an adult but subject to sudden physical changes

Opposite page: Teen years are a time for experimentation so there are lots of new details that can be added to the character design

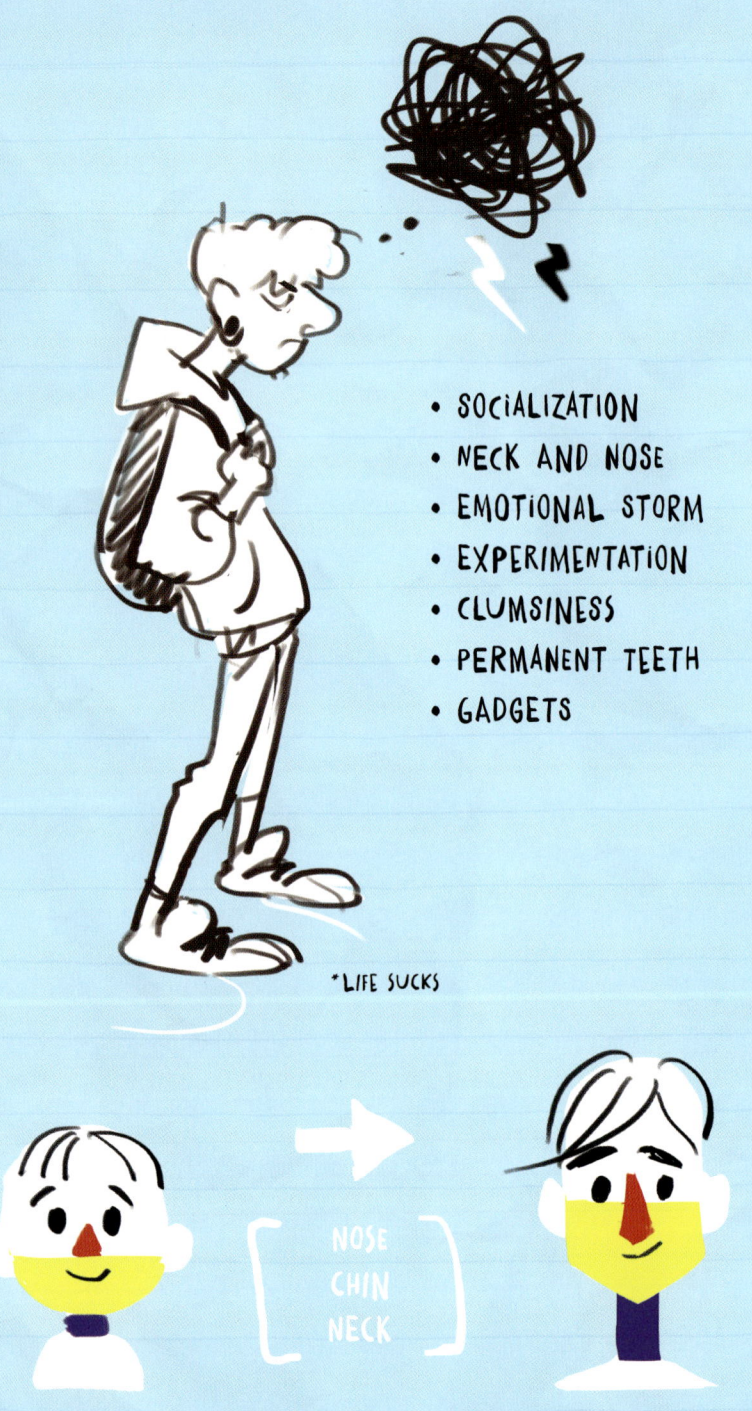

- SOCIALIZATION
- NECK AND NOSE
- EMOTIONAL STORM
- EXPERIMENTATION
- CLUMSINESS
- PERMANENT TEETH
- GADGETS

*LIFE SUCKS

NOSE
CHIN
NECK

SELF-EXPRESSION

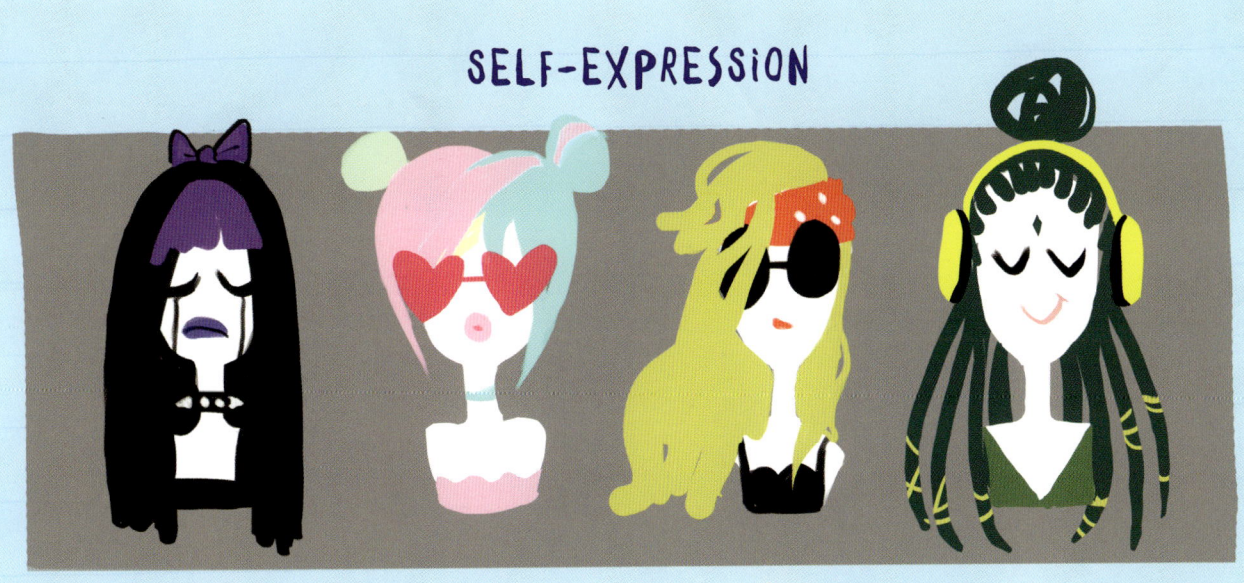

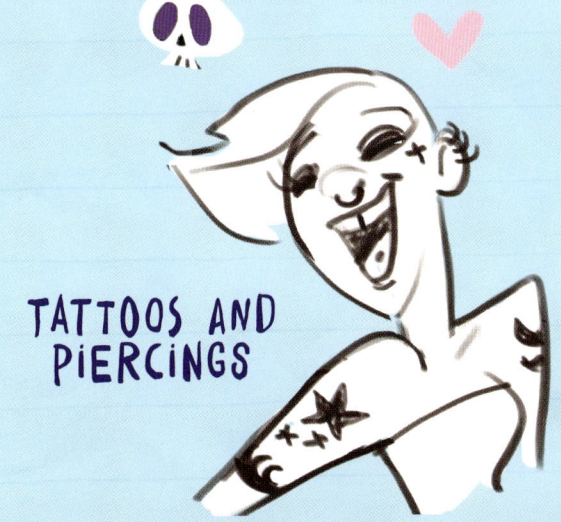

TATTOOS AND PIERCINGS

BRACES

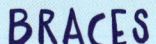
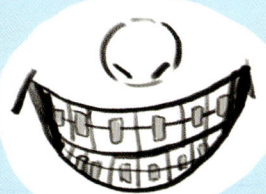

THE PERILS OF PUBERTY

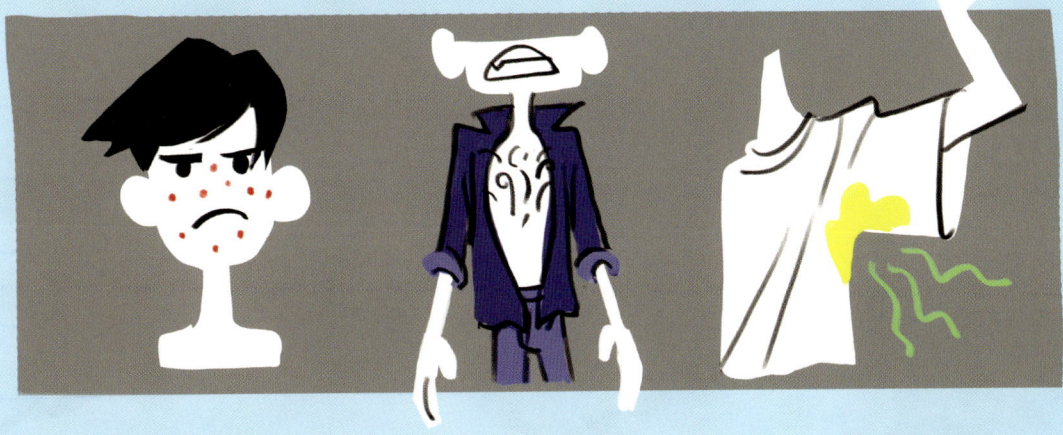

ADULT CHARACTERS

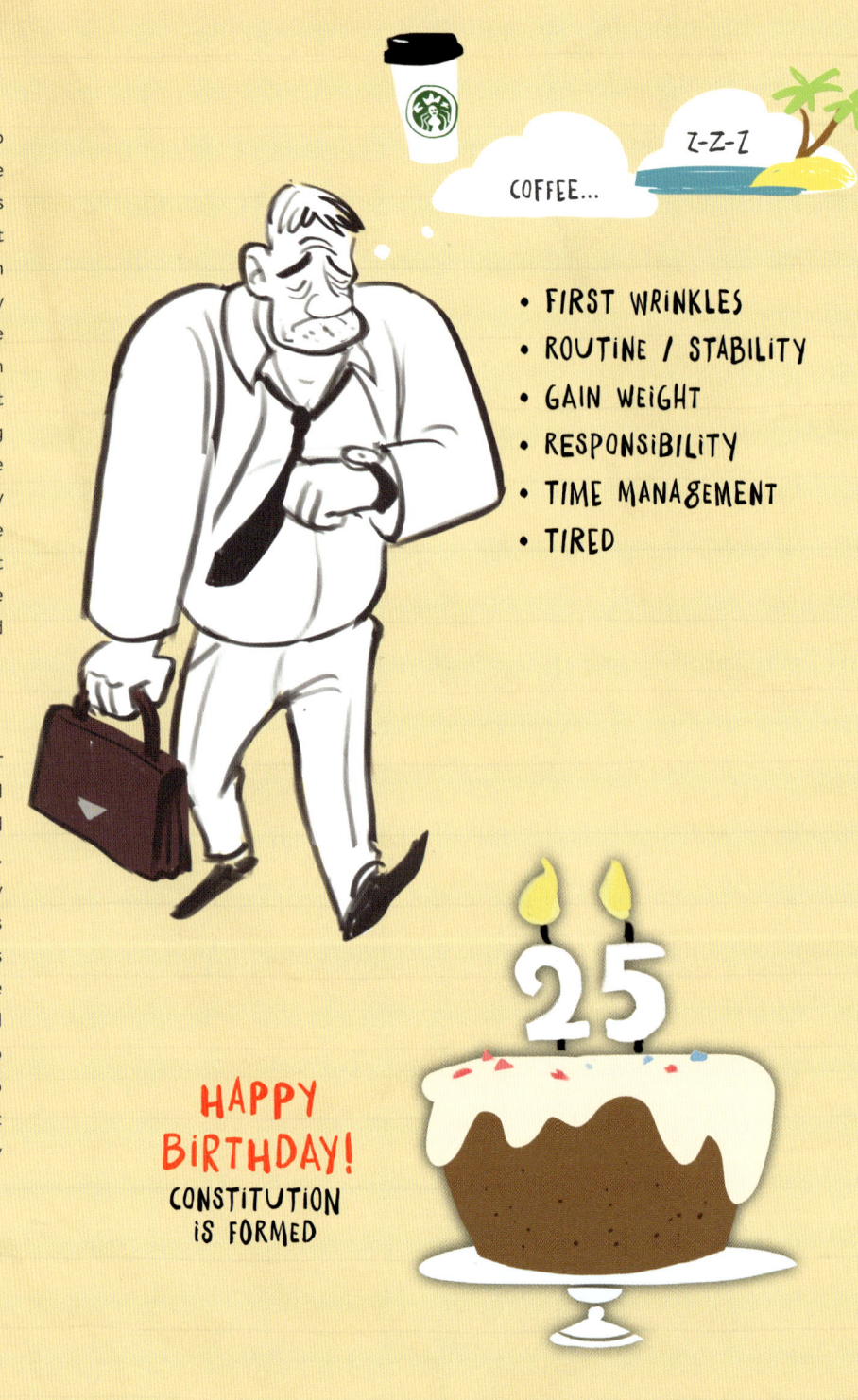

ONLY 24 HOURS IN A DAY...

Adult characters are interesting to design because you can show that there are differences between the character's internal needs and external actions. Most adults need to be responsible and often have to think about the future. They work a lot and in general their lifestyle features a lot of routine without much surprise or change. This is why adult characters are often presented as being tired or bored; especially when they have a lot of responsibilities such as a family and a mortgage. Adult characters can be conflicted because they cannot just quit an unloved job and have to find a balance between the things they want to do and the things they need to do.

BROAD DESIGN CHOICES

This period of compromise is heaven for character designers because the physical constitution of the character is formed and now starts to be affected by their lifestyle. So you can explore really different body types, clothes, and style choices. Adults tend to adopt different dress codes for each occasion so you can give one character multiple different clothing and accessory options. The main rule is to understand if your character prefers to live a healthy or unhealthy lifestyle; what their daily schedule might be, what they eat, and what their priorities are.

Top: Adult characters can be conflicted and the effects often show on their bodies

Bottom: After further education and training, adult life often becomes established from the age of twenty-five

Opposite page: Many choices about appearance, depend on the personality, lifestyle, and occasion

COFFEE...

Z-Z-Z

- FIRST WRINKLES
- ROUTINE / STABILITY
- GAIN WEIGHT
- RESPONSIBILITY
- TIME MANAGEMENT
- TIRED

HAPPY BIRTHDAY!
CONSTITUTION IS FORMED

25

FACIAL HAIR CHOICES

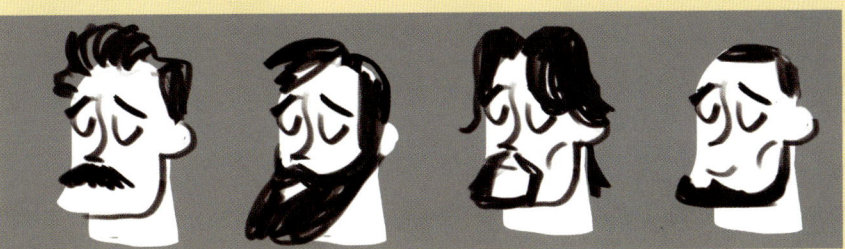

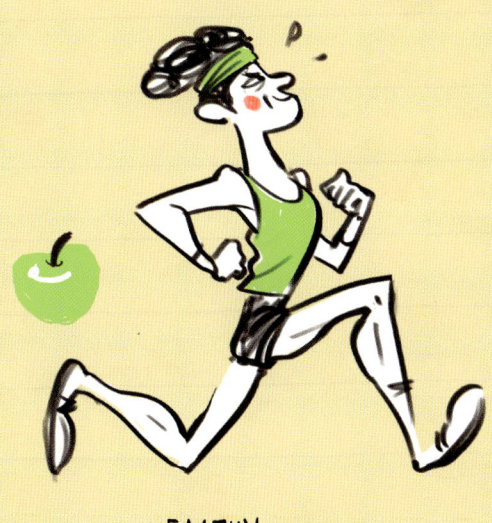

LiFE STYLE

- FOOD
- ALCOHOL
- SLEEP
- SPORT
- WORK

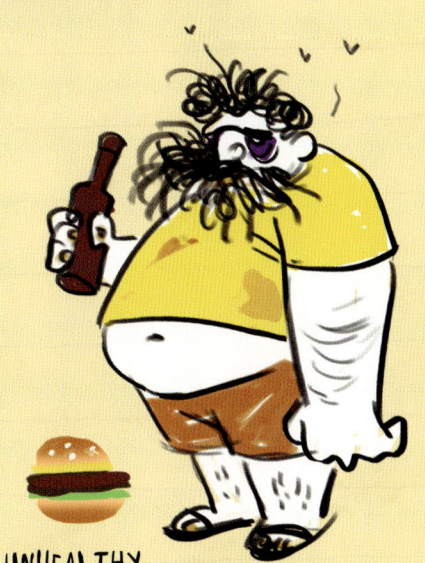

HEALTHY

UNHEALTHY

NAVIGATING DRESS CODES

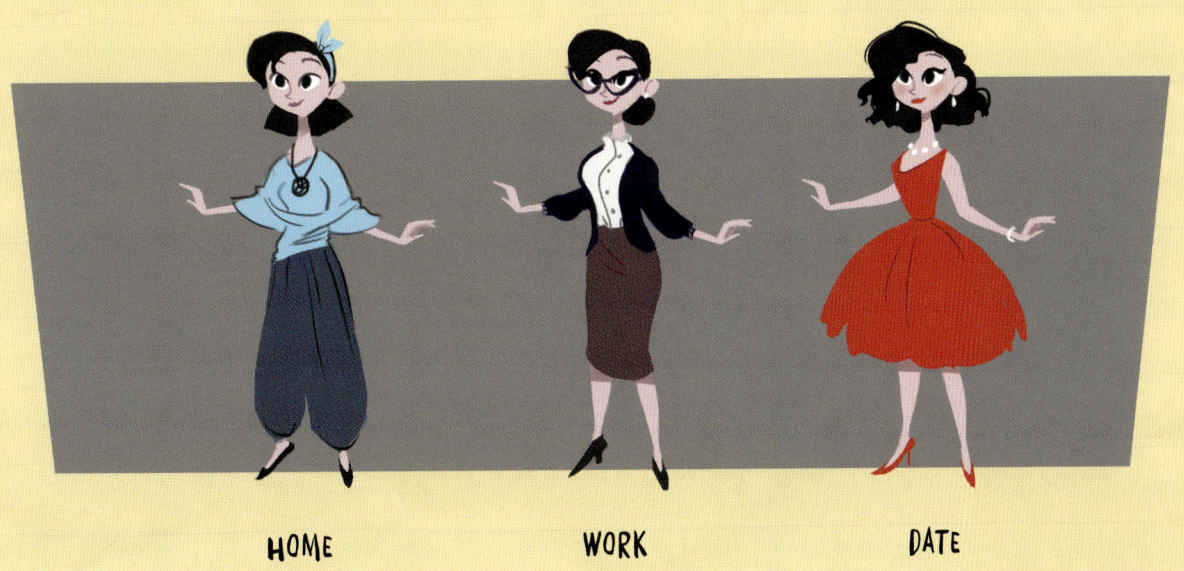

HOME   WORK   DATE

OLD AGED CHARACTERS

THEY NEED TO
EAT MORE

SUNSET

Some old people act like kids because they return to needing care, attention, and love. At this age a character can be wise or weak-minded, and this gives you some opportunities for different design experiments. As an old character's body begins to weaken, their posture and body shapes distort. Another impact on face wrinkles is gravity. When the person gets very old their skin and muscles get weaker and become affected by gravity which pulls the skin down.

PHYSICAL TRANSFORMATION

By old age the body hits the maximum level of deformation. Everything gets weaker and loses its elasticity so the character's general body shape will start to droop towards the ground. As there is less elasticity in the character's body their bones become more visible, particularly around the hands and feet.

Some body parts will keep growing such as the nose, ears, and feet so these can be exaggerated in the design. Old aged characters often have to support themselves with different equipment such as walking frames, medication, glasses, and so on. However, these different limitations can lead to creativity.

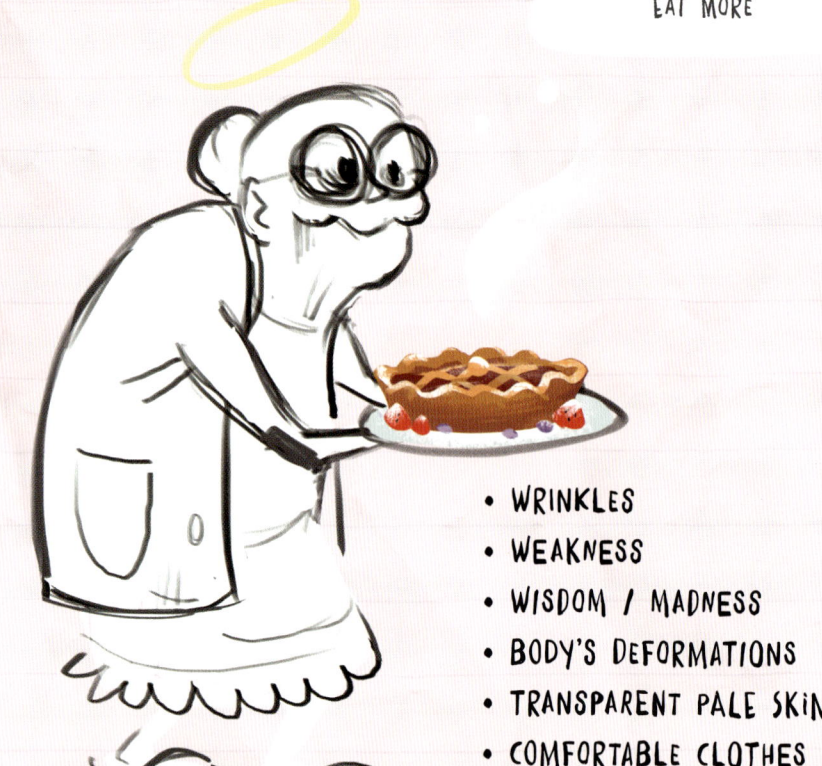

- WRINKLES
- WEAKNESS
- WISDOM / MADNESS
- BODY'S DEFORMATIONS
- TRANSPARENT PALE SKIN
- COMFORTABLE CLOTHES
- TIGHT TENDONS

FACIAL TRANSFORMATIONS

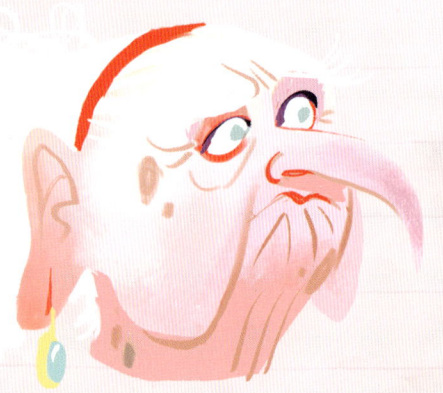

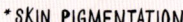
*SKIN PIGMENTATION

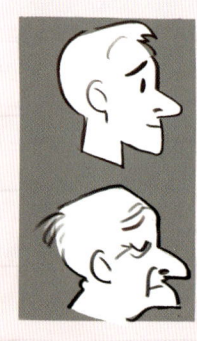

JAW OCCLUSION
CHANGES SHAPE

Top: Older characters can become childlike again but many also gain wisdom

Bottom: The face of old people changes significantly due to skin and muscle slackening

Opposite page: Physical challenges mean the chance to create props and accessories

MUSCLE CHANGES

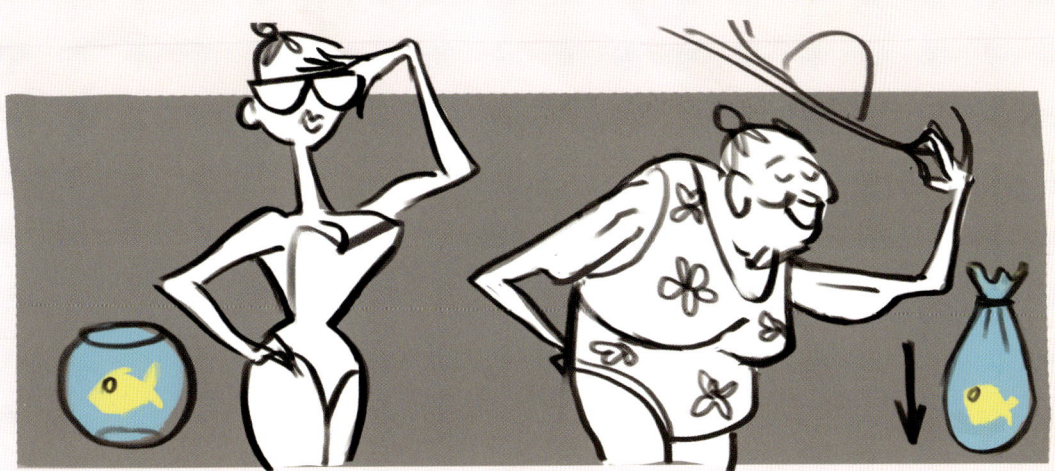

GRAVITATIONAL PULL

EXTRA SUPPORT

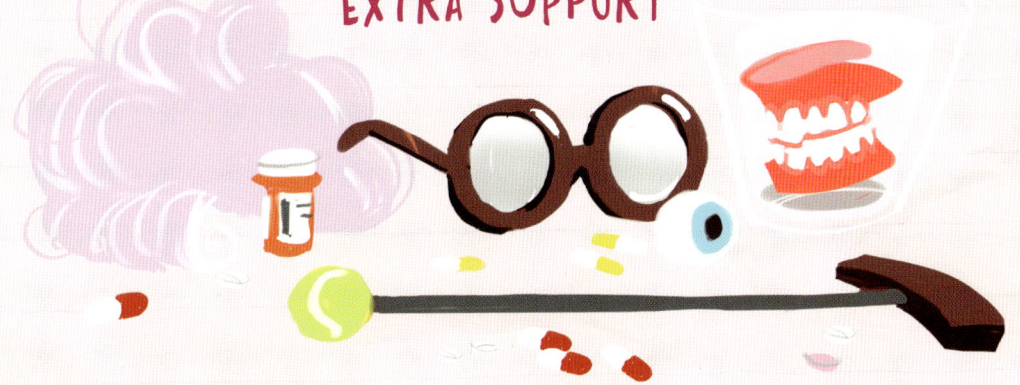

BONY EXTREMITIES

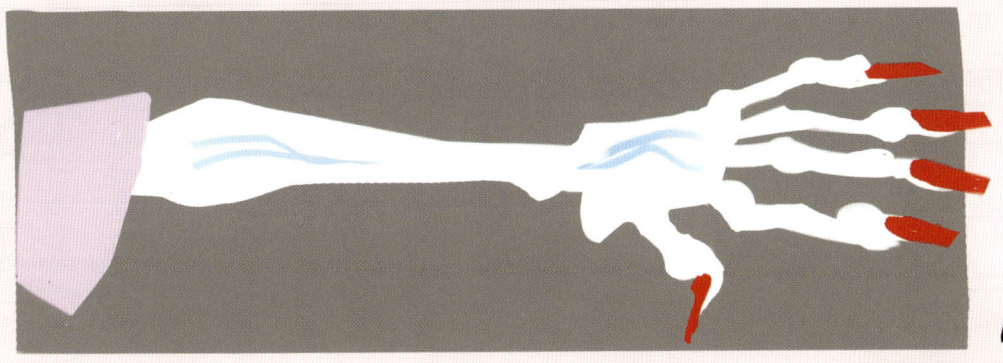

EARS AND NOSE GROW UNTIL...

CASE STUDY

THE STORY OF KATERINA

To demonstrate how a character might age and evolve throughout their life I create a "Soviet spy" character. I invent a story about a woman who has been through many changes at significant points in her life. From a young age she serves her country, believing in the "big idea" of her society, but as she grows older she has to play different roles and ends up losing herself. Every good story needs conflict so in this story it is based on the difference between the political and cultural atmosphere of the Soviet Union (USSR) and USA. My character, Katerina, is raised in the USSR with a strong ideology: being part of a community, working for the community, being willing to die for the community. She becomes a spy and is deployed abroad where she is introduced to another ideology. This inner opposition creates conflict.

THE INITIAL DESIGN

As a starting point for my character design I look at Katerina as a teenager. It is a time of self identification, when the character needs to make a choice based on her background. This choice also defines her future. I draw her in a graphic style that is similar to Soviet art and suits the theme well. I use edgy, sharp shapes that correlate to the dangerous role she will take on as a spy. As a young character she is under pressure from social influences and this makes her loyal, selfless, purposeful. By depicting her in a military-style uniform and pose I show that she is ready to start her spying career.

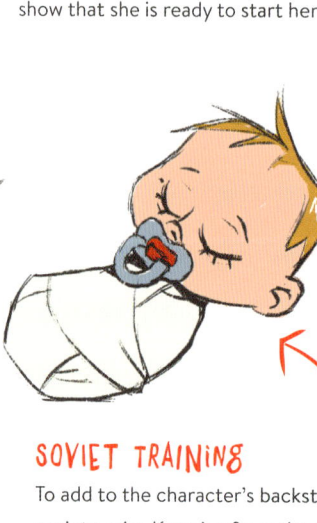

SOVIET TRAINING

To add to the character's backstory I look at Katerina as an infant next. I want to show how Soviet society grips Katerina from the very beginning and show that she has little choice in the direction her life takes. Therefore I add small red details and keep her tightly wrapped in swaddling to suggest a lack of freedom.

As a child her training starts with strong discipline: she has a uniform rather than play clothes, her hair is pulled tightly into bunches, and she has a lot of white clothes that need to be kept perfectly clean. There is no room for self identification. As a child she is taught to comply with the high standards expected of those associated with the Soviet red flag.

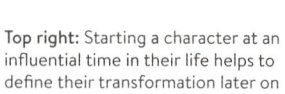

Top right: Starting a character at an influential time in their life helps to define their transformation later on

Above and right: Exploring the character as a child helps to build a back-story

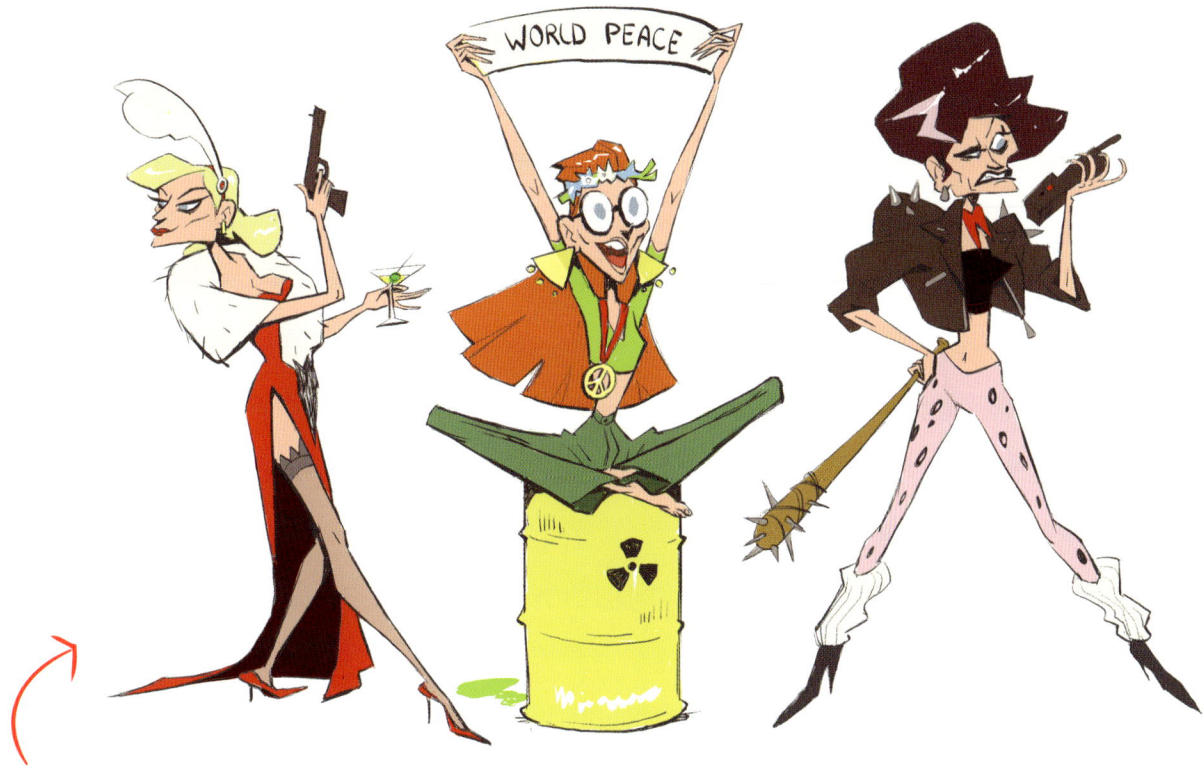

PERFORMANCE

Now looking at the character in adulthood, the center of my story, Katerina's spy career has started and she is sent to the USA. She is shocked by the different culture and experiences a new sense of liberty and opportunity. Her mission as a spy is to break in to her enemy's lair and over a long period she performs different roles to achieve this. First I show her as a glamorous sophisticate, then as a hippie, and finally as a fierce gangster. Not only does she perform these roles but she also experiences the lifestyles for herself and creates her own identity. Those roles are very contrasting and create inner conflict, which will eventually lead to Katerina's self destruction.

Designing this very mixed period of Katrina's life I use different costumes that suit her roles and social status, and suggest the passage of time by borrowing styles from different eras. I maintain the angular lines and shape language of the teenage design to maintain the sense of Katerina as a single character, but use different acting and posing to match the roles.

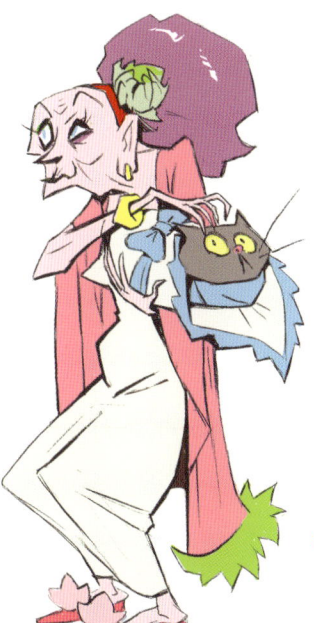

LOST

Time flies and the Soviet Union falls apart, and with so many conflicting missions, so does Katerina. Having lived through such a large number of different lives, she has lost a sense of her own identity and is stuck in a fictitious life. She is unstable, and cannot accept that the USSR ended, so I maintain the hint of red that she has had in every design.

I imagine Katerina still playing this spy game but now she is spying on her tenants so I use the "crazy old cat lady" stereotype in the design which works well. She is no longer attractive; she looks weird and out of place. Her costume does not support her former roles but the repetition of the shape language keeps some consistency with the other designs.

COLOR

SYMBOLISM AND STORY

Reviewing the group as a whole I check that the color palette will support the story and serve each character's individual role. The starting point of this story is the conflict between two different worlds and this conflict can be seen in my color choices. The world of the USSR is severe, and the colors for this period of Katerina's life are limited and monochromatic, the only bright color is red, that symbolizes the "great idea" of the society. The world of the USA however is shocking with colors, so the color pallet has a lot of variation. However, red still remains in small details as a reminder of the ideology Katerina has at heart.

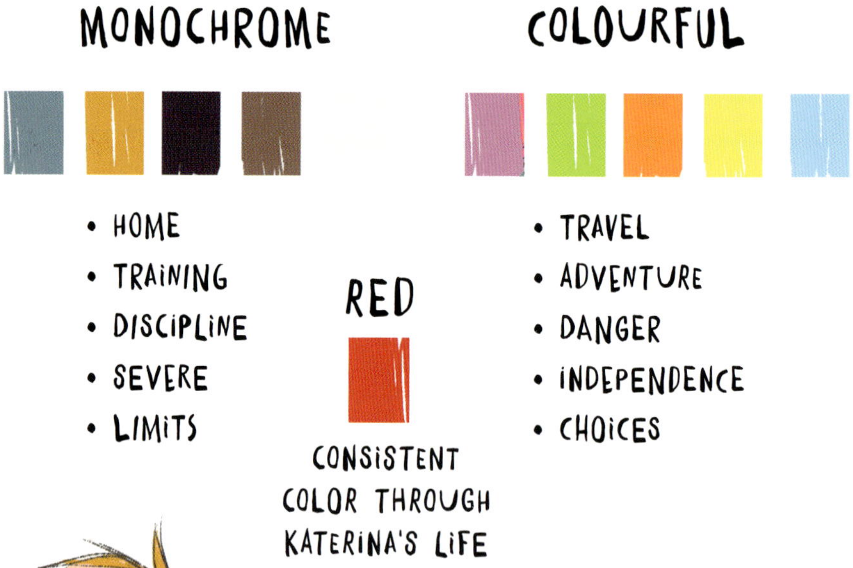

This spread: Reviewing the designs together shows that the color palette matches the conflicts the character faces

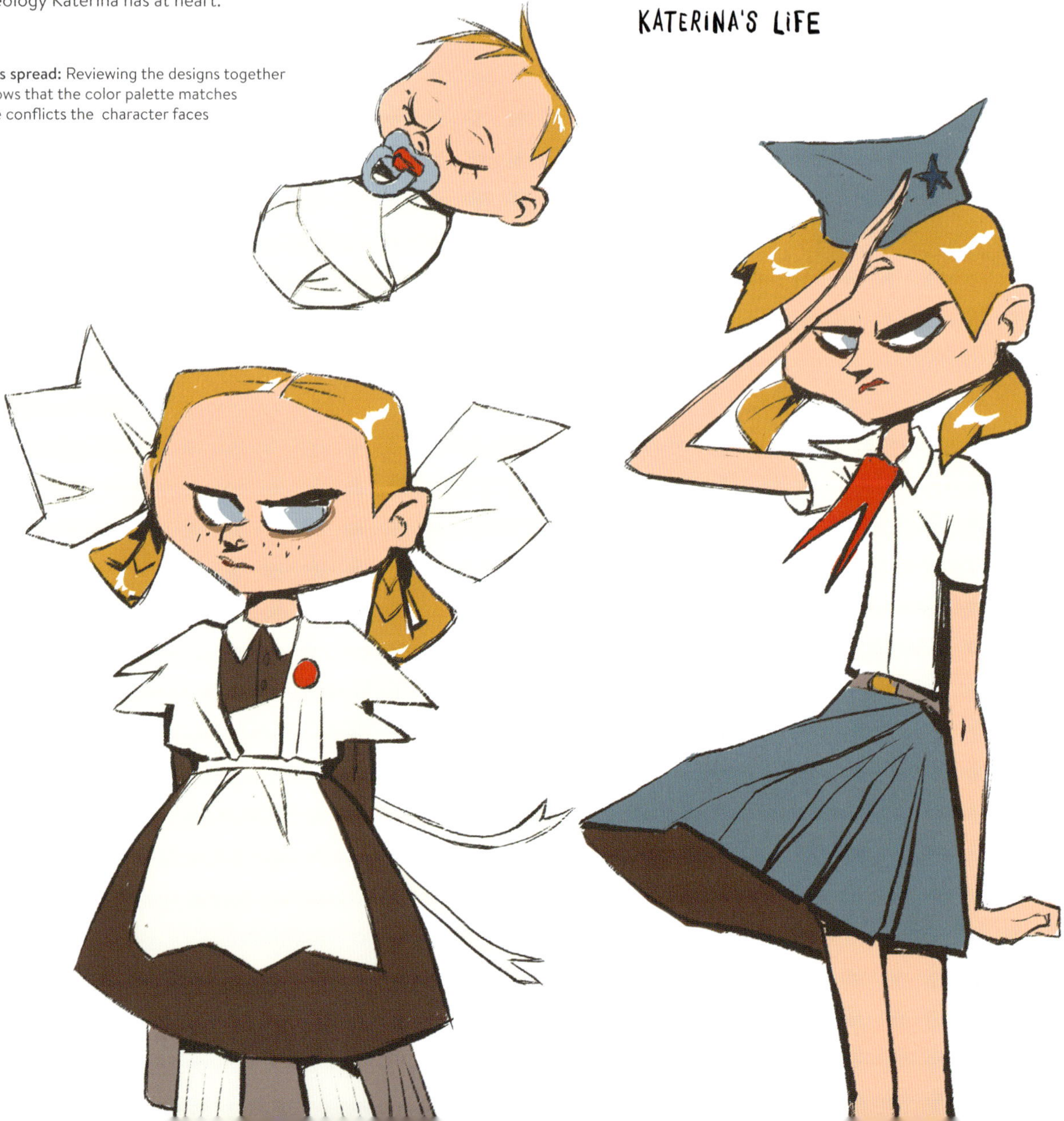

MONOCHROME

- HOME
- TRAINING
- DISCIPLINE
- SEVERE
- LIMITS

COLOURFUL

- TRAVEL
- ADVENTURE
- DANGER
- INDEPENDENCE
- CHOICES

RED

CONSISTENT COLOR THROUGH KATERINA'S LIFE

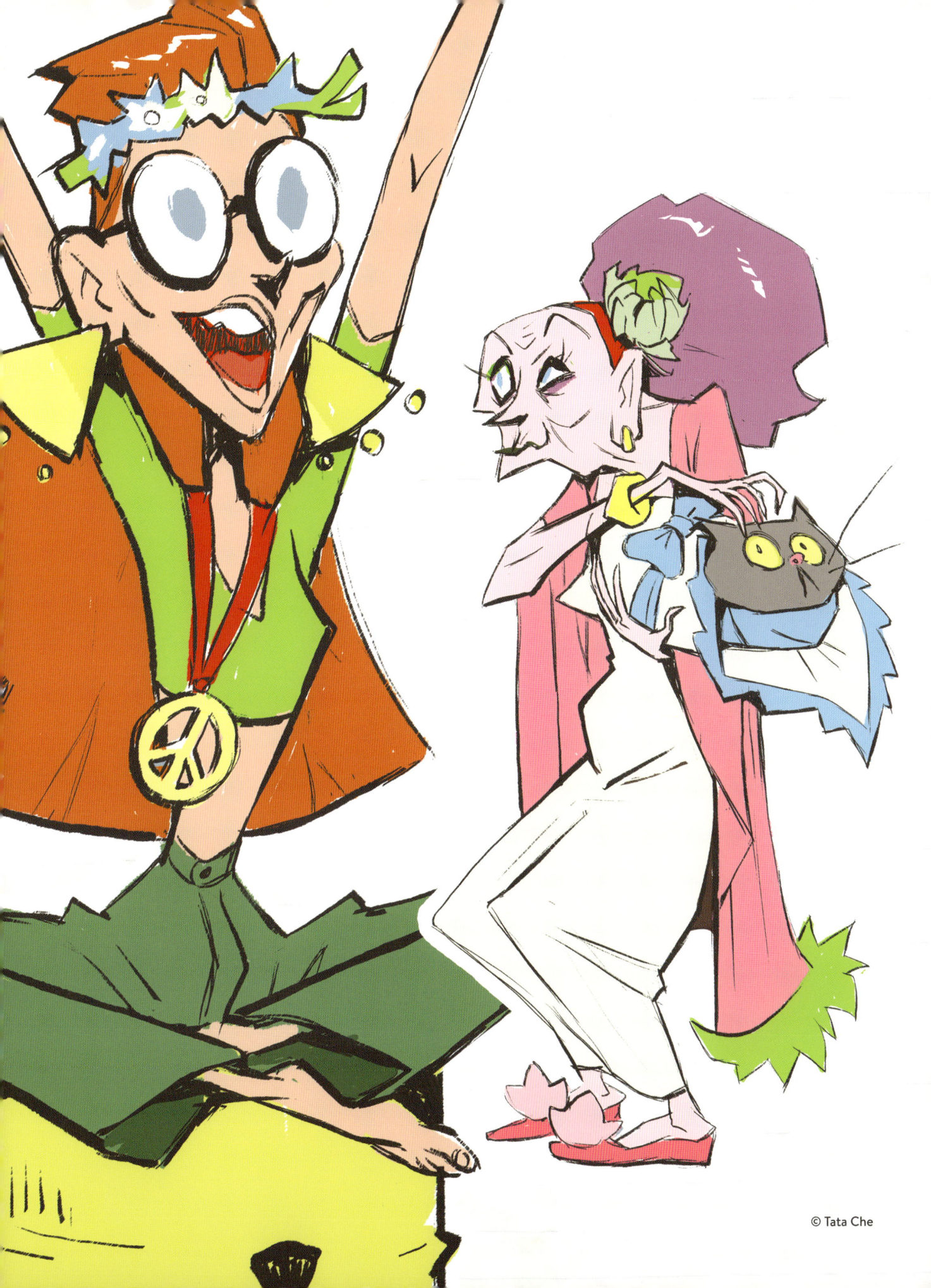

CONTRIBUTORS

LOIS VAN BAARLE (LOISH)

Digital Artist, Animator, and Character Designer
loish.net

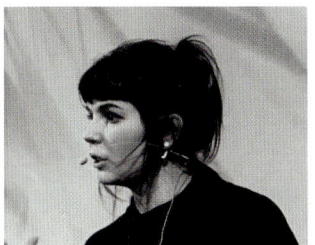

Lois has been drawing since she was old enough to hold a pencil. Her past clients include Psyop, Sony, and Guerrilla Games.

JAMES A. CASTILLO

Art Director & Character Designer
murfishart.com

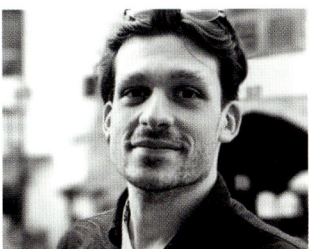

Working from his base in London, UK, James designs for companies such as Psyop, Paramount Pictures, and Illumination Macguff.

TATA CHE

Freelance Character Designer
tatacheart.com

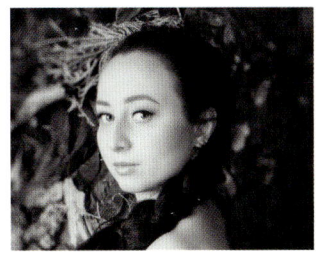

Tata is a passionate character designer focusing on animation. She currently lives in Russia but works with companies world-wide.

JULIA CHRISTIANS

Freelance Graphic Designer and Illustrator
juliachristians.de

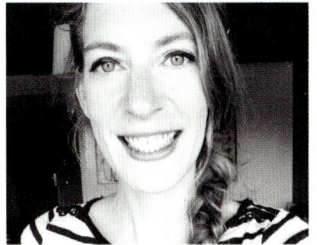

Julia is an illustrator from Germany. She studied communications design and now works freelance on editorial and children's books illustrations.

LUIS GADEA

Character Designer and 2D Animator
luisgadea.com

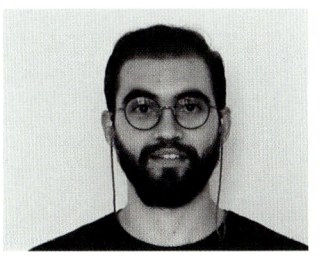

Luis has worked on animated commercials, TV series, and feature films. He often uses preschool art supplies to challenge himself.

VICTORIA KOSHELEVA

Freelance Illustrator
yavi.pro

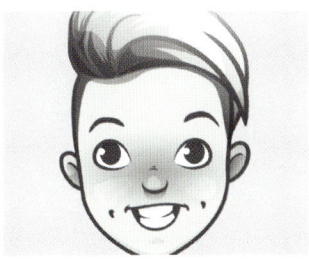

Victoria has previously created illustrations and character designs for the web, advertising, children's books, and games.

AMANDA MACFARLANE

Freelance Artist
Instagram: @theanimatedlife

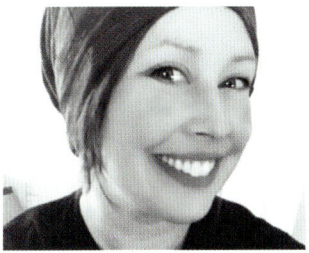

Amanda is a self-taught artist who works from home. She started drawing as soon as she could hold a crayon and hasn't stopped since.

FLORIANE MARCHIX

Visual Development Artist at DreamWorks Animation
florianemarchix.tumblr.com

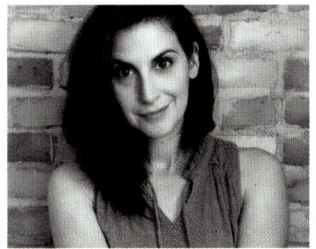

Floriane graduated from Gobelins and has since worked for Ubisoft, Aardman, and now works on feature films for DreamWorks Animation.

HOLLIE MENGERT

Freelance Character Designer and Illustrator
hollie-mengert.squarespace.com

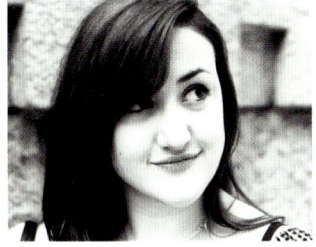

With a background in animation, Hollie has worked on children's books, games, and comics. She loves animals and telling a good story.

IVAN SHAVRIN

Freelance Comic Artist and Illustrator
artstation.com/shavrin_ivan

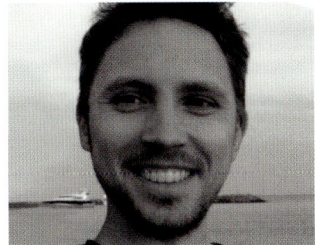

Born and raised in Omsk, Russia Ivan has worked for impressive clients including Ankama, Disney, LucasArt, and Axis Animation.

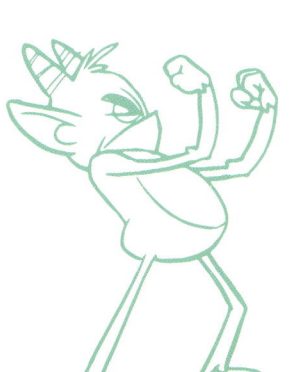
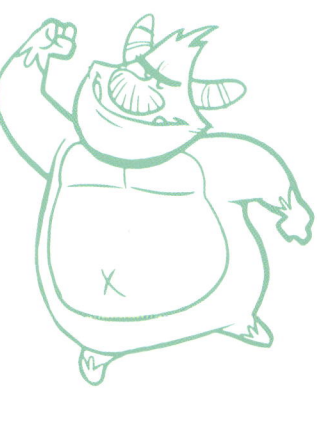

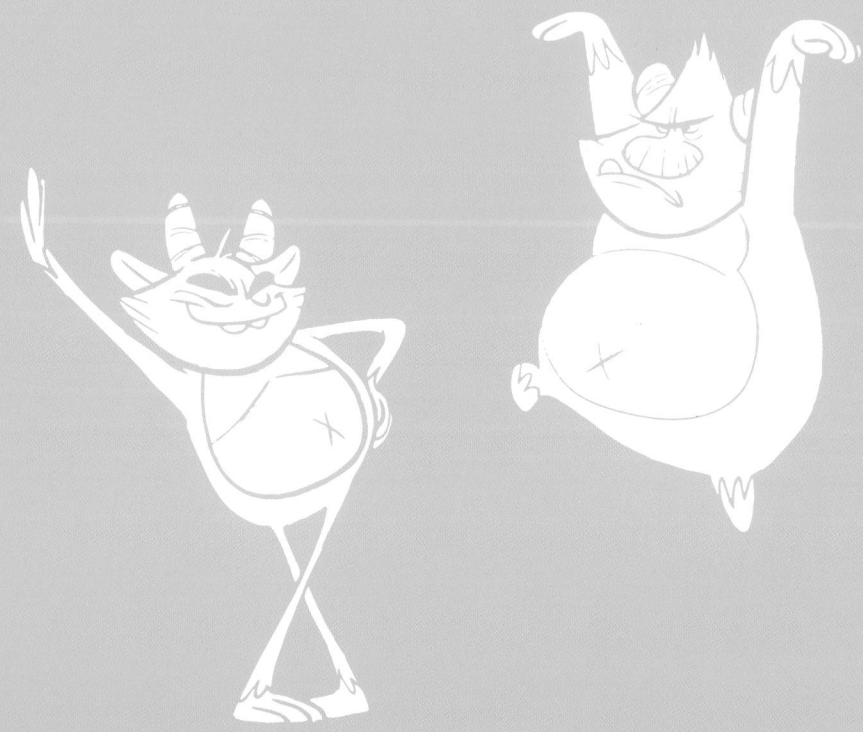